BOTTOM LINE

B A S I C S

UNDERSTAND & CONTROL BUSINESS FINANCES

By Robert J. Low

Edited by
Linda Pinkham

The Oasis Press® / PSI Research
Grants Pass, Oregon

031596

Published by The Oasis Press®/PSI Research
© 1995 by Robert J. Low

The following have generously given permission to the use of quotations from
copyrighted works: Reprinted with permission of the publisher from *The Mana-
ger's Book of Quotations* by Lewis D. Eigen and Jonathan P. Siegel © 1989
The Quotation Corporation. Published by AMACOM, a Division of the American
Management Association. All rights reserved. Reprinted by permission from C.
Charles Bahr, Bahr International, Inc., Dallas, TX © 1988 from speech, "Sick
Companies Don't Have to Die."

This publication is designed to provide accurate and authoritative information
in regard to the subject matter covered. It is sold with the understanding that the
publisher is not engaged in rendering legal, accounting, or other professional
service. If legal advice or other expert assistance is required, the services of a
competent professional person should be sought.

> — *from a declaration of principles jointly adopted by a committee of
> the American Bar Association and a committee of publishers.*

Editor: Linda Pinkham

Editorial Assistant: Erin Wait

3 2280 00518 5525

Book Designer: Constance C. Dickinson

Typographer: Jan Olsson

Please direct any comments, questions, or suggestions regarding this book to
The Oasis Press®/PSI Research:

> Editorial Department
> 300 North Valley Drive
> Grants Pass, OR 97526
> (541) 479-9464
> (800) 228-2275

The Oasis Press® is a Registered Trademark of Publishing Services, Inc.,
an Oregon corporation doing business as PSI Research.

Library of Congress Cataloging-in-Publication Data
Low, Robert J., 1957–
     Bottom line basics : understand & control business finances / by
Robert J. Low ; edited by Linda Pinkham. -- 1st ed.
       p. cm. -- (PSI successful business library)
     Includes index.
     ISBN 1-55571-329-7 (binder) : $39.95. -- ISBN 1-55571-330-0 (pbk.)
: $19.95
     1. Corporations--Accounting   2. Business enterprises--Accounting.
3. Managerial accounting.   I. Pinkham, Linda.   II. Title.
III. Series.
HF5686.C7L654   1994
657--dc20   94-24774

Printed in the United States of America
First edition 10 9 8 7 6 5 4 3 2 1 0

 Printed on recycled paper when available.

Table of Contents

Preface

If it's boring and dull and soon to be forgotten, continue to learn until you love double-entry bookkeeping. You should love the mathematics of business.

— Ken Olsen[1]

My goal in writing this book has been to communicate that effective financial management in smaller businesses is both critical for success and involves much more than just accounting. By focusing on the practical uses and benefits of accounting, planning, and control, rather than the mechanics, I also hope to motivate nonfinancial managers to take a more active interest in financial management.

For most people, financial management is not the most interesting aspect of running a business. You probably find it more stimulating to design a product than compute its cost, more enjoyable to close a sale than collect payment. But these financial tasks are critical.

Recently, the first major study of leadership skills of entrepreneurs was conducted, surveying several hundred of the top entrepreneurial CEOs in America. The goal of the survey was to identify the key leadership skills of entrepreneurs. What skills were perceived by entrepreneurs themselves as most important for guiding their businesses through previous stages of development and for achieving the next level of success?

At the top of a list of 34 skills, by a wide margin, was financial management. This was defined as acquiring and maintaining adequate capital, plus using the acquired funds wisely. The latter included anticipating cash needs, controlling spending, collecting receivables, and monitoring cash flow. The necessary skills for doing these tasks were seen as general accounting knowledge and the ability to apply it.[2]

At the other end of the spectrum, much of my consulting experience has been dealing with companies in financial distress. A recurring theme in nearly all of these companies has been the lack of financial discipline and control, specifically:

- Lack of planning and forecasting;
- Late and uninformative financial reporting;
- Failure to collect past due accounts receivable;
- Lack of basic controls, including bank reconciliations and transaction logs; and
- Excess and poorly controlled inventory.

These recurring themes have led to some of the symptoms of poor financial management including strained cash flow, poor customer service, seat-of-the-pants operating decisions, and strained banking relations.

The job of implementing the controls suggested in this book rests with you and your financial managers — your bookkeeper, accountant, controller, or chief financial officer. You have no need to become an accountant to ensure financial control. But a working knowledge of accounting and control will help you communicate with financial staff, so that you can direct and understand their work. This book is intended to provide that working knowledge for both smaller business owners and managers of large corporations.

This book should also be helpful to financial professionals. While the mechanics of accounting are familiar, if you are an accounting professional, you must look beyond the numbers and play a more proactive, operating role. This book illustrates how to apply financial skills to not just report, but actually improve, the bottom line.

I believe this book is the first to focus on the practical, management applications of financial accounting and control. By presenting applied knowledge, rather than just mechanics, and providing specific tips on achieving financial control, I hope I have made this book both interesting and rewarding. Not all topics will be equally relevant to you, though, and I encourage you to focus on the sections you feel are most important and skim over the other material.

I also welcome your comments and suggestions. Your feedback will help strengthen future editions and help better communicate the techniques and benefits of effective financial management.

Bob Low, August 1994

Acknowledgments

The content and organization of this book were shaped by the comments of Florence Graves, Bart McAndrews, Andy Dumaine, and Charles Markham. They reviewed my earliest outlines and chapters and provided much needed encouragement.

I would also like to thank Andy Bangs, Brad Howe, Fred Kofman, Mike Quattromani, Ed Simches, and Dave Tenney, who agreed to be interviewed for this book and referred me to additional sources.

Much of my personal experience and perspective on management are owed to working with Ron Lang and Roy David. Their skills at operating companies have provided a model for applying my skills in finance and have helped develop my management skills.

I thank my editor, Linda Pinkham, for her work in converting my draft into a finished manuscript. Her reorganization and revision of my text have made the book easier to read. In addition, I commend Constance C. Dickinson for her design of the book's page formats.

I would also like to thank the rest of the PSI Research/Oasis Press staff and owners Emmett and Ardella Ramey, for sharing my belief in this book and contributing their expertise to its preparation and marketing.

Endnotes

1. Quoted in THE BOSTON GLOBE, August 1, 1993, p. 80.
2. Eggars, John and Raymond W. Smilor. "Leadership Skills of Entrepreneurs: Resolving the Paradoxes and Enhancing the Practices of Entrepreneurial Growth," Unpublished study sponsored by the Center for Creative Leadership and the Ewing Marion Kauffman Foundation Center for Entrepreneurial Leadership.

How to Use this Book

The numbers tell you how your business is going, not why.

— Jonathan Siegel[1]

Overview of this Book

This book is not an accounting text or a controller's desk reference. Rather, it provides an overview of the critical issues concerning financial management and accounting in smaller companies. The goal is not to turn you into an accountant, but to illustrate the impact effective controllership can make on a company. Accounting has a reputation for being boring and much of it is. This book minimizes the amount of technical information and includes what is needed for a working knowledge of controllership — which ultimately helps make you money.

Part I

Bottom Line Basics is divided into five major parts. Part I of this book, The Accounting Primer, contains chapters that survey the current practice of accounting and controllership, and the basics of accounting for nonaccountants. Part I concludes with a chapter that explains the benefits of going beyond financial accounting. Don't be overwhelmed by the details of accounting, but just strive to understand the basics presented in chapters 3 and 4.

Part II

Part II – Beyond Financial Accounting begins with a detailed job description for a modern controller. This job description provides the outline for the remainder of the book, including chapters on one aspect of controllership — management accounting.

Part III – Managing Your Assets concerns yet another aspect of controllership, asset management. Chapters in this section go into detail on two of the most critical areas for the majority of businesses — controlling inventory and increasing cash flow. **Part III**

Part IV – Taking Control covers a number of topics related to effective controllership, including planning, budgeting, computer systems, and internal controls. The concluding chapter of this section contains a ten-step plan to help you get started right away with effective financial management. **Part IV**

Part V – The Appendix contains a useful glossary of terms used in accounting. A comprehensive index is next, followed by the Related Resources section at the end of this book. If you want to find more detailed or technical information on specific topics, refer to the Related Resources. **Part V**

Overall, the chapters are organized in a logical sequence, but feel free to skip around to topics that are most relevant to you. Of course, not all sections will apply to, or interest you. For example, service businesses have no inventory to manage and retailers may not offer credit. You can skim, or skip past, any section that is not relevant or use some of the more detailed chapters as if part of a desk reference. **Other Features**

This book has several handy features to make it user-friendly, including the topic headings that appear at the outside page margins, making it quicker and easier to find or relocate the information you need.

Examples of actual businesses are set apart in the text by a checkmark icon (✓). You will also find sample financial statements, forecasts, and more. Several useful worksheets are included in the book:

- The Net Present Value Project Evaluation worksheet can be used to determine the value of a project.
- The Break-Even Analysis worksheets can help you calculate the amount of sales needed to break even on a project or business.
- The Internal Control Questionnaire for Cash Disbursements can help you decide whether your internal controls for cash are adequate.

Included in the chapters are formulas, tables, and illustrations, to help you understand the material and allow you to put it to work for your business.

Endnote

1. Quoted in the *Manager's Book of Quotations*, p. 393.

Part I

The Accounting Primer

Chapter 1

Why Understand Controllership?

*Is it not impossible that a merchant should be prosperous without being
a thorough-pac'd Accountant ... as that a mariner should conduct
a ship to all parts of the globe without a skill in navigation?*

— anonymous London Merchant, circa 1700

A story is told about a balloonist who gets lost and is forced to make an emergency landing in an open field.

The balloonist flags down a passerby and asks him, "Where am I?"

"You are in a balloon basket in the middle of a field," is the reply.

"You must be an accountant," says the balloonist. "The information you just gave me is perfectly accurate and of absolutely no use."

"And you," replies the passerby, "must be a CEO [Chief Executive Officer]. You are operating a craft over which you have no control and want me to tell you where you are going."[1]

This story depicts the gap that can exist between business owners and accountants. Accountants often focus on providing accurate numbers, which may not be relevant or timely. Many business owners and managers, though, steer their businesses using a seat-of-the pants style and could benefit from financial know-how and controls.

As a small business owner or manager, you will want strong communication and support between you and your financial staff.

Effective accounting, planning, and control often mean the difference between success and failure for smaller companies. Yet, many smaller business owners, although skilled providers of a service or product, often operate with little background in financial management. Poor accounting methods, however, often contribute to:

- Shortsighted management decisions
- Misallocation of resources
- Failure to anticipate crises

Whether you are the owner of a smaller business or manager of a larger corporation or division, you can avoid these costly mistakes if your company has an accounting and finance department that plays a dynamic and diversified role in management support. As you will see in this book, accounting statements are only one part of financial management, yet they frequently receive the most attention. Ironically, these statements are designed to serve the information needs of investors, not management. The other aspects of accounting and controllership, which support internal management and decision making — management accounting, planning, asset management, and internal controls — are at least as important. These other aspects need to be implemented, preferably with business-savvy input from both you and your financial staff.

The number and types of financial advisers and staff members you employ will vary depending on the needs of your business. Your accounting department may consist of only a bookkeeper, an accountant, or both. On the other hand, you may employ a Chief Financial Officer (CFO) or controller, plus an entire support staff. You will likely rely on an outside certified public accountant for tax work and, perhaps, financial statement audits or more. While the next chapter goes into greater detail about the types of financial and accounting players, the main distinctions between the different job titles you might encounter are:

- Bookkeepers and accountants usually do the mechanical work of daily transactions and the compiling of financial statements.
- Controllers oversee accounting, but also have operating responsibilities, including interpreting financial information, controlling expenses and cash flow, planning, and implementing internal controls. See Chapter 6 for more information about the controller's role.
- CPA firms are outside advisers who specialize in tax preparation and auditing.
- CFOs usually supervise the controller, but also have responsibility for the financing, treasury, and administrative activities of a company.

No matter how small or large your business is, and no matter how many and what kind of financial advisers you employ, your leadership and direction of your accounting department are the important factors for having the information you need to become a hands-on manager.

This introductory chapter provides you with an overview of the issues you, as a smaller business owner or a CEO, need to be aware of to successfully operate your business. It discusses why it is critical for business owners and financial advisers to work well together and why, in practice, they don't.

Financial Information Gap

In many, if not most companies today, a wide gap exists between the needs of business owners and managers for financial information, systems, and control, and what is being provided by their internal financial managers and CPAs. This gap creates a serious vulnerability, particularly for smaller businesses, which operate with less margin for error than large corporations.

While the risk may not be easily quantifiable, it seems hard to overstate. Several authors have blamed 60–80% of business failures on financial problems, including poor recordkeeping and factors linked to cash flow.[2] On the positive side, a recent study has established the existence of a direct relationship between the financial and quantitative skill of entrepreneurs and the sales and bottom lines of their companies.[3]

The sources of financial management problems that can cause business crises are diverse. Consider some of the following examples:

✓ An industrial heating and air conditioning system installer was losing money. Essentially, three separate businesses were operating under one roof: installation of systems, service contracts and maintenance, and sale of replacement parts.

  Management needed to know how each product line was performing to make decisions on pricing, staffing, or whether to divest the line entirely. Because sales, expense, and time sheet data had always been aggregated, rather than collected by business line, this information was unavailable and the company was eventually unsuccessful in designing a turnaround strategy.

✓ A furniture manufacturer with annual sales of five million dollars was forced to write off $500,000 of receivables from customers unable or unwilling to pay. Lack of credit controls, applying payments randomly to invoices, and incomplete records all contributed to the problem. The company was forced to file bankruptcy.

✓ A moving company, modestly profitable but with flat sales, failed to aggressively collect past due accounts. The company experienced write-offs that threatened to wipe out the accrued profit and suffered a surprise cash squeeze. Operations were hastily slashed to conserve cash and, because the company was an S corporation where profits are taxable to the stockholders, the owner ended up without the cash to pay a $50,000 personal income tax obligation.

✓ A jewelry manufacturer suffered with a manual order entry system that was redundant and paper laden. Seven separate forms were used to track orders, beginning with the receipt of the order, to issuing a production order, to shipping, and finally to invoicing. Five different people set up individualized files, procedures, and double checks as the paper worked its way through the office and plant. In addition to the costs of redundancy, the process was costly in terms of lost orders, poor customer service, and an inability to track historical information for management.

Sometimes these types of management problems can lead to one of the most critical problems a business can face. Joe Namath once said he never lost a football game, just ran out of time on a few occasions. Similarly, entrepreneurs often blame their demise on simply not having enough cash. Unfortunately, running out of cash is usually just a symptom. The problem may be failing to anticipate a crisis, waiting too long to take action, or taking the wrong action.

No matter how good a company's employees, products, or services, strong financial management is a critical ingredient for success.

Turnaround expert C. Charles Bahr, author of *How Not to Go Bankrupt in the First Place*, had this to say in a 1988 speech:

> "Although the famous 'bottom line' is our agreed upon measuring stick, financial difficulties are usually the result of other ignored warning signs rather than the cause of them.

> "But in troubled businesses, we observe the top executive has marginal numbers skills and won't admit it. He lacks personal grasp of the numbers and their meaning in his own business. He may claim that his understanding of the numbers is 'good enough,' when in fact it is not good enough. This leaves him at the mercy of the skills and diligence of others. It is [like an airplane pilot with] iced-up windows and disabled instruments. It is remotely possible to 'talk down' a blinded pilot, but the expected outcome, shall we say, is likely to be suboptimal.

> "Numbers are just a means of communication, projection, and planning. In troubled companies, we see a lot of numbers, but they are too complex, too simple, mismatched to the requirements or just ignored. And they are nearly always late. Indeed, I don't believe you have to be a financial wizard to run a company today .... I just want a CEO to understand basic addition and subtraction and to do it."[4]

Controllership

Unexciting and underestimated, the controller's role is more important than you may think. Avoiding and steering through problems like those mentioned above is the joint task of you and your controller. If a business owner or CEO is a company's navigator, the controller is the map maker. Yet, time after time, companies drift because these two key players fail to address vital financial and control issues. Why? From the perspective of a business owner, two related reasons are apparent.

- First, smaller businesses usually owe their initial success and growth to an entrepreneurs' skill in producing a product, delivering a service, or selling. However, these entrepreneurs usually do not have commensurate experience, skill, or interest in financial management and administration. Though finance is, arguably, the most common route to the top in large companies, few smaller business owners have such backgrounds. They find financial management tedious and are happy to leave the details to their accountants and concentrate on sales, production, or research and development (R&D).

- Second, and more important, business owners can underestimate the scope and potential contribution of sound financial management. Financial management is often thought of in a very narrow sense, perhaps not much more than basic bookkeeping. Little is demanded of the accounting department beyond paying and collecting bills, producing regular financial statements, and filing tax returns.

This narrow perception of the controller's responsibilities falls well short of the mark. Just as most businesspeople today have no trouble distinguishing between sales and marketing, it is beneficial to understand that controllership is distinct from accounting. True, controllership encompasses basic accounting, but it also includes:

- Management accounting
- Cash planning and management
- Credit and collections
- Inventory management and control
- Planning and budgeting
- Internal controls
- Information systems

In a small company, if limited resources preclude having two top financial managers, a controller may also handle financing and treasury functions, which in larger organizations would be reserved for the chief financial officer (CFO). Controllers also frequently handle a variety of administrative functions, such as payroll, and may also be responsible for tax work.

In addition to underestimating the scope of the controller's job, business owners and CEOs also underestimate the job's potential impact. Accounting is often viewed as a necessary evil, an overhead function, whose costs should be minimized. It may even be seen as constricting if paperwork or other procedures interfere with managers' day-to-day freedom of action. As a result, rather than investing in information systems, controls,

Owner's Side of the Gap

or planning, companies run in more informal, even haphazard, seat-of-the-pants styles.

Nonetheless, even when business owners seem to devote too little time and resources to the controllership function, they are usually aware a gap exists. Many business owners admit to not fully understanding the finance function and are uneasy at not having a better understanding or handle on it. But this vague feeling of concern does not provide enough impetus for the owner to dive fully into financial reporting and control.

What these business owners and CEOs often do have is a strong instinct for the type of critical or sometimes "soft" information they need to stay on top of operations. Such information could include bookings to shipments ratios, the number of customer complaints, employee headcount, or sales by square foot. Each business is a bit different, each business owner zeroes in on different indicators, and little of it is routinely picked up by traditional accounting systems. Where the controller fails to provide this feedback through systematic means, the business owner is forced to collect it in a hit-or-miss manner, perhaps on scraps of paper or in an endless stream of special reports.

Controller's Side of the Gap

On the other side of the gap, many accountants lack the training, desire, or perspective to get involved in management issues. As a result, the shortcomings in financial management do not get met from the controller's end either.

To begin with, most companies work with two very different sets of accountants — CPAs and internal financial staff, including bookkeepers, accountants, and controllers. On the outside, the company may engage a CPA. Though CPA firms, particularly the large, national firms, have expanded the breadth of their services in recent years, their focus is on tax work and auditing or reviewing financial statements. Day-to-day issues are beyond the normal scope of a CPA's work, even in very small companies where a CPA may be called upon to actually compile the financial statements, perhaps sitting down with the bills and checkbook at the end of a month.

On the other hand, working with management day-to-day are the internal controllers, accountants, and bookkeepers. The experience and training of these people can vary widely, making it important to properly match the skills to the job. Expecting people trained only in bookkeeping or basic accounting to assume full controllership duties is unfair.

Even a well-trained controller may not have significant general management expertise. Differentiating between accurate and useful information, and anticipating needs rather than reporting after the fact, are skills not easily taught.

Personality also plays a role. The stereotype of all accountants as unimaginative, rather humorless souls who spend their day poring over figures, is unflattering. Nonetheless, people who are comfortable working with figures may not be as comfortable working with people. A controller needs to work actively with you and your managers. A controller who is shy and unaggressive will be ineffective.

Similarly, a controller who prefers to work with figures and stays rooted to the accounting offices cannot establish needed contact with other departments. And if you do not seek out the controller, you may discover that he or she is very happy to be left alone. Instead of building a strong working relationship, you and your controller work in separate spheres, coming together only to discuss monthly financial statements and routine issues in collections, invoicing, and payments.

Just as business owners get wrapped up in day-to-day crises, a controller can get bottled up by daily processing and the monthly accounting cycle. When times get hectic, the controller may fail to sit in on management meetings, and emphasis is given to getting invoices out, payroll processed, and statements issued. Important tasks that provide needed checks and balances can get pushed aside and time is not taken to analyze information. Reconciliations fall behind and collection calls aren't made.

In short, you will need to have a controller or accountant who has the ability to anticipate needs, as well as provide financial information; be aggressive and willing to meet with you and your managers; and have the skills and background that best fits your business' needs.

Financial Accounting Hindrances

Financial accounting, the accounting used to prepare standard financial statements, should form just a cornerstone of the controller's job. Unfortunately, it often dominates, squeezing out the other, vital aspects of controllership, such as planning, asset management, and internal controls. In subtle ways, financial accounting also influences how nonfinancial work is performed by creating pressure for profits — as opposed to cash flow — or imposing a rigid reporting calendar. As much as any factor, the dominance of financial accounting interferes with effective communication with, and support for, management.

An interesting note is that before the 20th century, management — not financial — accounting prevailed. The focus was on collecting information relating to internal operations and their effectiveness. Managers knew if they could do certain operations effectively, they would be successful over the long haul. The need to measure profit, particularly over defined periods, was far less important.

That emphasis changed with the need to raise financing and to report results to outside investors. The demand for objective standards that outsiders could use to evaluate and compare companies led to the rise of financial reporting and generally accepted accounting principles (GAAP). The needs of internal managers for information on the efficiency of their organizations did not disappear. But those needs were eclipsed by the demand for financial statements complying with GAAP.

Nevertheless, financial accounting is an impressive discipline. While financial accounting has some crucial weaknesses, which are discussed in Chapter 5, the ability to summarize the financial performance of even the largest corporations on a few, short reports is noteworthy. In general, investors are well served by financial reporting standards and the institutions that support them. But the reporting, which is highly aggregated and prepared well after the fact, is of much more limited use to internal management, whose decision making depends on current, detailed, often nonfinancial information.

So why are GAAP statements frequently the only statements produced by a company? First, most accountants are given little impetus to push beyond financial accounting. Financial and tax reporting are required; management accounting, budgets, and detailed cash flows are not. A conscious decision is needed to push beyond the required accounting into those other aspects of controllership such as management reporting, not to mention planning and asset management. Second, the training of most accountants is in financial accounting. Management accounting, at best, ranks a distant second in an accountant's education, together with tax. Other controller skills may not be taught at all. Finally, CPAs, who are relied on heavily by small companies, are specialists in taxation and compliance with GAAP, not controllership. A certified statement says little about efficiency or the quality of management; so, what satisfies a CPA may not help you directly with the operational decisions of your business.

Of all the aspects of the controller's job, financial accounting is probably the least interesting to business owners and their top managers. Financial accounting is the most technical aspect — this is where debits and credits are spoken. While business owners are interested in seeing the final numbers, the numbers have little direct impact on running the business. So if GAAP reporting dominates a controller's activity, is it any wonder a business owner or CEO takes little interest?

A Language Gap

The mention of debits and credits is a reminder of the language barrier that can exist between business owners and accountants. Beyond just knowing whether a debit goes on the left or the right side of the ledger page (the left) and when a credit balance is a good thing, accounting can introduce terms and concepts that are alien to business owners.

For example, business owners intuitively understand cash flow; accountants talk in terms of profit. Owners want to know what something is worth; accountants talk of cost and value assets based at what was paid for them (historic cost) less depreciation. Business owners spend money on R&D and advertising to get long-term benefits; accountants assign no future value to these expenditures. The list goes on. Dual definitions may be unavoidable since they serve different but necessary purposes, but it helps communication when both business owners and accountants can translate back and forth.

The difference in language also highlights a difference in focus. You may have noticed that accountants always seem to present the balance sheet first, while you instinctively flip to the income statement — note that the balance sheet comes first in audited statements and annual reports. This observation demonstrates how accountants often focus on the more static "snapshot" the balance sheet provides and less on the more dynamic "flow" of the income statement.

When asking for input on operating issues, an owner may think to him or herself, "Don't think like an accountant." The implication is that accountants tend to be unimaginative, their thinking narrowed by perceived rules and guided by the numbers. Put another way, although putting a financial dimension on problems is important, not everything a company does can be translated into numbers.

Bridging the Gap

For you and your controller to work together, your dialogue must move beyond financial reporting. You both must understand the dynamic role accounting and controllership can play in your company and dedicate the time and resources needed to realize it.

A controller is in a position to know more about a company's operation than anyone except the president or owner. This doesn't mean that he or she will know more about sales than the sales manager or more about production than a foreperson. But being in a position to see the transactions from all departments and work with managers throughout the company, the controller is exposed, in great detail, to the entire operation. As a result, your controller has an opportunity to contribute insights and information and improve the quality of overall management. So don't focus just on the bookkeeping aspects of the controller's job.

At the same time, the controller is usually the specialist in reducing company costs, managing assets, implementing systems, performing financial analysis, and planning for future goals. These skills contribute directly to your company's profitability, and you need to put your controller's skills to work.

From an owner's or manager's perspective, you have no need to become an accountant. However, a basic knowledge of accounting is needed to properly interpret financial statements. And, while no business can be "run by the numbers," an instinctive feeling for what the figures mean and which numbers are relevant is valuable.

The bottom line is knowing how to make a controller accountable. To accomplish the bottom line means understanding not only accounting, but key financial operating issues, such as:

- Why do profitable businesses run out of cash and what can be done to prevent that?

- How should accounting information be used to set prices or perform production or buying decisions?

- How can cash be wrung out of receivables and inventory?

- How do you know everything shipped is invoiced or that nothing is paid for twice?

Armed with a basic knowledge of the controller's role and responsibilities, you can be part of a true dialogue on financial management. More importantly, you can truly take control of your company's "balloon" and steer it in the proper direction. While this introductory chapter has generally highlighted some of the problems businesses face, many solutions and preventive measures can be implemented, starting in your accounting department.

The rest of Part I provides you with background material to help you understand the fundamentals of basic accounting, beginning with a more detailed description of the accounting industry. If you already possess a good background in accounting, you may want to jump ahead to Chapter 5, for a discussion of how traditional financial accounting fails to provide all of the information necessary to successfully manage your business. Chapter 6 describes the modern controller's function and leads in to the remainder of the book.

Endnotes

1. Schiff, Jonathan and Lee Berton, eds. *Wall Street Journal on Accounting.* Dow Jones-Irwin, 1990. p. iv.

2 Branch, Shelly. "Go with the Flow — Or Else." BLACK ENTERPRISE November 1991: 77.

3 Eggars and Smilor, p. 22.

4. Bahr, C. Charles. "Sick Companies Don't Have To Die," speech given in Houston, Texas, 14 June 1988, printed in *Vital Speeches of the Day*, 1 September 1988, p. 687.

Chapter 2

Who the Players Are

*When you have mastered the numbers, you will no longer be reading numbers
any more than you read words when reading books.
You will be reading meanings.*

   Harold Geneen, former CEO of IT&T [1]

The accounting profession enjoys an exalted, but somewhat misunderstood status in the business world. While accountants are considered the most trusted professional group in America,[2] large numbers of executives and small business owners are unclear on what accountants do and how to purchase accounting services. And, while accounting is often called the language of business, few nonfinancial managers are fluent in it.

Most smaller business owners place a lot of faith — at least partly due to the stellar reputation CPAs have for not disseminating information — in their internal and outside accountants.

Not only do managers need to trust the people that handle their financial affairs, they may also use them as confidants. A few CPAs even feel like religious confessors for clients, frequently hearing not only about business affairs, but of family and marital problems.

But underneath this faith is a lack of understanding about what accountants do. In a survey of 632 executives, 40% were confused about the scope and purpose of an audit.[3] Another survey of very small business owners — fewer than 20 employees — found that the majority failed to recognize the difference between a CPA, accountant, or bookkeeper.[4]

This last study by Emmett D. Edwards concluded that small business owners frequently fail to differentiate among the skill levels of professionals offering accounting services and are ineffective in defining the services to be provided. Not only can you end up overpaying, but you may get incompetent help. According to Edwards:

> "Popular misconceptions about competency in accounting and failure to realize the impact accounting and financial management areas have on success often lead owners of very small businesses to hire less-than-competent external providers.

> "Failure by owners of very small businesses to recognize the impact of accounting and finance activities on their business and, as a result, to master even the most rudimentary concepts of accounting applications almost certainly is a contributing factor to the high incidence of failure among that group."[5]

Accounting practices are largely self-regulated, guided by several key institutions. To clear up any misconceptions you may have, this chapter discusses the different types of accounting methods in use, what kinds of services are available, and who the players are — both industry organizations and the kinds of accountants associated with each.

Types of Accounting

The first step in becoming an educated customer of accounting services is understanding that there are several different types of accounting. The four main branches of accounting are financial, tax, management, and nonprofit accounting. Accountants specialize in different areas, so you will want to hire accordingly. This often means using multiple accountants.

For example, CPAs are experts in tax work, but may lack the operating experience and be too expensive to use for internal reporting. In addition to distinct branches of accounting, there are two main methods for recognizing expenses and revenues — accrual accounting and cash method accounting.

Financial Accounting

Financial accounting is used by for-profit businesses to prepare financial statements and is probably the most familiar type of reporting. All public companies are required to issue regular financial statements that conform with GAAP, and most private companies do so voluntarily. Pick up a textbook on accounting or take an introductory class and it will almost certainly be about financial accounting. This topic is covered in more detail in the next two chapters.

The standard reports of financial accounting are an income statement, balance sheet, and statement of cash flows. Companies usually prepare these reports on an accrual basis. In other words, revenue is recorded when it is earned and expenses are recorded when resources are used or obligations incurred, which is not necessarily when cash is exchanged. For example, a sale shipped on account would usually be counted as revenue, even though the payment might come in several weeks later.

While accrual accounting is nearly always required to comply with GAAP, it is possible to prepare other types of financial statements on a cash basis. Cash based accounting is what most individuals use to compute personal income for tax purposes. It is also used by very small businesses and professional service firms who have no inventory and few long-term assets.

Cash Method Accounting

Cash based accounting is as simple as a checkbook register. Cash in is income and cash out is expense. This is adequate in simple situations, but accrual accounting is usually needed to get a true picture of profits as businesses get more complex. For example, if you are a retailer and make a $48 cash sale, recording the sale that day is all right. However, if you sell a year-long service contract or subscription for $48, recording the entire sale right away is misleading.

You get a more accurate picture of what your business actually earned with an accrual system that recognizes $4 of revenue per month over the course of the year. As is discussed later in Chapter 11, however, profit is not the same as cash flow, and accrual based statements do not eliminate the need for tracking cash flow.

Tax accounting has its own set of rules, laid down by the Internal Revenue Service (IRS). Figuratively speaking, businesses may keep two sets of books for operating and tax purposes. There are two main reasons for this. First, the timing of some expenses and revenues differs under GAAP and tax laws. Examples include:

Tax Accounting

- Capital lease payments — These are deducted for tax purposes in most cases, but for GAAP are treated as if they were installment payments on long-term debt with a portion allocated to interest expense and a portion to principal.

- Unrealized losses on marketable securities — GAAP requires that the expense be recognized, but the securities must be sold to take a loss on your taxes.

- Reserves for anticipated inventory write-offs and markdowns — These are expenses under GAAP, but no tax write-off is allowed unless the inventory is actually disposed of.

Second, a company may want to show as little taxable income as possible, while issuing public statements with healthy profits. For some items, like depreciation, a company can choose different accounting methods for tax and book purposes. By using accelerated depreciation for tax purposes, while spreading the costs more slowly for book purposes, a company can reduce taxable income while limiting the hit to net income.

No matter who performs your company's internal accounting or what conventions are used, consult a tax specialist on how to minimize your tax payments. A little advanced planning can save you a significant amount in taxes, plus an expert can help make sure you take advantage of available tax credits, avoid double taxation on funds removed from the business, and prevent extra costs from rules such as the alternative minimum tax.

Management Accounting

Financial and tax accounting satisfy the needs of outsiders. While the information can be useful internally, it is highly aggregated and usually prepared well after the end of the period it reports on. Management accounting — also called cost accounting, especially in manufacturing businesses — is a separate discipline that addresses management's need for current, detailed, internal operating information, which might include unit costs of production, sales by store, or profitability of individual projects. Chapters 7 and 8 cover management accounting in more detail.

Nonprofit Accounting

Nonprofit organizations, such as governments, universities, and some hospitals, have different accounting standards. In some cases, the distinctions are slight. If a hospital that operated for profit were suddenly changed to one that was nonprofit, but still got all its revenue from sales, the only accounting changes might be to recognize that there are no shareholders and that success is not measured by profit. Instead of net income, the bottom line would be "excess of revenues over expenses." The shareholders equity section of the balance sheet might simply be called "equity."[6]

At organizations such as universities and hospitals, funds are received from nonsales sources such as donations and grants. Much of this is earmarked for special purposes. If alumni donate money specifically for a school's endowment or to finance a new building, it is inappropriate to use the funds for operating purposes. The funds are segregated and the accounting system must track the revenues and expenses for each fund separately.

Accounting for state and local government often gets extremely difficult to understand. One problem is that they carry fund accounting to an extreme. Funding comes from multiple revenue sources, such as bonds, taxes, and fees, and many of these, such as gas taxes and highway tolls, get earmarked for specific purposes. Some agencies use encumbrance accounting, which tracks contractual obligations, as well as actual expenditures. Others incorporate budgets into their accounting to track actual results against projected revenues and appropriations.

Finally, many nonprofit organizations do not use accrual accounting. Rather than record expenses when a resource is used, they record when the expenditure was made. For service organizations, where payroll is the main expense incurred and is paid for in the same period, not using accrual accounting may make little difference. But for organizations with large amounts of capital spending, expensing purchases immediately rather than recording them as assets can make a sizable difference.

Who Makes the Rules

Two primary bodies regulate accounting. The Securities and Exchange Commission (SEC) was set up by Congress in the 1930s and holds the authority for setting accounting standards for the financial statements of publicly traded companies. For the most part, the SEC has delegated this responsibility to the accounting profession. However, the SEC has released more than 200 opinions in its *Accounting Series Releases* and occasionally exerts its power by disagreeing with positions taken by the accounting profession.

Before 1973, accounting principles were developed by committees of the American Institute of Certified Public Accountants (AICPA). The Committee on Accounting Procedure was active from 1938 to 1959 and the Accounting Principles Board (APB) from 1959 to 1973.

The Financial Accounting Standards Board (FASB), formed in 1973, is an independent organization with full-time members having a wide range of backgrounds in industry, academia, and public practice. The FASB has issued more than 100 standards and continues to be the primary standard-setting accounting body.

The IRS has a strong influence on financial accounting practice even though tax and financial accounting have different objectives and principles. IRS regulations are not GAAP and, technically, good financial accounting practice should be independent of tax accounting. In practice, though, to minimize taxes and avoid the need to keep duplicate records, managers often adopt the accepted accounting practice that results in the lowest taxable income.

The Cost Accounting Standards Board (CASB) is authorized by Congress to establish cost accounting standards for contractors negotiating federal defense contracts over $100,000. Like IRS regulations, CASB standards influence financial accounting practice where the FASB has not established a principle.

Industry Organizations

Although the AICPA no longer establishes GAAP, this organization of accountants is still the largest, with more than 300,000 members, and is the most influential. In addition to certifying accountants, the AICPA is an influential adviser to the FASB. The AICPA is the leading force in establishing and maintaining a professional code of ethics and in continuing education. The AICPA is also the leader in developing auditing standards, issued through one of its committees.

A rapidly growing organization is the Institute of Management Accountants (IMA), formerly the National Association of Accountants. The IMA has close to 100,000 members and focuses on management accounting. Since 1972, it has sponsored an exam for the certified management accountant (CMA) designation. More than 10,000 certificates have been issued, and those who pass the exam become members of the Institute of Certified Management Accountants (ICMA).

Other organizations are the American Accounting Association, which is primarily for accountants in academic work, and the National Society of Public Accountants, which is a trade organization providing benefits, support, and some education.

Certification of Accountants

The certified public accountant (CPA) is the best known, and most popular, professional accounting designation. Certification requirements are fairly stringent, but vary slightly from state to state. A four-part exam is administered nationwide by the AICPA, presently covering:

- Business law and professional responsibilities;
- Auditing;
- Accounting and reporting — taxation, managerial, governmental, and nonprofit; and
- Financial accounting and reporting for business enterprises.

All four parts must be passed; however, this can be done over several sittings. In addition to the test, accountants must work a specified time in public accounting. Sometimes, general accounting experience can be substituted for part of the time required. To maintain certification, continuing education is necessary.

In sharp contrast to the CPA exam, the CMA exam covers topics such as economics, ethics, management motivation, and corporate decision making, as well as financial and management reporting. Candidates must be members of the IMA, have two years of management accounting experience, and meet continuing education requirements to remain certified. The examination's recognition and popularity are rapidly increasing. The IMA and ICMA are aggressively promoting the CMA program in corporate and academic arenas, which is where most CMAs are employed.[7]

CPA Firms

CPAs work in both public and private practice. Public accounting firms range from one person shops to the omnipresent "Big Six." The Big Six firms are:

- Arthur Andersen & Company
- Coopers & Lybrand
- Deloitte & Touche
- Ernst & Young
- KPMG Peat Marwick
- Price Waterhouse

The Big Six are all international firms with a presence in most major American cities. They offer a full range of accounting and consulting services. However, because they are required to maintain objectivity, their ability to expand into other financial services is sharply limited. Also, to ensure objectivity, if a CPA firm is auditing your statements, there are limitations on the services it can perform for you.

The primary tasks of CPAs are tax and audit. Most companies and wealthy individuals don't — and should not — venture into tax planning or preparation without the aid of a CPA.

One caveat: while a CPA is likely to be skilled in minimizing your taxes and will usually assist you if an IRS audit occurs, you are still responsible for any return you sign, whether or not it was prepared by a CPA. You cannot escape penalties and interest just by using a CPA.

Choosing a CPA

If you compare large and small CPA firms, you will find that their professional credentials are pretty much the same. Your decision is more likely to be driven by investor requirements, cost, service, and personality factors. A Big Six firm makes sense for companies with aspirations of going public — or being acquired by a public company — or where required by investors. The larger firms also offer a broader scope of services. However, they tend to cost more and you may find yourself dealing with different staff members each year.

Small CPA firms may provide more long-standing and personal service. But if you need fairly specialized expertise, the chances are less that a small firm will have it. In addition, some CPA licenses don't allow work on public companies. The same is true for nonprofits for which CPAs need special training and certification.

In all cases, be sure to get an engagement letter that spells out the scope of any audit or tax work. Get a breakdown of the proposed fee and see if you can save money by shifting some of the work in-house. A capable controller, or even a temporary worker, can usually prepare many of the audit schedules at a lower cost than the CPA firm. You may also find you can do without some of the proposed services or can substitute less expensive audit personnel for high-priced partners and seniors.

Not All Accountants Are CPAs

While CPAs are the only professionals who can certify financial statements, they are not the only ones who can prepare tax returns or contract accounting services. This is both good and bad news. Using a tax preparation service or a bookkeeping service to compile — but not audit — financial statements may be an opportunity to save money. The down side is that few states regulate who can call themselves accountants. Distinguishing how qualified a practitioner is may be difficult.

Most professionals in the accounting field have no certification; however, lack of certification does not mean they are unqualified. Nor does using a CPA or CMA guarantee a correct match up for a company's needs. A CPA, for example, is a somewhat narrow designation. The designation demonstrates skill in tax, audit, and theory, but says nothing about management skills or cost accounting.

A CPA is likely to be an overkill for a bookkeeping job. An accountant with significant industry experience may not be a CPA, but could have valuable experience dealing with operating issues. But, even if an accountant holds a CMA, that person's experience may be limited to a few companies and he or she is probably not current on tax issues.

Minimizing what is spent on accounting is often tempting. But the contractor doing basic accounting work for a low fee may not be the right person to give financial advice or ensure proper controls. A bookkeeping service does different work and promises a different level of expertise than a part-time controller. Accountants who are moonlighting or doing temporary work can have a wide range of experience. Failing to sort out the qualifications can lead to inadequate reporting and controls.

CPA Reports

CPA firms can provide several different types of financial statement preparation and examination services — such as audits, reviews, or compilations — depending on what your business needs are. Review the following descriptions of services to determine the differences between the services and which ones you may need. Included at the end of this chapter are samples of both qualified and unqualified audit opinions and a review opinion.

Audits

Auditing consists of examinations of a company's financial statements and internal controls. An audit by a CPA is required of all public companies — companies whose ownership shares are publicly traded — and the audit opinion is an important part of the financial statements. The audit opinion includes a description of the scope of the audit, an opinion on whether the financial statements were prepared in accordance with GAAP, and any qualifying remarks.

If you manage a private company, do you need an audit? Although audits may be perceived as suitable only for large corporations, some compelling arguments can be made for smaller company audits. Some of the reasons for which you may want an audit are listed below.

- If your company has, or anticipates having, outside investors or a loan from a bank, you will almost certainly need to obtain an independent opinion.
- Audited financials may facilitate your dealings with vendors and customers.

- If your company is considering going public or being acquired, you will want a history of audited statements.

- The CPA's assessment may provide you with peace of mind over the soundness of your accounting systems and procedures, plus an opportunity to get an objective viewpoint of your management practices.

On the other hand, if you have no internal requirement for an audit, you may want to avoid the expense. Expect to pay at least $10,000 for a company with sales of $500,000–1,000,000, increasing up to $50,000 and higher for a $20 million company.

Actual costs will vary depending on:

- The type of CPA firm used — the Big Six are usually more expensive than local companies;

- The amount of work performed internally;

- Whether the CPA also does the company's tax work; and

- The extent of testing required.

Don't be afraid to negotiate price. CPAs will often offer lower rates to lure customers. However, don't jump from CPA to CPA without a compelling reason, as this not only disrupts a potentially rewarding long-term relationship, but it is also frowned upon by investors.

The independent CPA examination results may take one of two forms — an audit or a review opinion. The audit requires testing of internal procedures, reviewing of certain transactions, and verification of account balances — specific procedures are discussed in more detail in Chapter 4. After the audit, the CPA issues a formal report on the company's financial statements that states the following:

- Whether the statements conform to GAAP;

- Whether accounting principles have been consistently applied from year to year;

- Whether disclosure is adequate — assumed so, unless otherwise stated; and

- An expression of an opinion or the reasons why an opinion cannot be given.

In addition, a description of the scope of the audit is included. A sample of a typical unqualified audit opinion is located at the end of this chapter. Even though each CPA firm adopts its own language, the three paragraph format shown is fairly standard.

If the auditor fails to express an opinion, issues a qualified opinion, or, rarely, an adverse opinion, serious problems exist and can be a major setback to a company. Reasons why an auditor may not issue a favorable opinion include:

- Uncertainty over whether the company is financially stable — in other words, survival over the next year may be in doubt;

- GAAP, including adequate disclosure, have not been conformed to;

- Sufficient data cannot be gathered or tested; or

- Statements may be subject to resolution of a significant uncertainty, such as a major lawsuit.

The formats of qualified and adverse opinions differ from the normal three paragraph format, making them easy to spot. A sample qualified audit opinion is located at the end of this chapter, so that you can compare the qualified and unqualified opinions with each other.

Adverse opinions are only issued if the departures from GAAP are so severe that the financial statements as a whole cannot be relied upon. A disclaimer of opinion might be made if an auditor is unable to collect enough data to form an opinion.

What an Audit Is Not

Audits do not guarantee that financial statements are accurate. Rather, the scope of the audit is to determine whether material differences exist. The definition of what is material will differ from company to company. A discrepancy of $100,000 will be material to a small company but is probably immaterial to the statements of a billion dollar corporation. Considerable professional judgment is exercised by the auditor in deciding what is material for a particular audit. In addition, because the main purpose of the audit is to protect outside investors, greater emphasis is usually put on possible overstatements of income or net worth than understatements.

In addition, an audit or review is not intended to detect fraud. Uncovering fraud may be a by-product of the audit, but fraud is not specifically searched out. If you suspect fraud, alert your CPA. Chances are good the CPA will detect it, but doing so requires a different set of procedures than normal.

To get a specialist in fraud investigation, call on a forensic accountant — someone who seeks out evidence of cheating or theft, whether by insiders or outsiders. According to *CFO* magazine, "The forensic accountant is to a regular accountant what the pathologist is to the family doctor."[8] Forensic accounting is a rapidly growing field. The National Association of Certified Fraud Examiners — founded in 1986 and the sponsor of a four-part, ten-hour certification exam — has more than 10,000 members today.

Reviews

A less rigorous and less expensive alternative to a full-blown audit is a review. A review is similar to an audit in that it involves steps in examining the accounting system, transactions, and balances. However, a CPA relies on a much smaller volume of information. The purpose is to determine whether major deviations from GAAP exist. Where a problem is suspected, the auditor may decide to expand tests to the same level as an audit.

As with an audit, the CPA expresses an opinion, but the opinion states that the auditor is "not aware of any material modifications that should be made" to conform with GAAP.[9] Contrast this with the much more positive assertions made in the audit letter. A sample review opinion is included at the end of this chapter.

The cost of a typical review is about half that of an audit. Since being endorsed by the AICPA in 1979, reviews have grown in acceptance. Check if your bank or investors will accept a review before opting out of an audit. If they will, the review is a cost-effective alternative.

Compilations

For very small businesses, a compilation is a third alternative that is available. For a compilation, a CPA simply assembles the company's data into a statement, but gives no opinion or assurance about the statements.

Industry Crisis

In recent years, the CPA profession has faced a serious crisis stemming from an onslaught of liability cases brought by investors and government regulators. Accounting firms in 1992 faced 4,000 lawsuits, double the number from 1985. Nearly two-thirds stem from the savings and loan (S&L) scandals. Price Waterhouse was hit with a $387 million judgment for its role as auditor in a 1987 bank acquisition.[10] One of the industry's largest firms, Laventhol & Horwath, filed for bankruptcy in 1991 due to litigation. In 1991, the Big Six spent 9% of their auditing fees on related legal costs.[11]

Most of the lawsuits — 60% — stem from the auditing function and the CPA's certification of statements. Where work has been sloppy, auditors can certainly be held liable. However, because fraud is beyond the scope of a standard audit, to shift the blame for undetected fraud to the auditors is unfair. Auditors rely heavily on the assertions of management and clever management can usually conceal fraudulent activity, at least for a short time.

How auditors should respond to fraud once they come across it is controversial. While many people feel CPAs should blow the whistle on clients when they uncover fraud, auditors often prefer to simply walk away quietly from these accounts. If that happens to a publicly traded firm, the client must file a report with the SEC explaining why the auditors resigned. However, the details are typically played down.[12]

The financial pressure introduced by the lawsuits will certainly lead to changes in the industry. Legislative proposals have already been introduced in the wake of the S&L crises and increased regulation of accounting firms is possible. Clients are likely to face higher fees and accounting firms are becoming more selective about who they service.

Some companies with risky profiles — those that have fired previous auditors, for example — may be unable to hire an auditor at any cost.[13] In addition, most accounting firms, including the Big Six, are expected to shift their legal form of ownership from partnerships to corporations, limited liability partnerships, or limited liability companies to gain limited liability status.[14]

A Word about GAAP

Part of selecting the right accounting services is understanding the role of financial and tax reporting. This book repeatedly stresses how this required reporting is only part of financial management. Most experienced bookkeepers and accountants can do the mechanics, and your CPA can provide insurance that they are done properly.

Accounting skill does not imply financial management and operating savvy. Audited financials do not guarantee proper controls or provide detailed information. Sound financial management also demands attention to costs, planning, controls, and asset management. Whether hiring internal or external financial people, look for those with experience beyond basic accounting. The importance of financial accounting is not to be diminished. It is fascinating how the myriad activities of any business can be captured by accounting transactions, then be summarized in financial statements comprehensible by readers inside and outside a company. Like a picture, financial statements are worth at least a thousand words.

But GAAP reporting is primarily intended to meet the needs of investors and other outsiders. While the statements are still valuable to management, they provide an overview rather than a detailed picture. And, in protecting the interests of investors, trade-offs in GAAP make the statements more objective but less informative. In the next three chapters, issues of financial accounting are examined.

Endnotes

1. Moscow, Alvin, with Harold Geneen. *Managing*. New York: Doubleday, 1984. p. 185.

2. Edwards, Emmett D. Jr. "What Financial Problems." MANAGEMENT ACCOUNTING August 1992: 54.

3. Siegel, Gary. "Public Accounting Report." 1993 survey of 632 executives by U. DePaul.

4. Edwards, p. 56.

5. Ibid. p. 57.

6. Anthony, Robert N., Regina E. Herzlinger, and Richard D. Irwin, Inc. *Management Control in Non-Profit Organizations*. Homewood, Illinois, 1980. p. 134.

7. Bulloch, James. "The CMA is 20 Years Old." MANAGEMENT ACCOUNTING April 1992: 23–27.

8. Mintz, S. L. "The Fraud Detectives." CFO MAGAZINE April 1993: 29.

9. Miller, Merton C. *Miller's Comprehensive GAAP Guide.* New York: Harcourt Brace Jovanovich 1986. p. 40.62.

10. The judgment was later thrown out and a new trial ordered.

11. Ehrenfeld, Tom. Gerald A. Polansky, Chairman of the AICPA, quoted in "Survival of the Fittest." CFO MAGAZINE Aug. 1992: 7.

12. McCarroll, Thomas. "Who's Counting?" TIME 13 April 1992: 49.

13. Woolley, Suzanne. "The Big Six Are In Big Trouble." BUSINESS WEEK 6 April 1992: 78.

14. Clolery, Paul. "LLPs/LLCs: Bulletproofing Your Firm." THE PRACTICAL ACCOUNTANT Sept. 1994: 24.

Unqualified Audit Opinion – Sample

Unqualified Audit Opinions typically have the following sections:

- An introductory paragraph identifying management's responsibility for the financial statements, giving a brief description of what an audit is, and stating that any opinion is based upon the audit work;
- A scope paragraph describing the work performed during the audit;
- An opinion paragraph asserting that the statements are in accordance with GAAP; and
- The auditor's signature and the date of the report.

Report of Independent Auditors

Stockholders and Board of Directors:

We have examined the balance sheet of XYZ Corporation as of December 31, 1994 and 1993, and the related statements of income, stockholders' equity, and cash flows for the years then ended. These financial statements are the responsibility of the Company's management. Our responsibility is to express an opinion on these financial statements based on our audit.

We conducted our audits in accordance with generally accepted auditing standards. Those standards require that we plan and perform the audits to obtain reasonable assurance about whether the financial statements are free of material misstatement. An audit includes examining, on a test basis, evidence supporting the amounts and disclosures in the financial statements. An audit also includes assessing the accounting principles used and significant estimates made by management, as well as evaluating the overall financial statement presentation. We believe that our audits provide a reasonable basis for our opinion.

In our opinion, the financial statements referred to above present fairly, in all material respects, the financial position of XYZ Corporation at December 31, 1993 and 1992, and the results of its operations and its cash flows for the year then ended in conformity with generally accepted accounting principles.

[Date] _____   [Signature] _____

Qualified Audit Opinion – Sample

Qualified Audit Opinions typically have the following sections:

- An introductory paragraph as shown in the unqualified opinion;

- A scope paragraph as shown in the unqualified opinion, unless the qualification results from the scope being limited. In that case the words "except as explained in following paragraph" are added to the start of the paragraph;

- An explanatory paragraph describing the reasons for the qualified opinion and the potential impact of the qualification on the financial statements;

- An opinion paragraph similar to the unqualified opinion, but containing the phrase "except for" or "subject to" and referring to the explanatory paragraph; and

- The auditor's signature and the date of the report.

Report of Independent Auditors

Stockholders and Board of Directors:

We have examined the balance sheet of XYZ Corporation as of December 31, 1994 and 1993, and the related statements of income, stockholders' equity, and cash flows for the years then ended. These financial statements are the responsibility of the Company's management. Our responsibility is to express an opinion on these financial statements based on our audit.

We conducted our audits in accordance with generally accepted auditing standards. Those standards require that we plan and perform the audits to obtain reasonable assurance about whether the financial statements are free of material misstatement. An audit includes examining, on a test basis, evidence supporting the amounts and disclosures in the financial statements. An audit also includes assessing the accounting principles used and significant estimates made by management, as well as evaluating the overall financial statement presentation. We believe that our audits provide a reasonable basis for our opinion.

As more fully described in Note A to the financial statements, the Company is involved in continuing litigation relating to patent infringements. The amount of damages, if any, resulting from this litigation cannot be determined at this time.

In our opinion, subject to the effects, if any, of such adjustments as might have been required had the outcome of the uncertainty discussed in the preceding paragraph been known, the financial statements referred to above present fairly, in all material respects, the financial position of XYZ Corporation at December 31, 1993 and 1992, and the results of its operations and its cash flows for the year then ended in conformity with generally accepted accounting principles.

[Date] _____ [Signature] _____

Review Opinion – Sample

A review opinion has the same sections as an audit opinion. The wording is modified to reflect the lesser scope and the auditor is does not express an opinion as to whether the statements conform with GAAP. Rather, the opinion states whether the auditor is aware of any material modifications that are needed.

Report of Independent Auditors

Stockholders and Board of Directors:

We have reviewed the balance sheet of XYZ Corporation as of December 31, 1994 and 1993, and the related statements of income, stockholders' equity, and cash flows in accordance with standards established by the American Institute of Certified Public Accountants.

A review consists principally of inquiries of company personnel and analytical procedures applied to financial data. It is substantially less in scope than an examination in accordance with generally accepted auditing standards, the objective of which is the expression of an opinion regarding the financial statements taken as a whole. Accordingly, we do not express such an opinion.

Based on our review, we are not aware of any material modifications that should be made to the accompanying financial statements in order for them to be in conformity with generally accepted accounting principles.

[Date] _____ [Signature] _____

Chapter 3

Debits and Credits Primer

Few have heard of Fra Luca Pacioli, the inventor of double-entry
bookkeeping; but he has probably had more influence on
human life than has Dante or Michelangelo.

— Herbert J. Muller[1]

"I don't want to be an accountant." This is the refrain of most business
owners when trying to choose an accounting software package, read
financial statements, or keep financial records. While there is certainly no
need to learn to write journal entries or pore over FASB pronouncements,
a basic understanding of financial accounting can help you wade through
the bombardment of financial information you get from internal and
external sources.

Admittedly, accounting is not the most fascinating subject to study. However, accounting principles assume that readers of financial statements
are knowledgeable, and provide little guidance for the unsophisticated
user. Therefore, a basic knowledge of accounting is needed to properly
interpret statements. The ability to interpret financial statements is a skill
with a wide range of applications, from analyzing internal statements to
gleaning competitive information from the statements of rivals, to reading annual reports for personal investing.

More importantly, since many companies devote a disproportionate amount
of financial management resources to GAAP accounting, knowledge of
this field will help you sort out unneeded activity. And when terms and statistics, such as gross margin, book value, and various ratios, are bandied

about by accountants and investors, you will understand how relevant each measure actually is.

If the bad news about accounting is that it is, indeed, boring, the good news is that the basics are nearly all you really need to know. Once you have learned the underpinnings, the rest of accounting is mostly just clarification, interpretation, and application of these rules. In addition, most smaller businesses deal with only a small variety of transactions, so most transactions are repetitive and many accounting rules are not applicable.

The nuts and bolts of accounting are covered in this one basic chapter, which explains debits and credits, types of financial statements, and the underlying principles of financial accounting. Dry as accounting may be, learning basic accounting principles is worth the effort. If you would like more detailed information, you can take an introductory accounting course or read a basic accounting book, such as The Oasis Press' *Business Owner's Guide to Accounting and Bookkeeping*. For information on how to order this and other books, see the Related Resources pages at the back of this book.

Financial Statements

Financial accounting is simply the recording of transactions and events that can be objectively measured in monetary terms. Transactions of a nonfinancial nature and events with an unmeasurable future impact are not recorded.

Accounting results are generally summarized in a few standard formats — the balance sheet, the income statement, and the statement of cash flows. Statements may include footnotes and a management discussion to clarify or add to the information presented. Samples of these statements are included at the end of this chapter.

The Balance Sheet

The balance sheet presents the financial position of a company at a single point in time. Since the balance sheet is a snapshot as of the end of the accounting period, it may or may not be representative of the entire period. A change in the timing of events immediately before or after the end of the period, such as a large loan payment, the sale of securities, or collecting a major account receivable, can dramatically alter a company's balance sheet.

Numbers on the balance sheet are listed in two columns. By convention, the assets of a company are presented first. Depending on the presentation format, this will be either on the left side of the page, with liabilities listed on the right; at the top of the page, with liabilities listed afterward; or on the first page of a two-page layout. Assets are defined as resources of the business, items that provide future economic benefit. These include cash; accounts receivable; inventory; and property, plant, and equipment. An expense is an expired resource.

Listed after the assets are the liabilities and owner's equity. Where assets are the available resources of a company, liabilities and owner's equity are the sources of assets, such as earnings, equity invested, borrowing, and payables. Liabilities are the future obligations of the company, such as accounts payable, taxes due, and debt. Owner's equity includes the capital contributed by the company's owners, plus the cumulative earnings, less any dividends paid.

Typically, assets and liabilities are listed from the most liquid to the least. They are further grouped as:

- Current — assets expected to be converted to cash, and liabilities due, within one year; and

- Noncurrent — assets expected to be in service, and liabilities due, beyond one year.

While the balance sheet is a snapshot of a company, the income statement presents the performance of a company over a distinct period of time. Net income or loss, which is shown on an income statement, equals the net change in assets versus liabilities during a period, or the increase or decrease in a company's value.

The Income Statement

A convention underlying financial statements is that a one-year period is used to measure performance. The twelve months chosen by a company for its fiscal year do not have to conform to the calendar year. Car companies, for example, set their fiscal calendar so that year-end coincides with the end of a model year. Retailers typically choose a January 31 year-end, which enables their peak sales season to be captured in one period and is probably more convenient for taking year-end inventories. Many companies simply start their fiscal year with the date they were founded. In addition to annual statements, most companies also prepare interim monthly or quarterly reports to provide more timely information.

By convention, the income statement — also called a profit and loss statement or P&L — starts with revenues or income, then lists expenses. Companies that produce or sell products, list the cost of sales as the first expense category, including the purchase of goods and any manufacturing expenses. Revenue, less the cost of sales, equals gross margin, which is often shown as a subtotal on the income statement. Refer to the sample income statement included in the financial statements at the end of this chapter for an illustration of this calculation.

Operating expenses related to sales, marketing, research, development, and administration follow. A subtotal at this point is called operating income or earnings before interest and taxes (EBIT).

Interest, taxes, and any other items that are ongoing, but not part of the main operations of a company, are listed next. Although part of continuing operations, these are often labeled as nonoperating income and expenses. For most companies, these are the last categories. In the unusual circumstance that a company experiences a gain or loss by discontinuing an operation, having a one-time or extraordinary item, or changing an accounting principle, that results in a paper gain or loss, these events appear in that order, separate from the other items on the statement. Net income is the total of the expenses and revenues.

Public companies must also publish earnings per share (EPS). This calculation can get complex, particularly when a company has issued convertible securities, such as options and warrants; however, EPS is basically calculated by dividing net income by the number of shares of common stock outstanding. If a company pays dividends, these are shown last and not included in calculating net income.

The Statement of Cash Flows

The third basic financial report is the statement of cash flows, which provides a fuller picture of a company's sources and uses of cash and equivalents. In recognition of the importance of cash to companies, this report has evolved from the statement of sources and the uses of funds report — which reported on either a cash or working capital basis.

Many activities of a company generate or use cash without affecting net income. Examples include raising debt financing, issuing new stock, or acquiring fixed assets. Since it is cash, not net income, that is critical to a company's survival, and investors need to know the ability of a company to finance operations, additional information beyond the income statement is needed. The statement of cash flows attempts to meet that need by reconciling between net income, recorded on an accrual basis, and actual cash flow.

Required Reporting

The Securities and Exchange Commission (SEC) requires public companies to publish annual financial statements that include these three reports. The statements must be audited by certified public accountants. Public companies must also file quarterly, unaudited statements. These are familiar to anyone who owns common stocks and receives annual and quarterly reports.

Private companies are not subject to the SEC requirements, but often choose to adhere to the practice of preparing annual and interim statements. Outside lenders and investors may require this practice as well. Unlike public companies, privately held businesses may be able to save on cost and effort by opting for less formal reporting formats. Rather than an audit, they may elect to have their CPAs do a review, which is less extensive, as discussed in Chapter 2.

Double-Entry Accounting

Did you ever look at balance sheets and wonder why the assets and liabilities always came out exactly equal? Did you wonder what amount had been plugged to force everything to balance? Of course, there are no plug numbers. What is really responsible is the simple elegance of double-entry bookkeeping.

Basically, every transaction that changes a company's assets, obligations, or equity has a simultaneous and equal impact on another account, or accounts. An increase in cash has to come from somewhere, just as a payable to a vendor must arise from the receipt of some goods or services.

Double-entry bookkeeping is the process of determining what the two or more accounts affected were when a transaction has occurred, and the process of recording the results.

A Simple Example

Suppose your cash on hand increases from $100 to $200. You will make an entry to increase the balance on your records by $100. However, you cannot stop there; in accounting, nothing is ever an isolated event. The $100 had to come from some source.

One possibility is that another asset was reduced, which might occur if you collected an outstanding customer invoice. Another possibility is that you incurred an increase in obligations or liabilities, as would be the case if you borrowed the $100. If you acquired the $100 through a sale of stock, you would show an increase in owner's equity.

Possibly all or part of the $100 was profit. Perhaps it was interest earned on a savings account or a royalty payment. You would make an entry to your income statement increasing revenue by $100. Your balance sheet is kept balanced because net income is a component of owner's equity.

The increase in cash may be from a combination of changes in more than one account, which may increase the complexity of your bookkeeping entry, but the basic concept is the same. Say the $100 cash came from the sale of equipment that cost you $60. You would still record the $100 increase in cash. Then you would have to show a decrease in an asset — equipment — of $60. The remaining $40 would be recorded as an increase in profit.

All accounting entries work on this basic symmetry. Walk through a few simple transactions and you will quickly see this point. Buy inventory on credit and an asset (inventory) increases as does a liability (accounts payable). Pay the bill, and both cash and accounts payable are reduced. Ship the inventory to a customer as a warranty replacement, and inventory is reduced, as is net income.

Debits and Credits

As mentioned earlier, the balance sheet has two sides, with assets listed on the left and liabilities and owner's equity on the right. The accounts on each side total to the same figure and, through the symmetry of double-entry bookkeeping, stay in balance at all times. See the sample balance sheet at the end of the chapter.

By convention, balances that appear on the left side of the balance sheet are referred to as debits and those on the right as credits. The terms are rather arbitrary and can seem misleading if you expect all debits to be bad and credits good.

Since assets are listed on the left side of the balance sheet, their normal balance is a debit balance. This means that increases to asset accounts are debits and decreases are credits.[2] Similarly, since liabilities and equity are listed on the right side of the balance sheet, the normal balance is a credit balance. So, for liabilities and equity, increases are credits and decreases debits. Since net income is part of equity, revenue is a credit entry and expenses are debits.

A debit to one account must be offset by a credit elsewhere, either a decrease to another asset or an increase in liabilities or owner's equity. In the example above, if the $100 came from a collection from a customer's outstanding invoice, your entry would be a debit of $100 to your cash account and a credit of $100 to accounts receivable, as is illustrated in the samples below. The first example shows what is called a T-account, a common tool that helps in visualizing the bookkeeping process. The second sample shows the entry in a journal entry form, a common way of writing out entries.

Entry Using T-Accounts

Checking Account				Accounts Receivable	
Debit	Credit			Debit	Credit
$100					$100

Entry Using Journal Entry

Account #	Account Name	Entry Description	Debit	Credit
1100	Checking account	To record payment	$100	
1200	Accounts receivable	Received on account		$100

If debits and credits seem hard to keep straight, do not worry. They are simply the accountant's ways of referring to left and right. And even many accounting students only survived their classes by using the rule that "debits are toward the door" — a rule that works in about 50% of classrooms. As long as you understand that double-entry bookkeeping always affects at least two accounts — one as a debit and the other as a credit — you will be able to comprehend your financial statements and the general bookkeeping and accounting that goes into them.

What Gets Recorded?

Now that you have a better understanding of the basic mechanics of bookkeeping and financial statement preparation, the next questions to ask are at what point is a transaction recorded and how is the amount determined? Six broad principles underlie how accounting entries are recorded.

Historical cost. Assets and liabilities are initially recorded at their acquisition cost — as opposed to market value, replacement cost, or other possibilities. In most cases, they will remain valued at historic cost until they are disposed of.

Revenue realization. Revenue is not recognized until performance of services is virtually complete and measurable compensation, cash or receivable, has been received. In most cases, revenue is recognized at the point of sale, when product is shipped, or a service is completed.

Matching. Expenses should be recognized in the same accounting period as the revenues associated with them. Expenses not directly connected with revenues are recognized in the period they occur.

Consistency. The accounting principles used by a company should be consistent over time. Consistency helps ensure that useful period-to-period comparisons can be made.

Full disclosure. Financial statements must include sufficient information for a prudent, knowledgeable reader to make informed judgments. The information can be in the form of the account balances or included in footnotes and parenthetical notations.

Objectivity. The information should be based on fact. Some discretionary judgment is inevitable, but the basis of the judgment should be verifiable by outside parties.

In addition, these principles are modified and may vary according to several accounting conventions:

Materiality. When a particular disclosure is material, it must be reported only if it is likely to affect a decision of a reader. Where this line is drawn varies from company to company and requires a judgment; what may be material to a business decision may not be material to an outsider evaluating a company. During an audit, materiality is a key factor in deciding the scope of testing done by the outside auditor.

Industry practices. Companies in certain industries that have unusual processes or procedures are allowed to make departures from convention. One example is the inventories of meat packers, which, because of the impracticality of tracking the costs of individual pieces back to the cost of the animal, are valued based on market, not historic, prices.

Conservatism. When more than one accounting method is possible, the one least likely to overstate assets or income should be chosen. This rule is meant to be a guide to difficult decisions where more than one accounting treatment is possible. Conservatism does not mean income should be deliberately understated.

The six principles and three accounting conventions described above encompass the methodology your bookkeeper or accountant applies when taking care of your books. Throughout this book, you will discover over and over how these practices can affect your management decisions.

From Principles to Practice

Although knowing the underlying principles of accounting is a good basic step towards understanding your financials, you will need to translate these principles into how they actually are applied in practice. Before applying these principles, a few other general comments are needed. First, you must assume that a company is a going concern. Many valuations only make sense when an enterprise will be in business for the foreseeable future. If assumed otherwise, assets might need to be valued at liquidation prices and concepts such as depreciation, which take a long-term outlook, would be illogical.

Second, financial accounting only deals with transactions that can be clearly measured in monetary terms. Implementation of a quality improvement program, the resignation of a key employee or a change in the economy, are all events that affect a company's fortunes but, because their impact cannot be assessed, they are not recorded.

Occasionally, events such as the filing of a major lawsuit or loss of a significant contract arise that could significantly have an impact on a company's value, but the outcome is not yet known or the effect is unclear. Though these are not accounting events, they are not ignored. Rather, these types of events are disclosed in footnotes to the financial statements so that, even if the events cannot be quantified, readers have sufficient facts to make informed evaluations.

Another general rule is that a transaction must be essentially complete, or reasonably assured of completion, before being recorded. For most routine transactions, some exchange of money, goods, or services must take place before accounting recognizes an event. A customer placing an order is not recorded as a sale but shipment of the goods is; hiring an employee does not create an expense, but any actual time that employee works does.

Finally, as discussed earlier, GAAP accounting is accrual based. Cash or other assets do not have to change hands for a transaction to be complete. Conversely, a transaction is not necessarily complete just because cash has been received or paid. Revenue, for example, is generally recognized when goods or services have been delivered, which may or may not be when cash is received. Accrual entries are also needed to properly match expenses to the revenues with which they are identified.

Individuals and professionals, such as lawyers, who don't require audited statements can use cash accounting. Cash accounting is simpler and is generally used for tax accounting if inventory is insignificant. But GAAP accounting is accrual based and, as can be seen from the issues discussed below, differs substantially from cash reporting.

The following sections of this chapter discuss how the six principles and the factors that modify them are applied in practice to various parts of your financial statements. Take a look at the sample financial statements at the end of this chapter to familiarize yourself with the different parts.

Assets

Assets, the first component on the balance sheet, are defined as resources having a future value to a business and can present a variety of different issues when you try to quantify them. However, several conventions make asset valuation a reasonably standardized and consistent process.

The next several pages will show you how assets are recognized and valued. You will also understand how reserves, write-downs, depreciation, and amortization are used in this process.

Asset Recognition

Since accounting attempts to match expenses to the period they benefit, when an expenditure occurs, you must decide whether it applies to the current accounting period or has a future value. If the expenditure applies to the current accounting period, it is expensed — deducted from revenues — reducing income in the current period. If the expenditure has future benefit, though, it is capitalized — recorded as an asset — and expensed in future periods as it is consumed. In short, an asset is basically something that carries a future economic value.

Compare the following transactions to see how future economic value is determined:

- Payment of monthly rent is normally expensed. If it is being prepaid, however, it is recorded as an asset and then expensed in the month it applies to.

- Merchandise bought for resale is added to inventory and expensed when sold.

- Machinery is capitalized and, through depreciation, expensed over its useful life.

- Most wages are expensed in the same period they are earned. However, any labor that went into producing inventory would also be added to the value of inventory and expensed when the goods are sold.

As with any transaction, the value of an asset must be quantifiable in monetary terms and its acquisition essentially complete. Assets can be intangible, such as patents and trademarks. However, GAAP requires that expenditures for R&D and advertising, whose future benefit is hard to objectively determine, be expensed.

Asset Valuation

When an asset is purchased, it is valued at whatever was paid for it — its historic cost. For example, if you buy a new computer from a dealer for $3,000, either with cash or on credit, it is valued for $3,000. Any incidental costs of completing the acquisition or installation of the computer, such as shipping, handling, and sales taxes, are added to the base cost. Measuring value according to cost is objective and logical since an asset's value should be what you are willing to pay for it.

Notice, however, what would happen if a discrepancy arose between the historic cost and how the computer was valued on your books. For the entry to balance, a gain or loss would have to be booked to account for the difference between the cash paid and the value of the computer. But, this is not permitted under GAAP. The simple act of buying something, no matter how cheaply or dearly accomplished, does not, by itself, produce accounting income or losses.

Suppose a week later you buy an identical system from a discount mail order company for $2,500 and record it as an asset. Even though the two computers are identical, one will be valued at $3,000 and the other at $2,500. While this may seem like an anomaly, setting the two values equal is not a better solution. You would have to decide whether the $2,500 machine was a bargain or the other system over-priced before you could set the value.

What if your company is a reseller of computers and you can prove that customers are eager to buy these same machines at $3,500? Can they be valued at $3,500? No matter what you may think they are worth, until they are actually sold, no accounting transaction has occurred, so the computers are still valued at their historic cost.

With a few exceptions, historic cost is adhered to as long as the asset is held. Even though assets fluctuate in value due to obsolescence, scarcity, or inflation, their accounting value is fixed. Fluctuations from historic cost are not a problem for current assets, since they turn over fairly rapidly. However, some assets can remain on a company's books for years with no change in valuation. For example, many companies carry land on their ledgers at prices they paid decades earlier, regardless of the current market value.

Even marketable securities that have appreciated in value must be carried at historic cost, despite the fact their value at any point in time can be objectively determined from the stock tables and they are very liquid. Only when they are sold is a gain realized.

The use of historic cost arises from the desire for objective valuations and for profits to be realized only from completed transactions, not just holding onto assets. Another key reason for using this approach is because it satisfies the conservatism convention. The use of historic costs, rather than measures such as market values, is less likely to overstate asset values or net income.

Reserves and Write-Downs

Conversely, because of conservatism, if the market value of investments or inventory drops below historic cost, GAAP requires that you write down the value of the assets.[3] This rule, recording certain assets at the lower of cost or market, introduces a certain lack of symmetry. But the rule prevents asset values and, therefore, profits from being inflated. If the value of assets that you previously wrote down rise, you write them up, but no higher than their historic cost.

Similarly, you can expect that, over time, the full value of certain assets will not be fully realized. Some receivables may prove uncollectible and inventory may spoil or become obsolete. To account for these potential losses, GAAP requires that you establish reserves, so that the total asset value more closely approximates the expected realizable value.

You can calculate reserves by identifying specific uncollectible accounts or obsolete items. More frequently, you will make an estimate based on past history or other judgment. You may reserve for just a portion of an asset's value and not necessarily have to physically dispose of an asset in order to write off its value.

The reserve calculation is often a sticky issue in preparing financial statements. Inventory and receivables usually account for most of a company's assets, so reserves can create a large hit to net income. In addition, reserves are often required, even when no specific assets may be identified as overvalued.

Depreciation and Amortization

Assets are assumed to have a future value and the accountant's objective is to defer recording any expenses, or expired costs, until the periods when the value is realized. For assets such as buildings and equipment, which are used over a number of years, this is accomplished by calculating depreciation. Depreciation is a method of accounting that allows recognition of part of an asset's cost as an expense during each year of its useful life.

Of the several acceptable methods for calculating depreciation, the simplest is taking an equal amount every year for the asset's useful life, called the straight-line method. You may also use one of the accelerated depreciation methods, which book a higher expense in the earliest years an asset is in place. Theoretically, accelerated depreciation has some appeal. As can be seen with new cars, the greatest drop in value comes in the first year or two of use. Choice of an accelerated method, though, is usually driven by tax considerations, not theory, and the desire that write-offs be taken as soon as possible.

After you choose a depreciation method, the actual entry you make each accounting period simultaneously records an expense and reduces the asset's value with an entry to an account called accumulated depreciation. If your company buys a car for $20,000 and you choose to depreciate it over five years using the straight-line method, the entry each year will be $4,000 for depreciation expense and $4,000 for accumulated depreciation. At the end of five years, even though the car may remain in service, no further depreciation is taken.

Accumulated depreciation is a balance sheet account and the entry serves to reduce the company's assets. However, it does so, not by reducing the recorded value of the car, which remains at the historic cost of $20,000, but by creating what is called a contra account, which serves as an offset. Both the historic cost and the accumulated depreciation appear on the balance sheet — generally listed next to each other. So, together the $20,000 historic cost and the <$4,000> accumulated depreciation add up to a net book value of $16,000.

Amortization is similar to depreciation, but is applied to intangible assets such as patents and goodwill.[4] Unlike depreciation, amortization must be done using the straight-line method and no contra account is used. Rather, the asset account is reduced directly.

Inventory

In the previous example of the computer system, what if your company assembled the computer, rather than simply purchased the finished product? In this case, your cost of acquiring the computer would include all the materials used plus any labor. In addition, you would allocate to the cost of the computer a portion of any overhead expenses used in the assembly process.

Valuing inventory, whether for GAAP reporting, internal cost accounting, or taxes is one of the most complex accounting topics. Chapter 9 is devoted to this subject. In general, GAAP reporting is mostly concerned with the valuing of inventory in total, rather than the unit cost of each item. In addition, GAAP requires that the entire cost of manufacturing be allocated to the inventory produced in a period and the expense recognized in the period the items are actually sold. This treatment is consistent with the matching principle.

Liabilities

Liabilities, another component of the balance sheet, are the future obligations of a company. Refer to the sample balance sheet at the end of this chapter. Unlike assets, which are valued at historic cost, the values of liabilities are based on the future payout expected. In addition, where gains on assets must be realized to be booked, liabilities can be recorded when expectations change and the amount of change can be reasonably measured.

This method of accounting for liabilities satisfies both the matching principle, ensuring expenses are recorded when incurred rather than paid, and, notably, the conservatism convention. The aggressive approach to booking liabilities, particularly relative to assets that are carried at historic cost or below, once again serves to prevent income from being overstated. More importantly, this helps protect investors from being blindsided by unreported or unexpected corporate obligations.

Estimating liabilities is not always a straightforward process. If, in the computer example, you bought the first computer on 30 days credit, you would clearly have a liability, a trade payable, for $3,000. The transaction is complete at the time you receive the computer and the price and payment due date are clear.

Note that the computer has to be received before a liability is recorded. Though placing an order to buy the system may obligate a company to accept the computer, the transaction is not complete. Neither the buyer nor the seller has transferred any money or goods.[5] However, in the event that a future obligation that is not recorded as a liability is considered material, it must be disclosed in a footnote.

A tricky and controversial issue is raised if the computer is leased rather than purchased. In general, rental agreements, whether for office space or equipment, are also considered unexecuted contracts and no obligation is recognized until payment is due. However, many leases are more akin to installment purchases and the lease is essentially a financing vehicle. In these cases, GAAP accounting requires that the lease be treated as if two separate transactions were entered into: the borrowing of money — which creates a liability — and then using the proceeds to buy an asset. GAAP uses a complicated, four-point test for distinguishing between rentals and capital leases.[6]

If your company sells the computer, again, no liability is booked when a customer places an order. However, if the customer puts down a deposit, a transaction has occurred. Because delivery has not been completed, the cash received cannot be treated as revenue. Instead, the entire customer advance is treated as a liability, recognizing that you are now obligated to complete the transaction or return the money. Other types of prepayments made to you, such as for theater subscriptions, annual service contracts, and advance rent paid on property, are also liabilities. As services are actually delivered, the liability is reduced and revenue is recognized.

Selling the computer may create obligations to perform warranty work or accept returns. There is no way of telling if a particular machine will ever fail or exactly how much a repair may cost. However, if a reasonable estimate — normally based on past history — can be made of what total future expenses will be, you must record it. Usually this is computed as a percentage of sales. An entry is made to both warranty expense and a liability account for warranty work payable. As the work is actually performed, the liability account is reduced. This accounting helps match the warranty expense to the sale that gave rise to it and fully discloses an expected, if undetermined, future expenditure.

What if a company is being sued, is threatened with a product recall, or has signed loan guarantees of another entity? These events also are potential future obligations, but whether they ever need to be paid is uncertain, contingent on future events. In general, these are not recorded as liabilities unless the future expense is deemed probable — which is not defined in GAAP, but in practice is likely close to 90%[7] — and the amount can be fairly estimated. If the potential obligation is material, a footnote disclosure may still be required.

Equity

The final component of the balance sheet is owner's equity. Equity is the sum of contributions made by the owners of a company, plus cumulative earnings, less any dividends that have been declared. Owner's equity equals the difference between a company's assets and liabilities.

As such, net equity is also referred to as a company's net worth or book value. See the balance sheet example in the sample financial statements at the end of this chapter.

When new shares of stock are sold, equity increases. By convention, the actual entry is usually split into two pieces. The par value of the shares issued — the stated value of the stock — is booked to an account for either common or preferred stock. The par value is a minimal amount, such as $0.01, and has no relation to the market value of the shares. Any excess, which is usually the bulk of the proceeds, is recorded in another equity account such as paid in capital, or reflecting the amount of capital paid in excess of the par value. This split is done even though the concept of par value has become nearly meaningless.

As earnings are accumulated, these become part of retained earnings. Mechanically, entries are not normally made directly to the retained earnings account. Instead, they flow through the income statement. At year-end, when income statement accounts are reset to zero to start the new year, the difference between the revenue and expense accounts, which is net income, is closed out to the retained earnings account.

Earnings are often redistributed to owners through dividends. Cash dividends are not considered an expense, since they do not help generate revenue. Rather, dividends are a distribution of earnings and are recorded as a reduction of retained earnings.

A company sometimes chooses to issue stock dividends or declare stock splits. Though the number of shares outstanding increases, no cash is actually paid out and total equity is unchanged. However, accounting rules may require some shuffling between equity accounts.

Similarly, a company may buy back some of its own stock with the intent to retire it or redistribute it, perhaps as part of an employee stock purchase plan. Without going through the mechanics, these entries also are not considered expenses and, other than the cash actually paid, only involve transfers between equity accounts.

Revenue and Expenses

So far, the discussion has centered on the balance sheet accounts, which provide the snapshot view of a company's financial assets, obligations, and capital. As mentioned earlier, the income statement summarizes the flow of activity during a fiscal period and shows revenue and expenses.

As was seen above, decisions about entries to balance sheet accounts are inextricably linked to entries having an impact on the income statement. Most of the remaining issues in recognizing revenue and expenses have to do with questions of timing. At what point is a sale complete and what period's sales do expenses support?

Revenue

Basically, for revenue to be realized, delivery of goods or services has to be substantially complete and some measurable compensation received. For most transactions, this comes at the point of sale when:

- Product is shipped.
- Service is complete.
- Sale of a security is executed.

Simply having an order in hand is not sufficient. In addition, if a customer is entitled and is likely to return a product, such as when goods are sold on consignment, the sale should not be recognized.

One exception is when a company works on a long-term venture, such as a construction project, spanning several accounting periods. If progress and total costs for the project can be reasonably determined, a company can recognize revenue and expenses on a percentage of completion basis.

These calculations are independent of when cash is actually received. For example, a 25% upfront payment is not counted as revenue unless a proportionate amount of the total project expense has been incurred. In addition, if the last 20% of the project takes 80% of the cost, that portion of the project is also allocated 80% of the revenue.

Expenses

Expenditures — any purchase or spending — generally are classified as either:

- Period expenses, recognized in the period they are incurred; or
- Costs with a future benefit, or assets.

When buying a physical item, such as a computer, or something with a defined useful life, such as an insurance policy, this distinction is fairly straightforward.

Expenditures that go toward intangibles can be harder to classify. Consider sales and marketing expenditures, including advertising. A strong argument can be made that these carry a significant future benefit. However, because of the difficulty in sorting out the present and future benefits and matching specific efforts to product sold, GAAP requires you to expense them in the period they are incurred.

General and administrative expenses are also period expenses, since they cannot be closely associated with product sold. But how about research and development expense? Unsuccessful R&D has little future value, but R&D that results in significant new products and patents enhances a company's value. Because of the uncertainty of the future value, these, too, are period expenses. However, as discussed earlier in the section about amortization, purchased patents are capitalized — treated as assets.

On the other hand, 100% of manufacturing expenses are added to the value of inventory and are only expensed when product is sold. Labor on projects started in one year, but not completed until the next, is also not expensed until the revenue is realized. In addition, expenditures made in constructing fixed assets, such as making leasehold improvements or building test equipment, are capitalized.

When relatively small dollar amounts are involved, the technical accounting rules can give way to expediency. For example, most companies establish dollar limits for capitalizing tangible assets. Rather than track every desk, phone, and chair that is bought, a company will decide to expense items costing less than $500 — or $250 or $1,000. Also, companies receive many invoices, such as utility bills, that span more than one accounting period. Instead of breaking them down by period, the entire amount is usually expensed in the current period. The amounts involved are not usually material and, because a bill is received every month, any discrepancies balance out over time.

Special Issues

So far, the discussion has covered how financial accounting principles are applied to everyday business transactions. However, not all business transactions will fit into a cookie cutter mold. Two such issues — errors and consolidations — are discussed below.

Errors

Errors that are not found until after a period has been closed are bound to occur in preparing financial statements. An invoice may be overlooked, the bad debt reserve may turn out to be too low, damages might be assessed on an old lawsuit that had not been accrued for, or some figures may simply have been added up wrong. Should you go back and correct financial statements from prior periods or take your lumps in the current period?

In general, GAAP calls for recording errors in the period they are found. Companies rarely restate any prior years' statements. Once again, if the amounts related to prior periods are considered material, they are disclosed in the footnotes.

Many companies, large and small, operate several separate legal organizations under common ownership and control. When one company owns more than 50% of another, the parent company will generally prepare a consolidated set of financial statements.

Consolidated Statements

Separate financial statements of each subsidiary are still important, but the consolidated statement is needed to properly present the performance of the entire entity.

In general, a consolidated statement is simply the sum of the separate statements. However, the impact of any transactions between the commonly owned companies must be eliminated.

For example, if one subsidiary sells to another, it records the sale on its books. From the corporate viewpoint, though, the item only transferred from one pocket to another and no profit was really created. Therefore, the intercompany sale gets offset as part of the consolidation process, so only sales to independent entities are included in the consolidated sales number.

Similar adjustments are made for any intercompany receivables, payables, and profit.

Even where a parent company owns less than 100%, a subsidiary's results are fully consolidated. However, the portion of profit and net worth belonging to minority owners, allocated as a percentage of stock they hold, is listed separately.

More Art than Science

More advanced accounting deals with how to handle the complications — seemingly endless — that can arise in business transactions. The theory, though, remains fairly consistent throughout. Understanding the basic principles of accounting presented here not only covers most transactions seen in a smaller business, but provides the essence for understanding even advanced topics.

Double-entry bookkeeping has a certain elegance and GAAP standards help ensure consistency across companies. Nonetheless, accounting remains more art than science.

While this chapter has discussed the theories and practices your accountant follows, the next chapter deals with the basic recording of the day-to-day information about your business.

Endnotes

1. Herbert J. Muller in "The Uses of the Past." Quoted in *Money Talks,* p. 43.

2. It is possible for an asset to have a negative, or credit balance. One example is if a company uses float in its bank account to write checks for more than what has been deposited. Rather than being printed on the right side of the balance sheet, the account remains listed on the left, but with a negative balance.

3. This calculation can be done in aggregate, not item by item. For example, if a few marketable securities drop in value but the entire portfolio's value rises, no entry is made.

4. These intangibles only arise though external purchases. Goodwill is the simple difference between what is paid for assets and their market value and comes about when one company buys another for a price greater than the value of its assets. Virtually all internal expenditures, such as R&D, that go toward developing intangibles must be expensed in the period they are incurred. Note how this treatment is both objective and conservative.

5. In nonprofit accounting, where staying within budget constraints may be critical, contractual obligations are often tracked using encumbrance accounting.

6. Though the rules, enacted in 1976, may seem complex, they ended a period in which companies regularly used leases to keep financing "off the balance sheet." They were such an accounting dilemma that 8 of the first 30 FASB Statements dealt with leases.

7. Davidson, Sidney, Clyde P. Stickney, and Roman L. Weil. *Intermediate Accounting.* Hinsdale, Illinois: The Dryden Press, Hinsdale, Illinois, 1980. p. 15-4.

Financial Statements

Financial Statements – Sample Balance Sheet

Balance Sheet

XYZ Corporation

Year-End – December 31

Assets	1994	1993
Current Assets		
Cash and equivalents	$ 6,908,026	$ 8,756,427
Investment in marketable securities	2,525,309	—
Receivables	4,992,962	4,586,095
Inventories	8,602,173	7,583,079
Prepaid expenses	901,968	634,380
Total Current Assets	23,930,438	21,559,981
Property, Plant & Equipment		
Leased land & building	7,153,896	4,367,591
Leasehold improvements	3,105,954	3,098,496
Machinery & equipment	10,093,714	9,402,344
Construction in progress	83,698	110,453
	20,437,262	16,978,884
Less: Accumulated depreciation	<11,869,714>	<10,614,599>
	8,567,548	6,364,285
Deferred Charges		
Income taxes	861,997	919,378
Other	189,929	21,152
	1,051,926	940,530
Other Assets	302,770	323,800
Total Assets	33,852,682	29,188,596

Financial Statements – Sample Balance Sheet (continued)

	Year-End – December 31	
Liabilities & Equity	**1994**	**1993**
Current Liabilities		
Accounts payable	$ 1,007,034	$ 938,972
Accrued wages & benefits	1,181,373	1,016,614
Accrued taxes	542,311	821,149
Accrued dealer incentive	1,050,000	760,422
Accrued warranty expense	485,170	444,790
Other accrued expenses	763,891	609,488
Current portion of long-term debt	666,118	843,098
Total Current Liabilities	5,695,897	5,434,533
Capital Lease Obligation	4,743,801	2,499,200
Long-term Debt, Net of Current Portion	630,000	945,000
Stockholders' Equity		
Common stock	13,553,890	13,553,890
Additional paid-in capital	1,604,184	1,604,184
Retained earnings	13,048,115	10,595,039
Less: Treasury stock	<5,423,105>	<5,443,250>
	22,783,084	20,309,863
Total Liabilities & Equity	33,852,782	29,188,596

Financial Statements – Sample Income Statement

Income Statement

XYZ Corporation

Year-End – December 31

	1994	**1993**
Net sales	$45,812,436	$42,156,980
Cost of sales	28,712,589	27,565,874
Gross margin	17,099,847	14,591,106
Other operating expenses		
Sales & marketing	5,897,421	5,401,723
Research & development	684,597	542,136
General & administrative	6,452,141	6,021,458
Allowance for doubtful accounts	84,000	66,000
	13,118,159	12,031,317
Other income (expenses)		
Interest	<175,842>	<178,650>
Gain on disposal of assets	46,054	25,401
Loss on discontinued operations	—	<50,000>
	<129,788>	<203,249>
Income Before Taxes	3,851,900	2,356,540
Income taxes	1,395,624	978,524
Net Income	2,456,276	1,378,016
Earnings per share	$ 1.13	$ 0.65

Financial Statements – Sample Statement of Cash Flows

Statement of Cash Flows

XYZ Corporation

	Year-End – December 31
	1994
Operating Activities	
Net income	$ 2,456,276
Adjustments to reconcile net income to net cash provided by operating activities:	
Depreciation & amortization	1,697,966
Deferred income taxes	57,381
Provision for doubtful accounts	84,000
Gain on disposal of assets	<46,054>
Changes in operating assets & liabilities.	
Receivables	<406,867>
Inventories	<1,019,094>
Prepaid expenses and other assets	<465,163>
Accounts payable	68,062
Accrued expenses & other payables	193,302
Net cash provided (used) by operating activities	2,619,809
Investing Activities	
Property & equipment purchases	<1,044,904>
Proceeds from sale of assets	39,729
Investment in marketable securities	<2,429,351>
Net cash provided (used) in investing activities	<3,434,526>
Financing Activities	
Principal payments on capital leases	<823,684>
Principal payments on long-term debt	<210,000>
Net cash provided (used) in financing activities	<1,033,684>
Increase (Decrease) in Cash & Equivalents	$<1,848,401>
Cash & equivalents at beginning of year	8,756,427
Cash & equivalents at end of year	$ 6,908,026

Financial Statements – Sample Notes

Notes to Financial Statements

XYZ Corporation

December 31, 1994

1. Significant Accounting Policies

Recognition of Revenue: Revenue is recognized at the time a customer order is shipped.

Cash Equivalents: The Company considers all highly liquid investments with a maturity of three months or less when purchased to be cash equivalents.

Investment in Marketable Securities: The investment in marketable securities is recorded at cost, which approximates fair market value.

Inventories: Inventories are stated at the lower of cost or market using the first in, first out (FIFO) method.

Property, Plant, & Equipment: Property, Plant, & Equipment are stated at cost. Depreciation and amortization are computed using the straight-line method over the estimated useful lives of the assets. Lease amortization is included in depreciation expense.

Federal Income Taxes: The Company provides for deferred income taxes applicable to timing differences in the recognition of certain items of income and expense for tax and financial statement purposes.

2. Inventories

Inventories at December 31, 1994 consisted of the following:

Finished goods	$4,012,570
Work in process	1,245,855
Raw materials	3,343,748

3. Debt Arrangements

Long-term debt consists of a note from First State Bank. The note bears interest at a rate of 90% of prime rate which resulted in a rate of 6.30% at December 31, 1994. All property, plant, and equipment are pledged as collateral under the terms of the loan agreement.

4. Leases

The Company has a capital lease for land and building from Realty Associates. The lease expires June 30, 2002, and the company has an option to purchase the property at fair market value as determined by appraisal or renew the lease for an additional ten year period.

Financial Statements – Sample Notes (continued)

Future minimum lease payments under the capital lease and noncancelable operating leases consisted of the following at December 31, 1994:

	Capital Lease	Operating Leases
1995	$1,000,000	$117,000
1996	1,000,000	41,000
1997	1,000,000	6,400
1998	1,000,000	
Thereafter	4,657,700	
Total	$8,657,700	$164,000
Amounts representing interest	3,264,224	

5. Related Party Transactions

The Company has a management consulting service agreement with ABC Associates, a firm owned by a certain stockholder of the Company. Payments to ABC of $65,000 and $50,000 were made in 1994 and 1993 respectively.

6. Income Taxes

Income tax expense differed from that computed on income before taxes at the current statutory federal income rate as follows:

	1994	1993
Statutory federal income taxes	$1,130,695	$819,323
State income taxes	231,114	152,935
Nondeductible business expenses	42,455	11,687
Other	<8,640>	<5,421>
	$1,395,624	$978,524

Financial Statements – Sample Notes (continued)

Components of income tax expense are as follows:

	1994	1993
Current		
Federal	$1,185,262	$794,258
State	236,989	157,541
	1,422,251	951,799
Deferred		
Capital lease	9,658	8,740
Accelerated depreciation	<45,781>	<69,655>
Vacation & bonus pay	<21,779>	<18,253>
Other	2,605	11,053
	<55,297>	<68,115>
Total (current & deferred)	1,366,954	883,684

The Company made income tax payments of $1,452,247 and $901,865 in 1994 and 1993 respectively.

7. Export Sales

Export sales were approximately 15% and 14% of the Company's gross sales for 1994 and 1993 respectively.

Chapter 4

How Day-to-Day Entries Get Made

The higher mind has no need to concern itself with the meticulous regimentation of figures.

— Winston Churchill[1]

You may think that most accounting is done at the end of a period when your accountant sits down to record adjustments, allocations, and accruals needed to prepare financial statements. However, most accounting data is gathered in a daily stream of routine, repetitive transactions.

Every time you pay a bill, write an invoice, or issue payroll checks, you generate an accounting transaction. The quality and integrity of information in your accounting system is derived from day-to-day processing.

An accounting system, whether manual or automated, should mirror the natural flow of activity in a business. For example, a customer order moves from a salesperson to fulfillment, invoicing, collections, and customer service. At each step, transactions are generated. These flow through the accounting system, allowing each department to have current information about the order while simultaneously updating financial records.

At the end of an accounting period, the routine does get interrupted so that financial statements can be produced. Cutoffs are observed, accrual entries are made, and inventories may be taken to ensure that revenues and expenses are booked to the proper period. But, just as the work of the company doesn't stop, the day-to-day routine of the accounting system quickly resumes. This chapter discusses how the daily information from your business is collected and summarized. Topics discussed include:

- General and subsidiary ledgers;

- Month-end closing cycles and procedures; and

- Year-end closing procedures, including audits.

A critical, but often missed, first step to having numbers to manage by, is making sure the right information is collected. By choosing the right chart of accounts, you can develop a versatile account structure that provides you with the right information. After you have determined the kinds of information you need, you will then want to establish when you should receive it.

In addition to supplementing the knowledge you gained about financial accounting in the previous chapters, this chapter will show you how to overcome the roadblocks to getting accurate and timely inputs.

The General Ledger

The heart of the accounting system is the general ledger (G/L), as illustrated by the flowchart below. A ledger is simply a group of accounts listed in an organized fashion. The accounts that make up the G/L, collectively referred to as the chart of accounts, are used to produce the financial statements of a business.

Accounting System Workflow

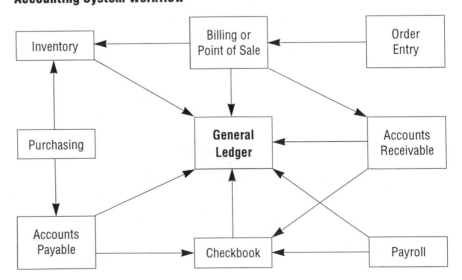

The G/L is the highest summary level of financial information. Detail supporting the numbers is supplied and maintained by subsidiary ledgers or records. For example:

- The actual detail on unpaid customer invoices is tracked by an accounts receivable (A/R) system. Transactions summarizing A/R activity are posted to the G/L. If you compare your aging accounts receivable — unpaid accounts classified into 30-, 60-, 90-, and 120-day periods — to the G/L, the total of outstanding invoices should match the balance of the receivables account on the G/L.

- All checks are recorded in a register. During the month, the activity is summarized and posted to the G/L. A bank reconciliation ensures that the cash balance on the G/L is accurate.

- Purchases and shipments of inventory are posted to the G/L through billing and purchasing transactions. Either through a perpetual inventory tracking system or periodic physical counts, the value of stock on hand is compared to the G/L total.

Except for very small companies that operate entirely out of a checkbook, there are usually distinct activities, even departments, for billing, payables, payroll, and inventory control. These functions have independent routines and reports that can seem autonomous, but they actually form a network of activity. Each takes information from other areas, generates additional transactions, and then shares the results with other departments and the general ledger.

If you have shopped for computerized accounting software, you will recognize how the modules in the software mirror the workings of an accounting department, with modules for payables, billing, G/L, inventory, and payroll.

Not all companies will need each function and many modules can stand alone. But they are designed to work as an integrated unit and are the most effective when they do. Similarly, the ideal way for your company's departments to work is as integrated units.

The first step in setting up an accounting system is defining the chart of accounts. Like a series of buckets into which information is dropped, the chart of accounts defines how your accounting information is categorized, collected, and reported.

Setting Up the General Ledger

If your company is just starting out, a very elementary chart of accounts will probably suffice. As your company grows, the number of accounts can grow with it. The layout of the accounts, though, will become more complex as the number of departments and reporting structure change.

Define the chart of accounts to fit your organization and report information in a meaningful fashion. If information is too aggregated, poorly organized, or misclassified, meaningful analysis can become impossible. Consider the following example:

✓ A jewelry maker operated three distinct businesses under one roof. One business manufactured colorful beads, pins, and earrings. The primary value added for these products was the labor-intensive painting process. The second business had a line of pins and earrings that used purchased metals and stones with only polishing and packaging done in-house. The third business operated an independent subsidiary in a corner of the plant; the subsidiary shared some of the labor, but none of the materials.

Unfortunately, the company had an overly simple chart of accounts: single accounts for sales, purchases, and labor. This structure was adequate for GAAP reporting, which only requires that aggregate sales and expense information be reported. But trying to analyze what each line of business contributed to net income was impossible. The information was so mingled that a breakdown of sales and costs by product line could not be done. When the company fell on hard times, it was impossible to accurately say which, if any, of the product lines was profitable.

Defining your accounts is only part of the battle. Once the structure is in place, data has to be put in the right buckets.

One of the best techniques for coding expenses is to push as much as possible out to the line managers and not leave it all to accounting. The advantage of this tactic is that many expenditures may be foreign to the accounting clerk being asked to make an entry. For example, a supplier invoice may only say that you bought part number XYZ-60. Was this a raw material or a supply? Was it used in manufacturing or in new product development? An accounting clerk can take a guess, but the person ordering the item will know for sure.

While some managers may resist the added clerical task, others will recognize that it serves their own interests. They want to know how to better manage their departments and may be evaluated on performance versus budget. Not only do they want accurate information on how money is being spent, but assurances that expenses for other departments aren't being billed to them by mistake.

Requiring managers to include the accounting code on purchase orders for items and services will greatly assist your accounting department. When the invoice and purchase order are matched, the accounting clerk can see the proper coding. If no purchase order exists, have the appropriate manager approve the invoice and indicate the proper coding at that time. All coding should be reviewed by you and your controller as a routine procedure when reviewing vouchers prepared for payment or when signing checks.

Chart of Accounts

Both manual as well as automated systems require that you set up a chart of accounts first when creating your accounting system. Setting up can be a doubly daunting task if you are installing a computerized system for the first time. But while you should take care in setting up the accounts to design an account structure that suits your company, the process is not difficult.

A sample chart of accounts, located at the end of this chapter, shows a basic chart of accounts. While assigning account numbers is as much art as science, the basic numbering convention illustrated is fairly standard. Assets, liabilities, equity, sales, cost of sales, and operating expenses are grouped and numbered in distinct sequences. For example, assets start with "1," liabilities "2," and so on. Note that this sequence corresponds to the typical order in which the balances are presented on the financial statements. If your company is just starting out, you may be satisfied with a chart of accounts very close to this.

Accounts are often structured in a hierarchy. Usually, only the lowest level of accounts — often called sub, posting, or child accounts — can have transactions posted to them. Their balances are consolidated and summed into various higher level accounts — often termed parent or summary accounts. In the sample chart of accounts, for example, the balance in the raw materials account is aggregated into inventory, then current assets, and total assets.

The length and structure of account numbers varies by company. Many companies find four-digit numbers adequate, while others have numbers more than ten digits long, or may even vary the length from account to account. Some companies segment the number to contain distinct department or company codes. While account numbers are easier to remember when there is some logic to the numbering and digits have consistent definitions from category to category, it is not a requirement.

If you computerize, your software package will probably impose some constraints. The length of the numbers may be defined and certain digits may take on specific meanings — for example, department codes. Don't get locked into an inadequate numbering scheme. Decide on your account structure first, then select a software package that can handle it. Some checkbook accounting packages, such as *Quicken*, have eliminated the need for account numbers, though they still group accounts by asset, liability, expense, and so on.

Most software packages also come with a sample or default chart of accounts. Although using the sample charts provides a shortcut to getting started, resist the urge to use these as is. Take the time to tailor an appropriate account structure, either by starting from scratch or editing one of the samples provided. Be sure to do this before posting any transactions, since it can be difficult to delete or rearrange accounts that have activity posted to them.

Technical Tips

A basic philosophy in setting up a chart of accounts is to define as many accounts as you want as long as they have distinct meaning to you. For instance:

- Should advertising and promotion be separate accounts?
- What about travel and entertainment?
- Is it useful to distinguish sales by product line?
- How about by territory?
- Should personnel, payroll, and accounting be separate departments?

If the differences have meaning to you, or you think they might in the future, then set additional accounts up.

Your accounts should be sufficiently detailed to allow reporting by each significant entity. For example, if several different managers have the responsibility for assembly and packaging, create separate accounts. If you need profit information by product line, as well as territory, create as many detail accounts as you need. However, you do not need to duplicate details that can be obtained via your billing, payroll, and payables systems. For example, sales information by salesperson or customer can usually be pulled from your billing system; they do not have to be separate general ledger accounts. In addition, tax laws may influence your choice of some accounts. For example, tax laws treat meal expenses differently from other travel expenses. Separating these expenses upfront can save work at year-end.

When setting up your accounts, a little imagination can give you a way to capture some extra views of your data. If it is important to know how much inventory is purchased each month, do not book both inventory coming in and inventory going out to the same account. If a manufacturing company, for example, has just a single raw materials account, all issues and receipts get mixed in together during a month. In this case, if you want to know how much was purchased, you cannot determine it quickly. However, you can easily have this information by setting up a structure similar to the following:

Account #	Account Description
1300	Purchases
1301	Offset to purchases
1310	Raw materials

Each purchase is debited to the purchases account; all deductions are charged to the raw materials account. At month-end, the offset account (1301) is credited for the monthly balance in the purchases account and the raw materials account debited. Accounts 1300 and 1301 net to zero, but you know your purchases for the month just by looking at the 1300 account.

You can use a similar scheme to capture expenses for employee benefits. What if you want to know the totals spent for health insurance or FICA, but still be able to bill each department for its share? Rather than divide each bill as it comes in or throw it all into one operating department, set up a department to just capture each individual benefit expense, such as:

Account #	Account Description
7500	FICA
7510	FUTA
7520	Health insurance
7599	Offset to employee benefits

At month-end, if the total in accounts 7500–7520 is $1,000, make an entry for $1,000 in the offset account (a credit) and allocate the expense to your operating departments (a debit). The benefits department now has a net of zero, but each line item is intact, so you can see at a glance just what was spent on health insurance or FICA. The same scheme works for expenses related to occupancy. Accumulate rent, insurance, and utility expenses in their own accounts before doing allocations.

Journal Entries

While most data comes to the general ledger through subsidiary ledgers, some adjustments are posted directly to the G/L with journal entries. These are typically adjustments made at month- or year-end and not routine transactions like those discussed above.

Examples of where journal entries are used include:

- Correcting an error, such as a purchase posted to the wrong expense account;

- Recording monthly depreciation and amortization expense;

- Establishing a bad debt or inventory reserve; or

- Accruals (discussed in the next section).

In addition to preparing journal entries, like those above, your month- and year-end closings include a number of important routines and procedures to ensure that information is captured in the proper periods. You will also want to make sure that you receive financial statements on a timely basis. The next section discusses these period-end procedures.

Closings

Most companies close their books on a regular basis, producing annual and either monthly or quarterly financial statements. Part of the closing process is ensuring that expenses and revenues are booked in the proper period, requiring some modification of the day-to-day processes.

First, proper cutoffs must be established with a strict line between transactions that take place on the 31st and those on the 1st of the month. You have to watch out for transactions processed in one fiscal period that actually relate to another. For example, goods shipped December 31 are considered revenue, but may not be invoiced until January 2. Or, you might pay January's rent during the month of December.

Accruals

To ensure that entries are posted to the correct month, an accountant will book a series of accrual journal entries. An accrual is an entry that records revenue or expense, even though no cash transaction has occurred. The accountant analyzes actual and anticipated transactions and makes any needed adjustments. Some typical accruals include:

- Sales commissions, earned on the current month's revenues, but usually not paid until the following month;
- Liability for payroll taxes and employee benefits that are incurred when wages are earned, but may not be paid right away; or
- Property taxes, service contracts, and insurance that may be billed quarterly or annually, but should be allocated equally to each month's statements.

Usually, you will want to complete one month's payable and receivables processing before starting the next. For some software packages, it is a requirement. This cutoff allows agings to be balanced to the general ledger. Holding the old month open for three to four days is enough time for most bills to arrive.

Bills received after the cutoff date for payables can be accrued on a journal entry. This is best done using reversing entries. If you accrue an expense one month and reverse the entry the next, the reversal creates a negative expense that is exactly offset once the invoice is processed by accounts payable. The result is that while accounts payable processed the transaction routinely in the second month, the expense is recorded in the first.

Another solution for items like utility bills that recur every month for about the same amount is to simply record them the month they come in. It is more important that an electric bill get entered each month than to precisely allocate usage to the proper month.

In booking expenses, timing issues are among the most common sources of errors in smaller company financial statements. One quick method for detecting omissions or overstatements is to compare monthly expenses against the prior month or the year-to-date balances. If two rent payments slip into the same month or no electric bill was booked, it should be readily apparent. This type of side-by-side comparison is also one of the best ways for you to spot unusual expenses, shifts in performance, or changes in accounting. A good practice is to question any significant changes so you understand whether changes are permanent or temporary. In turn, you can also explain them to investors.

Smoothing, Spreading, and Estimating

Many accrual entries are made to spread large expenses evenly over several months, rather than taking an unusually big hit the month a bill arrives. For example, annual expenses, such as legal, audit, insurance, and heating, can often be estimated. But, because of seasonal and other factors, the bills may roll in irregularly.

To smooth their impact, many companies choose to book a flat amount each month. As the actual bills come in, no additional expense is booked. This is accomplished with entries to a balance sheet account, which is debited when a bill is received and credited when the monthly or quarterly expense is booked. Periodically, actual bills should be compared to the estimated annual total and the estimate revised, if needed.

A similar strategy may be used when an unexpected, large bill arrives. Rather than allowing a major hit to be incurred all at once, the expense is often spread over several months. Finally, a lot of numbers must simply be estimated. Accruals should be made regularly to allow for taxes, sales returns, bad debts, and inventory write-downs. You have to make a choice of how aggressive or conservative to be as, usually, a range of reasonable estimates is possible.

Closing Cycle

Whether your company is large or small, closing your books should be completed within five to ten business days from the end of the month or quarter. At year-end, this may take longer due to the added precision that is often desired. At that time a preliminary close within three weeks, with either a final close or start of an audit within four to five weeks, are good targets.

Any precision gained by taking longer than five to ten days at the end of a regular month or quarter usually isn't worth letting the statements get stale. But few companies can close in less than five days. One company that closed on the third day of each month did so by missing many month-end accruals. Not surprisingly, the owner didn't care about the accruals because the statements were considered "garbage anyway." To keep the closing on track, establish a regular closing schedule with departmental deadlines. A typical ten-day closing schedule for a small manufacturing company is shown below.

Typical Monthly or Quarterly Closing Schedule

At the end of the month or quarter, send all shipping documents to billing and send all receiving documents to accounts payable. Close checkbooks and complete all entries affecting cash.

Day 1 – Complete all billing. Run final receivables reports. Run sales reports. Begin processing new period.

Day 3 – Cutoff payables entry. Run final payables reports.

Day 4 – Accrue payroll expense for days unpaid at month-end. Accrue commissions.

Day 5 – Deadline for submission of sales and expense figures from subsidiaries.

Day 7 – Final close. Print all reports. Begin preparing financial analysis such as variance reports and updates of budget to actual.

Day 10 – Deadline for submission of statements and supporting schedules to management committee.

The closing schedule should include procedures for each department. For receivables and payables, all transactions for one month must be entered and desired reports run, before starting the next. Once payments and invoices for the next period are processed, the agings are updated and the "snapshot" from the end of the period cannot be recreated.

For the general ledger, closing one period before beginning to process for the next is not necessary.[2] However, special care must be taken to ensure entries are applied to the correct period.

Day-to-Day Cutoffs

Cutoff and closing issues apply to day-to-day processing as well. In many companies, the most important information provided by the accounting system is not financial statements, but statistics needed to run the company every day — how much of an item is in stock or what a customer's balance is. The need for this information creates its own demands for accuracy and timeliness that cannot be met by an accountant's journal entry.

For systems to work, users need to understand that if they make information demands on a system, they must be prepared to input data on a timely basis. Consider the following example:

✓ At one used car dealership with more than 30 locations, salespeople had the ability to see, on a terminal, the inventory on hand at all the other lots. This included cost information critical for setting resale prices. When a car was added to stock, it usually needed servicing before being sold. The service expenditures were added into the cost of the car. The accounting department promised same day turn-around processing paperwork so that the cost figures on-line would always be up to date.

Problems arose when the service department allowed paperwork to stack up and did not submit it to accounting. A car would be sold for what seemed like an $800 margin and then a $400 repair bill would float into accounting after the sale. Not only was the car priced too low, but the salesperson found out after the fact that his or her commission was halved. Even though the service department was responsible, accounting got the blame.

Sometimes getting cooperation requires a careful explanation of how the pieces fit together. The following example illustrates how the effort of a careful explanation can pay off.

✓ The CFO of the same car dealership told a story about a clerk who made numerous inaccurate entries and failed to understand why these errors were important. Rather than fire the clerk, the CFO sat down one day and asked the clerk to figure out how much new car inventory to order for the next two months for a particular model. First, the employee realized, some sales history was needed to predict future sales — information that came from an accounting report.

The next step was to see how many cars of that model were on hand. At this point, the clerk said, "Hold on. I have to make a few adjustments first." It turned out the prior day's incoming shipment had not been entered yet, and the report was five cars short. The clerk realized that without the updated figures, the company would have overbought by $50,000. Suddenly, the importance of the clerk's job was apparent.

If reports are unreliable or not timely, people stop using them and may start inventing personal systems, as shown in the next story.

✓ At one apparel manufacturer, the production manager stopped using daily computer reports and started keeping manual notebooks to plan each day's production. The reason for this was because the manager planned production at the start of the day at 6:00 A.M., while accounting collected the prior day's production reports at the end of each day and didn't start processing them until they came to work at 7:00 A.M. Updates were only available in mid-morning, too late for the production manager.

The problem was corrected by collecting production reports by 2:00 each afternoon, so data entry could be finished by 5:00 P.M. Because of the earlier cutoff time, reports were on the production manager's desk at the beginning of the day.

People responsible for data entry must also understand the sensitivity of the system to errors. A $400 error may be inconsequential to a financial statement, but a $400 error entering the cost of a used car could result in setting the resale price too low, costing the dealer money. Over time, these errors can add up, particularly if the source of errors isn't found and corrected.

Fiscal Years

Along with daily and monthly cutoffs, a company must choose a fiscal year. Most opt for a calendar year since this is the simplest to think about and the easiest to coordinate with payroll tax filings; however, income taxes can be reported on a fiscal-year basis, making it unnecessary to use a calendar year. Many companies select the anniversary of their founding or time their year-end to match the seasonality of their business. For example, many retailers choose a January 31 year-end to allow completion of the holiday season.

GAAP requires that financial statements be prepared on an annual basis and public companies generally must file quarterly statements. Otherwise, you have some freedom on when, and how often, interim statements are prepared. Whether you close quarterly or monthly depends on your need for information or investors' demands for reports. And at least one company, SKI Inc., which operates several ski mountain resorts, has used weekly closings to stay on top of operations.

Year-End Procedures

Fiscal year-end is sort of a grand finale to the accounting cycle. At this time, the books get their greatest scrutiny and additional steps are taken to ensure their accuracy. The fiscal year-end also places the greatest workload of the year on the accounting department.

Part of the work may be an audit or review by an independent CPA, as discussed in Chapter 2. Companies with outside investors are usually required to submit to an annual audit or review by outside CPAs. Knowing what is involved can help your company prepare and may even lower your audit fees.

An audit is not an adversarial process. Remember, the auditors are hired to provide assurance to you, your management, and investors that the financial statements have been fairly and consistently prepared and can be relied upon. Auditors often provide useful feedback on internal controls and interpretation of the numbers.

The objective of an audit is not 100% accuracy, but to ensure that financial statements are not materially misstated, meaning an auditor can work with a statistical sampling of data. The size of the sample is basically a function of the level of confidence the auditor has in the internal controls of the company and the magnitude of any discrepancies found. Typical items tested include:

- Cash — Ensure company records are reconciled to bank statements.

- Receivables — Request a confirmation of selected account balances shown on the company's aging directly from the customers.

- Inventory and fixed assets — Observe and test counts performed by the company.

- Payables — Review the aging, as well as payments, made several weeks beyond year-end.

- Loans and leases — Request confirmation of balances and terms directly from the lender.

- Capital stock — Match to legal records.

Where documentation is requested from outside parties, the auditors will insist that all correspondence be addressed directly to them to ensure the integrity of the responses. You will be asked to assist in requesting responses and in following up any delinquent replies. You may also be asked for a written representation letter, signed by either you or your top financial manager, covering a wide range of financial and operating issues relevant to forming the audit opinion.

The auditors will also ask any questions needed to comply with full disclosure or to deal with uncertainties and contingencies. These include possible lawsuits or other contingent liabilities, future obligations under contracts and leases, outstanding stock options or warrants, and resolving any possible concerns about the company's viability.

Audits are biased toward detecting possible overstatement of net income and net worth rather than understatement. The reason for this is mainly because financial reporting serves the needs of investors who are more concerned about inflated instead of understated earnings. Another factor that shapes audit procedures is the use of outside parties. Vendors and customers from whom confirming data is sought have an incentive to report information in a manner consistent with their self-interest.

Techniques

For example, confirmation letters are sent for receivables balances, but not payables. Management has little incentive to understate receivables and is more likely to want to overstate them — and therefore show higher sales and assets. However, a customer is almost sure to point out any overstatement of amounts owed on a confirmation. They may keep quiet, though, if invoices are omitted. The confirmation letters, therefore, can detect inflated receivables, but cannot be relied on to catch understatements.

For payables, the primary concern is that a company will understate them. Invoices may be omitted, and the auditor cannot send confirmations on invoices having no record. If payables are overstated, vendors who see an error in their favor cannot be relied upon to report it.

For the same reason, auditors diligently observe inventory and fixed asset counts and confirm bank balances. They do not go searching for assets that may have gone unreported. However, they will seek evidence that no liabilities have been omitted or understated. This task is, perhaps, the most difficult part of the audit and may involve a review of invoices received and checks issued following year-end; letters of inquiry to the company's attorneys; and careful review of contracts, leases, and loan agreements.

Preparation for the audit usually begins a few weeks before the end of the fiscal year. The auditor starts planning the audit procedures and gets updated by management about events during the year. At this time, the auditor may also evaluate internal controls, identify areas of audit exposure, and review any other items that impact the scope of the audit.

Timing

The auditor will also want to get a head start on correspondence needed for the audit, including requests for cutoff bank statements, minutes of board meetings, and letters to the attorneys concerning legal issues.

Generally accepted auditing standards (GAAS) require that auditors observe the taking of physical inventories, which for most companies occurs at year-end. Where internal controls are adequate, inventories can actually be taken on dates other than year-end, which may be desirable if a year-end physical would be costly or require a plant shutdown. Fixed assets may be counted at the same time. To ensure that proper cutoffs are observed, the auditors will likely request copies of shipping and receiving logs immediately prior to and following year-end.

The bulk of the audit work comes after a company has prepared a preliminary closing statement, typically three to six weeks after year-end. Even for small companies, this work will take at least one to two weeks. Depending on how many reconciliations and schedules you can prepare before the beginning of this round of field work, you could reduce the cost and difficulty of the audit. Work that can save you money includes:

- Preparation of lead and supporting schedules — fairly simple spreadsheets that list the income statement and balance sheet totals and trace the balances back to detail accounts;

- Bank reconciliations;

- Agings of accounts payable and receivable that match the balances on the general ledger;

- Listings of fixed assets, and other assets that all tie to the general ledger;

- An orderly summary and pricing out of the physical inventory; and

- Ensuring access to important records, such as payroll registers, journal entries, contracts and leases, and cash disbursement journals.

Once this field work is complete, the auditors will finish and review their work off-site. You may be required to do additional follow up. If this is the case, you may need to provide certain requested documentation, such as confirmations, that has not been received yet. Preparation of some footnote information, such as outstanding lease obligations and stockholder information, may be held off until now. Also, your financial statements must disclose any material events that occur after the close of the year, but before the issuance of financial statements. You will be asked to discuss these, if any.

The auditors will issue draft statements and discuss them with you to ensure their accuracy and resolve any outstanding issues. You may have preferences on how information is presented and how footnotes are worded. Often, some last minute negotiation may occur over the figures themselves, particularly judgment items, such as reserves for bad debts or inventory markdowns.

For public companies, audited statements are usually incorporated into the annual report. Auditors will generally provide bound copies of the audited statements to private companies for distribution.

Management Letters

An audit is supposed to formulate an opinion on a company's financial statements. Frequently, auditors are also requested to write a management letter. In this letter, which has no special format, the auditors discuss weaknesses in the accounting systems and any operating problems noted in the course of their work.

Although you should investigate and respond to the comments contained within the management letter, you are not required to do so. Have the auditors review the management letter directly with you, not the CFO or controller. Because the letter reports on the effectiveness of the financial systems, this type of review provides an internal control on the controller.

Whether you choose to have an audit or review, year-end is a good opportunity to clean up the books. Here are some items you can take care of at year-end. **If No Audit**

- Ensure that bank accounts are reconciled and long-standing reconciling items researched.

- Tie accounts receivable detail to the general ledger and write off or reserve for any questionable items.

- Take a physical inventory and revise standard costs for the new year.

- Count and tag all your fixed assets and update your perpetual listing of these assets.

- Recompute depreciation entries for the new year.

- Research the balances for prepaids, such as insurance or miscellaneous receivables from employee or insurance claims and either write them off or list them on a supporting schedule.

- Reappraise any reserves, such as for bad debts or inventory write-downs.

- Match accounts payable aging to the general ledger total.

- Make sure that miscellaneous liabilities, such as payroll, income and sales taxes, commissions, and contributions to employee benefit plans are in line with actual liabilities. Other accrued liabilities may also need to be recomputed. These include accounting and legal fees, employee vacation time accrued and not taken, warranty and returns reserves, royalties, and any possible surcharges for items such as common area fees or insurance premiums.

- Ensure that balances for principal owed on leases or loans agree with amortization schedules.

More than an accounting exercise, these reconciliations and examinations ensure that amounts owed by or owed to your company are not lost in the shuffle. You will also be confident that when the records show a balance for payables or receivables, it is accurate and backed up by supporting detail. Of course, you don't have to wait for year-end. You can routinely verify this supporting detail exists by asking your controller or accountant for reconciliations and agings.

What Is Ahead

The material discussed in the previous three chapters, including audits and closing the books, relate to financial accounting. As is stressed throughout this book, this is just one aspect of financial management. A clean audit opinion, for example, does not ensure your reporting system is complete or sound.

Having discussed how your external reporting needs are satisfied, the next chapter looks at how financial accounting, used alone, will fail you and your company. Chapter 5 will look at some of the weaknesses in GAAP reporting. Particular discussions will focus on how companies can manipulate financial reporting and why even properly prepared statements can be misleading. Later, Chapter 7 covers why management accounting is needed to supplement the information developed using GAAP.

Endnotes

1. Winston Churchill, quoted in *The Manager's Book of Quotations*, p. 2.

2. Unfortunately, some software packages do impose this artificial constraint. Many companies are unable to produce interim financial statements in the months following year-end because their audit has not been completed and their books are still open for the previous year.

Chart of Accounts – Sample

Account Numbering

Unless your accounting software limits your choices, account numbers can be any length; however, four to six digits are usually sufficient. Extra digits may be desired to track multiple divisions, subsidiaries, or projects. Some industries, like automobile dealers, have a standard chart of accounts. Most companies, though, are free to design their own. Typically, account numbers are grouped as follows:

First Digit	Type of Account
1	Assets
2	Liabilities
3	Equity
4	Revenue
5	Cost of Sales
6	Operating Expenses
7–9	Nonoperating Expenses, Taxes

Computerized systems usually require you to set up a hierarchy in which accounts either can be posted to or contain subtotals summing the accounts below the hierarchy. This is done to format your printed financial statements.

Chart of Accounts

Account Number	Account Description	Type of Account
1000	Current Assets	Summary
1100	Cash	Summary
1150	Cash on hand	Posting
1160	Checking account	Posting
1200	Receivables	Posting
1400	Other current assets	Summary
1420	Deposits	Posting
1450	Prepaid insurance	Posting
1500	Inventory	Summary
1510	Raw materials	Posting
1520	Work in process	Posting
1530	Finished goods	Posting
1600	Noncurrent Assets	Summary
1610	Fixed assets	Summary
1630	Equipment	Posting
1640	Building & improvements	Posting
1650	Office Furniture	Posting
1710	Depreciation	Summary
1730	Accumulated depr. – equipment	Posting
1740	Accumulated depr. – building & improvements	Posting
1750	Accumulated depr. – office furniture	Posting
1800	Land	Posting

Chart of Accounts – Sample (continued)

Account Number	Account Description	Type of Account
2000	Current Liabilities	Summary
2100	Trade payables	Posting
2200	Accrued payroll & benefits	Summary
2210	Wages and commissions payable	Posting
2220	State taxes payable	Posting
2230	Federal taxes payable	Posting
2240	Accrued benefits	Posting
2300	Other current liabilities	Summary
2320	Sales tax payable	Posting
2340	Customer deposits	Posting
2400	Short-term debt	Posting
2600	Noncurrent Liabilities	Summary
2700	Long-term debt	Posting
2800	Other noncurrent liabilities	Posting
3000	Equity	Summary
3100	Common stock	Posting
3200	Capital in excess of par	Posting
3300	Retained earnings	Posting
4000	Revenue	Summary
4100	Product sales	Posting
4200	Service sales	Posting
4300	Discounts & allowances	Posting
5000	Cost of Sales	Summary
5100	Direct labor	Posting
5200	Overhead	Posting
5300	Purchases	Posting
5350	Inventory change	Posting
6000	Operating Expenses	Summary
6100	Sales & marketing	Summary
6110	Salaries, commissions, and benefits	Posting
6130	Supplies	Posting
6150	Travel	Posting
6170	Advertising & promotion	Posting
6300	General and Administrative	Summary
6310	Salaries and benefits	Posting
6330	Supplies	Posting
6360	Professional fees	Posting
6380	Rent & insurance	Posting
7000	Other Income & Expense	Summary
7100	Interest income	Posting
7200	Interest expense	Posting
7500	Other nonoperating	Posting
9000	Taxes	Posting

Chapter 5

Financial Reporting Pitfalls

Accountants are the witch doctors of the modern world.

— J. Harman, English Jurist [1]

Figures are not always facts.

— Aesop [2]

Financial accounting is effective in providing outside investors with relevant, objective information. Boiling down the complex operations of entire companies to a few, simple statements that have a consistent presentation across companies and industries is an impressive feat. At the same time, major shortcomings in GAAP reporting severely limit its usefulness. Some of those shortcomings are:

- GAAP reporting is intended to meet the needs of external decision makers, not internal managers. Though properly structured statements can be useful to you, much of the information is too aggregated or not timely enough to help with business decisions. Management accounting is the accounting discipline that provides detailed information on internal operations. Management accounting is discussed in chapters 7 and 8.

- Financial accounting measures can be accurate, yet inadequate or misleading. Accounting concepts, such as profit, historic cost, and conservatism, are not the same as cash flow, market value, and accuracy. Many changes in a company's financial position or outlook are simply not fully recorded under GAAP. Accounting often fails to capture the true impact of events on a company's value or support current decision making.

- Creative accounting is a reality. Through methods that range from simply aggressive to fraudulent, companies can shape their financial statements. The reader of statements must beware.

Weaknesses in GAAP are not merely academic concerns. Investors must rely heavily on financial statements to make decisions. In addition, even though managers have other decision making tools at their disposal, they often let financial accounting be the tail that wags the dog. Rather than just reporting on a company's performance, the accounting actually influences it.

For example, management compensation tied to accounting measures can provide inappropriate incentives. Trying to "make the numbers" each month or quarter can chew up management time, create artificial deadlines, and cause long-term goals to be compromised. Standard financial analysis, used for decisions on credit and investment, places a lot of emphasis on ratios, earnings, and book value, even though these measures are often flawed. And creative accounting often masks poor management and distorts decisions by investors and creditors.

These faults do not mean GAAP should be replaced. Indeed, the need for objective and consistent financial reporting is clear and GAAP meets this need. Given the complexity of accounting issues and the different needs of internal and external readers, any set of rules are a compromise. However, the rules should not dictate how business owners operate or limit them from developing additional sources of information. The key is for both internal and external users of financial statements to be aware of the limitations of GAAP reporting and put it in proper perspective.

Costing methods, valuation, judgment, and creative accounting are factors that can create both intentional and unintentional distortions of the financial facts. This chapter concentrates on those factors and how they can affect your perception of a business.

Balance Sheet Pitfalls

The ideal balance sheet would reflect the value of your company at a given point in time. Your assets would be valued according to their future earning power and their ability to be converted into cash. In turn, your liabilities would fairly state all your company's future obligations. Unfortunately, the balance sheet does not come close to attaining this goal. Instead, it has a strange mix of historical, current, market, and depreciated values. The totals and ratios that result from these numbers often have little meaning on their own.

To illustrate this amalgamation, examine how the various asset and liability accounts are valued.

- Current assets, such as cash or receivables are valued at their historical cost, which generally coincides with current value.

- Inventory is recorded at the lower of either cost or market value. In addition, there are several acceptable methods for valuing inventory that can yield very disparate figures.

- Equipment, furniture, and fixtures are valued at historical cost, less some fraction for depreciation. The value can vary greatly based on the write-off method chosen. Fully depreciated assets have zero accounting value even though they may remain in service.

- Marketable securities are valued at the lower of cost or market value. Book value will equal market value if the investments have not appreciated.

- Land is valued at historical cost. The bookkeeping entry will usually differ greatly from market value when land is held for many years.

- Intangibles are only recorded if purchased and are ignored if internally generated.

- Liabilities are generally listed at market value. Liabilities may be difficult to value for obligations arising from events that are anticipated, but have not taken place.

Ratios and Book Value

Accounting statements add together all of the figures for the above-listed accounts to arrive at numbers such as total assets and net worth. Given the mix of valuation methods used, the totals by themselves have little meaning. They represent neither what was paid for assets nor what they could be sold for. While the individual accounting methods may be very logical and objective, combining figures, unless properly interpreted, is dangerous.

Even one of the most common tools of financial analysis, ratios, can be inaccurate. Outside analysts, such as lenders, place a high emphasis on ratios to judge a company's performance and make credit decisions. Loan covenants often specify earnings or liquidity ratios a company must meet. In addition, many business magazine articles instruct business owners to pay attention to certain ratios as key indicators of the financial strength of their companies and even suggest certain parameters these ratios should fall within.

While ratios, particularly changes over time, are useful, they also mix valuation methods and, therefore, can yield misleading results. For example, an earnings to book value ratio uses earnings, stated mostly in current values, and book value, which mixes several cost bases. The same is true of return on investment (ROI), return on assets (ROA), and debt-to-equity ratios.

Short-term measures of liquidity — the current ratio or the quick ratio — are more useful to you since all the inputs are valued currently. The current ratio is determined by dividing current assets by current liabilities. The quick ratio, also called the acid test, divides highly liquid assets — such as cash, receivables, and marketable securities — by current liabilities.

Finally, whether discussing ratios or the balance sheet in total, remember that the balance sheet is simply a snapshot at a point in time. Individual elements, particularly cash, can fluctuate greatly from day to day. As was discussed in Chapter 4, the timing of transactions close to the end of an accounting period can greatly impact elements of the balance sheet. Events, such as whether a large receivable is collected or a loan payment is made on December 31 or January 2, can affect the reported condition of a company.

Valuation Pitfalls

In addition to dealing with a mixture of costing methods, when reading a balance sheet, you must also be aware of different valuation assumptions and judgments that go into some of the figures. Even where a balance is objectively valued, an accountant has a choice of accounting methods. In addition, when accounting for future events, such as contingent liabilities or bad debt reserves, either a conservative or aggressive approach can be adopted.

For most current assets and liabilities, there is little problem with valuation. Assets are either cash or quickly convertible to cash, and liabilities will likely be settled at their face value.

Reserves

Reserves present a different problem, especially the establishment of a bad debt reserve. As discussed in Chapter 3, reserves are estimates of anticipated losses that are then recorded as expenses. The bad debt reserve may be based on specific troubled accounts or as a percentage of total receivables based on experience. Although the reserve only reduces the book value of receivables and does not mean collection efforts have been abandoned, business owners often are reluctant to record bad debt expenses. Even though, statistically, some accounts are likely to be uncollectible, particularly those aged beyond 90 days, as long as you are actively pursuing collection and feel the full amount is due, you may be reluctant to record a reserve. Where statements are audited, the amount of the reserve may be determined by negotiation between you and your CPA.

As is covered in more detail in Chapter 9, the largest variable for nonservice companies is usually inventory valuation. For example, because a company can make one of several assumptions about the flow of its purchases and sales, this choice can greatly affect the accounting value given to inventory. For example, the last in, first out (LIFO) method assumes a company sells its newest inventory first, so that the oldest units are still in stock. This inventory is valued at the prices in effect when this type of inventory was first purchased, perhaps five or ten years ago. In contrast, the first in, first out (FIFO) method assumes a company sells the oldest units first, leaving the most recently purchased units in stock, valued at reasonably current prices. In an era of rising prices, a large disparity can exist between LIFO and FIFO values.

As with receivables, reserves are generally established to anticipate the likelihood that some inventory will become obsolete. Again, you may be reluctant to admit that more than a small part of inventory may require a reserve and the final number is largely a judgment call. Usually, external readers will not know the basis of the reserve.

Inventory and investments are subject to a lower of cost or market test, which can be applied on an item-by-item basis or in aggregate. Not only is there a lack of consistency because asset values may be at historic cost, market value, or a combination, but determining market values for inventory is highly subjective. And even though the values of any publicly traded investments are published every day, accounting only recognizes changes in market value when the value drops below cost.

For noncurrent assets, the spread between accounting and economic value can be very wide. This spread is a recognized but not easily reconciled issue. In a 1993 speech, Walter Schuetze, the SEC's chief accountant, said:

Noncurrent Assets

> "The cost of many assets does not represent anything close to the 'probable future economic benefit' to be derived from the asset.

> "For example, the probable future economic benefit of a successful, direct-response advertising campaign may be many multiples of the cost.

> "The future benefit of a discovery of mineral deposits generally bears no relationship whatsoever to the costs of finding the deposits."[3]

One issue creating disparity is that many assets decline in value over time. To account for this, equipment, furniture, and fixtures are carried at historical value, less some fraction for depreciation. While the concept of depreciation is sound, the application can be troublesome. Just as there are several methods of inventory valuation, several different methods of depreciation may be chosen. If your company bought a truck with an expected useful life of five years, there is no trouble deciding that the cost should be spread over the five years of service. But how should the depreciation expense be distributed?

One choice is for you to depreciate an equal amount each year using the straight-line method. While this is the simplest technique, accelerated depreciation would recognize that better service is given early on — and would probably better approximate the actual resale value of the truck. In theory, depreciation could also be calculated based on new appraisals each year or on the basis of mileage.[4]

At the end of five years, the truck may very well still be in service or have a considerable resale value — yet the book value would stand at zero. Once again, there would be no mechanism for writing the value up to market value. Many traditional manufacturing companies have factories full of working machines carried at low or zero book values. Conversely, plants and equipment that are under-utilized may have little economic benefit, yet are carried at historic cost. For this reason, the stock of public companies sometimes sells below book value and may be a sign that write-offs are looming.

Land probably has the largest disparity between book and market value. While no depreciation is taken, neither is any adjustment made for appreciation. As the value of land tends to rise steadily over time, companies that have held property over several decades will seriously understate the value.

Intangible assets rarely have any relation to economic value. Goodwill, for example, does not represent any measurable asset. Goodwill is an accounting concept and arises only when one company purchases the common stock or assets of another and the price paid exceeds the market value of the assets acquired. Goodwill is simply the difference, presumably representing the management talent or market reputation that made paying a premium worthwhile.

A similar accounting treatment is used for patents. If purchased, they are carried for the purchase price. However, the research and development costs of internally generated patents, no matter how valuable, are expensed as they occur.

Liabilities

Unlike assets, which are mostly carried at historic cost, liabilities are generally carried at current values. Most of the difficult issues affecting liabilities are when to account for events that are anticipated but haven't taken place and how to judge the future cost. In other cases, a firm may have incurred a future obligation, but because the expenditure benefits those future periods, no liability is recorded. When you read financial statements, be aware that significant exposures may have been omitted or only disclosed in footnotes.

Where either the probability of a loss cannot be determined or the loss cannot be reasonably estimated, contingent liabilities are not recorded. Exposures for environmental cleanups, product recalls, or outstanding lawsuits are examples of major, potential obligations that may stay off the balance sheet.

Long-term lease obligations are another liability that can be kept off the balance sheet, even though rules for leases have been tightened over the years. For example, leases that cover most of an asset's useful life are treated as if money were borrowed to purchase that asset. A month-to-month computer rental usually is not considered a liability; however, a four-year computer lease probably is. Yet, a four-year lease on a building is not considered a liability, because the useful life of that building is much longer. However, the total of all lease obligations is disclosed in footnotes.

Another variable concerning liabilities and the balance sheet arises because companies usually use different accounting methods for income taxes and financial reporting. A controversial GAAP requirement is that the difference between financial statement tax liability and that on the tax return be carried as a liability. The assumption is that the tax savings one year will be offset in following years. This is true, for example, of depreciation where an accelerated method for tax purposes will reduce income in early years, but cause higher income later. However, a strong argument can be made that in many companies the liability will never be paid and has no place on the balance sheet; in a growing company, the liability is likely to continue to build as new assets with high depreciation outweigh older assets.

Liabilities concerning partially funded employee pension plans may also be stated inaccurately on the balance sheet. Companies often set up employee pension plans in which they are obligated to make payments to employees after retirement. If an employer has set aside at least 100% of the cash needed to fund the expected liability, then the plan is considered to be fully funded. If not, the pension liability is only partially funded. Partially funded employee benefit plans have many accounting complexities and create liabilities that are complicated to measure. Suffice it to say that this category is likely to be misstated.

Income Statement Pitfalls

While the balance sheet represents a snapshot of a company's value at any point in time, the income statement summarizes the flow of activity between two such points. Net income is the change in reported value during an accounting period. So, you can see how problems in valuing balance sheet accounts simultaneously affect the income statement.

Valuation

Several balance sheet valuation issues have an impact on income. When depreciation is recorded, half of the entry reduces assets; the other half is an expense. Selecting an accelerated depreciation method, as discussed in Chapter 3, not only reduces assets earlier, but also increases expenses in earlier years.

For inventory, using the first in, first out (FIFO) method of valuing inventory uses more recent prices to value inventory. But while FIFO seems to enhance the currentness of the balance sheet, it has the opposite impact on the income statement. FIFO results in sales being booked at current prices, but expenses — inventory shipped — at older, historical costs. During periods of rising prices, FIFO will tend to inflate profits. By contrast, the last in, first out (LIFO) method ensures that both revenues and expenses on the income statement are at current values, but causes the balance sheet to reflect outdated values.

The argument of whether assets and liabilities should be written up or down as market values change often revolves around the impact these entries would have on reported net income. While adjusting the values would help the balance sheet be more reflective of the actual value of a company, the adjustment would require that income and expense be recorded, even though no transaction has taken place.

At times, the current rules protect investors by limiting management's latitude in assigning asset values and recognizing unearned income or expense. At other times, the rules have the opposite effect. Deferring recognition of gains on marketable securities, for example, not only understates a company's net worth, but gives management control over when to recognize certain income. For example:

✓ One small public company with annual sales of approximately $10–15 million held a large portfolio of securities. For several years they ran small operating losses, and while there is no way to tell whether management did so deliberately, they always recognized just enough investment income to show a small positive net income.

As you can see, the rules concerning valuation do not offer any solid assurances.

The Matching Principle

In addition to valuation issues that have an impact on the income statement, another pitfall you will encounter on income statements concerns how revenue and expense transactions are timed. One key accounting principle — the matching principle — dictates that revenues are not recorded until all or a substantial portion of the services have been completed, and objectively measurable compensation has been received. A company may substantially increase its earnings power during a period by developing products and services, booking orders, or partially completing a sale, but until a sale is actually consummated, no revenues or associated expenses are booked.

Complicated timing issues and occasional period-to-period swings also affect reported income. The income statement is driven by the desire to match the revenues in a given period with the expenditures that supported and produced them. If a product is built in one year, but not sold until the second year, the costs of making the product are carried as an asset at the end of the first year, when the product still has earnings potential, and expensed in the second year, when those earnings are realized.

But how are period expenses and costs with a future benefit distinguished? Consider sales and marketing expenditures, including advertising. A strong argument can be made that these expenses carry a significant future benefit. However, because of the difficulty in sorting out the present and future benefits and matching specific efforts to product sold, accountants choose to expense these types of costs in the period they are incurred.

Likewise, general and administrative expenses are period expenses since they cannot be closely associated with product sold. But how about research and development expenses? Unsuccessful R&D has little future value, but R&D that results in significant new products and patents enhances a company's value. Yet, because of the uncertainty of the future value, GAAP requires that all R&D expenses be recorded as period expenses.

On the other hand, manufacturing expenses are included in the value of inventory and expensed as cost of sales. As discussed in more detail in Chapter 9, depending upon the assumption made about the flow of goods, the amount of cost of sales can vary significantly, leading to further potential inaccuracies on the income statement.

So what is the "bottom line" on the bottom line? Is it a useless muddle of values or can it be of value?

Using Income Statements

Like any financial accounting statement, interpreting an income statement requires an understanding of the assumptions and judgments that went into it. However, compared to the balance sheet, fewer items distort the income statement. Because income is a flow of revenues and transactions during an entire period, the income statement is more representative of your company than a snapshot on a single day — as you have with the balance sheet — and less subject to shifts at the end of a period.

Income statements have fewer valuation issues — most expenses are incurred and settled within the same period, so the basis of valuation is known. Period-to-period and trend comparisons also have more meaning as a result. Nonetheless, as is discussed below, substantial room still exists for manipulation of net income; so investors reading financial statements must still be cautious.

While most people are only concerned with net income, the very bottom line that encompasses all activity in a period, some lenders and investors may focus on slightly different measures. A common focus is earnings before interest and taxes (EBIT). This measure more accurately captures the earning power of a company by excluding the impact of taxes and capital structure. For example, a company that finances its operations with debt rather than equity has higher interest expense.

A further refinement contains a focus on operating income, which excludes all nonoperating items from EBIT, such as investment income from an unrelated business. Lastly, many analysts — particularly banks — prefer to remove from the income statement noncash items, such as depreciation and amortization, to see the cash generating capacity of a company.

Some common ratios are used to evaluate income. For public companies, earnings per share (EPS) is often the only measure widely quoted. For companies with different types of securities, this measure can seem extremely complicated to calculate, but it is basically just net income divided by the number of common shares outstanding. Return on assets (ROA), which is net income divided by total assets, and return on investments (ROI), net income divided by owners' equity, are also frequently used. However, because the denominators in these two ratios come from the balance sheet, they are subject to the same weaknesses as other balance sheet ratios discussed earlier in the chapter.

Emphasizing Profit

Confucius is quoted as saying, "The wise man understands equity; the small man understands only profit."[5] Indeed, a perfect income statement would reflect the period change in a company's equity. This change, of course, is a subjective measure that takes a long-term view of a company — a look that investors try to make when evaluating companies, and business owners often instinctively recognize. But accounting is objective, and net income often fails to record the true impact of events on a company, particularly in the short term.

What is worse is the high degree of reliance managers put on short-term profits. Fast-track managers rarely stay in jobs more than a few years, so accounting methods are chosen that improve current reported income. Focusing on short-term profits can destroy the incentives to make necessary investments in R&D and other long-term programs.

Focuses on short-term profits are reinforced further by compensation plans that pay bonuses based on current income. The bonuses and financial rewards give added incentive to boost current income and to devote unnecessary effort attempting to manipulate profits. Having accounting conventions that stress profit over equity reinforces this behavior even more.

Cash Flow

While profit is an important measure, it is still an accounting concept. Equally important and often critical is cash flow. A company showing a profit or positive book value can run out of cash and fail but, as former MCI Chairman William McGowan once said, "No company has ever gone bankrupt because it had a loss on its P&L."[6]

As a measure of performance, cash flow has another key advantage — it is an extremely objective measure of performance. Cash flow can be precisely measured and verified without a need for accruals and other judgment calls. Simply put, unlike net income, cash flow won't lie. Cash flow is discussed in more detail in Chapter 11.

Creative Accounting

Did you hear the joke about a CEO who asked people interviewing for a job the question, "How much is 2 + 2?" The man who used lengthy equations and finally deduced the answer as "4" was hired as the mathematician. The woman who drew a graph with intersecting curves and answered "5" became the economist. The last prospect drew the curtains closed and whispered, "How much do you want it to be?" This person became the new accountant.

Anyone who has worked long with financial statements, or has noted the many judgment calls that must be made in accounting, will not be surprised that there are many opportunities to finesse the numbers. A difficult but all too common dilemma for accountants is handling requests from the boss to improve the appearance of the income statement or balance sheet. Almost always, changes in estimates or procedures can be made to boost net income and yet stay within GAAP. A common perception is that any controller or accountant worth his or her weight always has money tucked away that can be used to dress up the financial statements.

Outside CPAs are not immune from this pressure, either. In part, their resolve to get tough about accounting issues is tempered by knowing the client pays their salary. Usually, the bending, not breaking of rules is involved or a change that is not material to the overall statements. Finally, the CPA often is forced to rely on the word of the client and is not in a position to contradict an opinion on the salability of inventory or credit worthiness of a slow-paying account. A company's net income often ends up being a negotiated figure between the client and CPA.

In recent years, however, CPAs have clamped down on such creative accounting due to the success of some shareholder suits. Even so, only annual statements are required to have audit opinions. Significant decisions are based on monthly and quarterly financials and these escape — at least temporarily — independent review.

Management Implications

A popular cartoon from several years ago can help illustrate how the bottom line can be manipulated. The cartoon shows an executive addressing his management team saying, "I am glad to report that once again we broke even on operations and pulled a profit on accounting procedures." Unfortunately, creative accounting techniques are common. If just the effort that went into manipulating the bottom line went into improving operations, companies would be better off, even if reported profit dropped off.

Accounting gimmickry may have peaked during the 1960s. Switches in accounting methods, run-ups in unfunded pension liabilities, and assorted other tricks temporarily inflated reported earnings. Eventually, FASB and SEC rulings closed these gaping loopholes. One article cited 1970 as "the year of the big bath" when in a single week, 60 companies reported write-offs and write-downs to their earnings.[7] Even so, many opportunities to shape financial statements remain.

One legitimate reason to manipulate income is for tax purposes, where it is desirable to choose accounting methods that reduce reported income. In the United States and most Western countries, it is perfectly legitimate to maintain two sets of books — one for financial accounting and one for taxes.[8] The benefit of doing this, however, will vary from company to company.

Ironically, some companies choose to pay higher taxes in order to report higher net income — a strategy that only makes sense if reporting lower income or losses would jeopardize operating needs, such as the ability to raise financing.

Reserve Account Method

The most common weapons in the creative accountant's arsenal that can manipulate the bottom line are various reserve accounts. The accounts include reserves for anticipated bad debts and inventory loss or obsolescence and are often fairly sizable and unspecific. For example, a company may simply establish a write-down reserve for a flat 10% of inventory rather than identifying specific items that may be subject to future write-downs. From period to period, simply changing the basis of the calculation or the percentage used will alter the reserve and, thus, net income.

Write-Off Method

The decision of when to actually write off an asset is another variable in creative accounting. Generally, an accountant will wait for an opportune moment to take a write-off, which reduces income. As long as a plausible case can be made for an asset having a future value, an asset can generally stay on the books. A common example is inventory of slow-moving products. The inventory may be first quality and, therefore, potentially salable, but if no one is buying or future products threaten to obsolete it, the inventory should be written off. Yet, if a case can be made that the inventory could be sold within one year, the inventory may be allowed to stay on the books at or near full value. A corollary to this is that accountants prefer to take their lumps all at one time. If you are going to deliver bad news to investors, you may as well make it a disaster and hope you are putting all the bad news behind. At this time, reserve accounts are fattened up, which just adds to what is already a disaster and provides a cushion for future periods.

Timing of Transactions

Timing the sale of assets is a commonly used method to manipulate income. GAAP does not permit companies to write up the value of assets when the market value has appreciated; assets that have declined in value must be written down to market value, however. A company that bought land 20 years ago may have a sizable, unrecognized gain. That gain is booked when the land is sold, thus having an impact on the financial statements.

Using a related method, some companies refinance to show profits. If a company has issued debt and market value has declined below book value due to rising interest rates, the company can buy back the debt on the open market — or swap it for equity — and book a profit by retiring the debt.

Yet another timing technique involves other types of transactions. Just as an individual can manipulate taxable income by moving forward or back certain transactions close to year-end, the timing of other transactions will have an impact on financial statements. The most familiar example is the push most companies go through to ship as much as possible at month, quarter, or year-end. Here, no question arises as to the accounting treatment, since revenue is recognized in the period the sale occurs. But the company exercises control over which period to recognize revenue by choosing whether to ship on December 31 or January 1. In a similar vein, companies often refuse incoming shipments at month-end, hold onto outgoing payments, or offer incentives for customers to pay in order to improve the appearance of the balance sheet.

This process is often stretched by holding months open. No matter what the calendar says, at some companies, months may last 35, even 40, days if that is what is needed to make sales projections. Companies will also get permission from customers to ship at month-end with an agreement that delivery will not be completed until several weeks later. One company routinely loaded product on its own trucks on December 31, booked the sale, then had the trucks return the goods the next day when a credit was booked — in the new year.

Opportunities and Choices

Many of the decisions an accountant must make provide opportunities to do some creative accounting. Accruals of certain liabilities and expenses must be estimated, creating difficult decisions for the accountant — plus the opportunity to bias the calculation. Some common problems include establishing a warranty or product guarantee reserve, deciding whether and how much to reserve for an unsettled legal suit, or predicting how large executive bonuses will be. Since no transaction has actually taken place, an estimate is made based on the likelihood of an event occurring and a guess at the financial impact.

The choice of accounting methods affects net income and can be used effectively in creative accounting. Faster depreciation reduces income in earlier years; LIFO inventory decreases income relative to FIFO if prices are increasing. The accountant is not free, however, to switch back and forth between methods; once a method is selected, it generally can't be changed and any changes in accounting method must be disclosed.

To a smaller degree, the choice of how to apply accounting methods to individual items can be manipulated to an accountant's advantage. If furniture costing over $1,000 is usually capitalized, how about the purchase of a set of ten chairs for $200 each? Should a computer be depreciated over five years or over three? Should the salary of the vice-president of manufacturing be included in the overhead — which is added to inventory costs — or expensed?

Balance Sheet Techniques

Some quick maneuvering on the balance sheet at year-end can greatly enhance a company's appearance. Most of the procedures that boost net income will also improve the appearance of the balance sheet. Higher sales increase receivables, a current asset, helping both net worth and various financial ratios. Higher inventory values and slower depreciation keep assets on the books, while limiting accrued expenses keeps current liabilities off.

Some shifting between balance sheet accounts can also occur. Most common is boosting cash balances by holding off paying vendors until just after year-end or by encouraging early customer payments. Deliveries can be refused in the few days before year-end to keep both inventories and payables down. Last-minute borrowing, particularly if the debt is classified as noncurrent, can improve stated cash positions.

Leasing assets, instead of buying them, used to give firms an opportunity to do "off balance sheet" financing; however, this loophole was closed. So now, any lease qualifying as a capital lease is treated as if money was borrowed to buy the asset. Essentially, if a lease covers 75% or more of an asset's useful life, or payments exceed 90% of the asset's value, it must be classified as a capital lease. However, to the extent that short-term rental agreements rather than capital leases are used, liabilities can be kept off the balance sheet.

The Case of IBM

The difficulty of making accurate decisions using financial statements and the considerable leeway management has in choosing accounting methods is illustrated by the history of International Business Machines (IBM) in the late 1980s and early 1990s. In an article in *The Wall Street Journal* on April 7, 1993, considerable evidence was presented indicating that IBM adopted increasingly aggressive accounting methods to prop up reported earnings during a period when business was deteriorating.

Although the article asserts that none of the changes were illegal or affected any of the underlying business problems, IBM's day of reckoning was probably delayed. During this time, executives were awarded large raises and bonuses that were partly tied to earnings, while investors who bought shares near their peak in 1987 saw the stock plunge more than 70% by 1993.[9]

✓ The changes in IBM's accounting practice fell into three broad categories. The first involved revenue recognition and determining when a sale was actually complete. While some high technology companies wait until a system is installed and running at a customer site, IBM chose to book revenue upon shipment.[10] In some cases, but only when installation at a customer was expected within 30 days, they even booked shipments to their own warehouses as sales. Another revenue issue was how to account for various sales gimmicks that offered customers liberal return policies or price protection refunds if prices later fell. IBM critics contend that full revenue was being booked at shipment despite evidence that payments received would be less.

The second category was the treatment of leases. Many of IBM's leases had revenue streams that fell short of GAAP requirements for capital leases. Instead of qualifying as sales when the contract was signed, with all the expected revenue booked at once, they would have to be treated as rentals, with the revenue only booked as payments were received. In an extremely unusual transaction, IBM purchased insurance that guaranteed the value of the computers at the end of the lease. This residual value, when added to the payments from the customer, met the GAAP test and allowed IBM to recognize the sales immediately.

Finally, starting in 1984, IBM began reducing the estimated cost of their retirement plans and to spread the costs of its factories further into the future. Though these changes were fully disclosed in IBM's financial statements and were common at other companies, critics maintained they were a shift away from IBM's traditionally conservative accounting.

How large an impact the accounting changes had on IBM's earnings is unclear. The company asserts that its actions were appropriate and agreed to by its auditors. Nonetheless, analysts seemed shocked when IBM announced layoffs and nearly $5 billion in losses in 1992 and its stock fell sharply.

Summary

If IBM, with traditionally conservative accounting practices, can be tempted to adopt aggressive methods to boost earnings, how many other companies are acting similarly? If the analysts who closely scrutinize IBM's books can be surprised, how cautious should a small business lender or investor be when analyzing accounting statements? And did IBM's officers fool themselves into thinking things were better than they were based on the accounting numbers? If so, they may have missed their chance to turn the company around.

The Bottom Line

Income should not be manipulated other than for tax reasons — and even then only within legal limits. Minimizing taxes should not be confused with cheating. Profits can only be propped up so long before a deterioration shows up in another business barometer, or the accumulated sins become too much to overlook. Even in fairly steady times, the artificial increase of one period's profits only detracts from the next period.

The situation becomes worse if management uses inflated profits to delay operating action, including hiding issues from investors or lenders — ostensibly to work out problems without interference. Open communication and "no surprises" are keys to good relations with investors, and the financial statements are generally the centerpiece of communication.

However, a company should not unduly punish itself by choosing an overly conservative accounting approach, making it difficult to attract financing when earnings lag or are negative. If accelerated depreciation, choice of a cost of sales method, or writing off rather than capitalizing prepaid expenses unfairly penalize earnings, you should consider changing methods. The same holds true of the balance sheet, where enhancing cash balances and current ratios can make your company more attractive in lender's eyes, and some "window dressing" may legitimately further your goals.

You also cannot ignore the realities of business. The manipulation of income seems to be a fact of business life and most users of financial statements understand this. An idealistic controller and CPA will not be able to resist for long the pressures of their clients or bosses to present statements in the most favorable light. Knowing the boundary between legitimate practices and unethical or even fraudulent accounting can be difficult, but is essential.

In using accounting statements, whether manipulated or not, one key factor is: Do not fool yourself. You need to be aware of the real operating trends and issues, regardless of reported income. As Mark Twain said, "Get your facts first, and then you can distort them as much as you please." [11]

Endnotes

1. J. Harman, English Jurist, Miles vs. Clarke, quoted in *The Manager's Book of Quotations*, p. 4.

2. Aesop, "The Widow and the Hen," quoted in *The Manager's Book of Quotations*, p. 386.

3. "FASB Asset Definitions at Odds with Historical Cost Model." ACCOUNTING TODAY 7 June 1993: 13–15.

4. Ross, Howard. *The Elusive Art of Accounting.* New York: The Ro Press, 1966. p. 44.

5. Confucius, quoted in *The Manager's Book of Quotations*, p. 3.

6. William McGowan, quoted in *The Manager's Book of Quotations*, p. 6.

7. Gerstner, Louis V., Jr. and M. Helen Anderson. "The Chief Financial Officer as Activist." HARVARD BUSINESS REVIEW Sept.–Oct. 1976: 100.

8. Stancill, James McNeill. "Managing Financial Statements — Image and Effect." HARVARD BUSINESS REVIEW March–April 1981: 181.

9. Miller, Michael W. and Lee Berton. "As IBM's Woes Grew, Its Accounting Tactics Got Less Conservative." THE WALL STREET JOURNAL 7 April 1993: 1.

10. In 1987, the SEC filed suit against another computer manufacturer, Storage Technology Corp., for recognizing revenue when product was shipped rather than installed. The SEC also charged that a major transaction had been backdated in 1983 to turn a loss into a profit. The suit was settled with no admission of wrongdoing.

11. Bohle, Bruce. Mark Twain, quoted in *Apollo Book of American Quotations*. New York: Dodd, Mead & Co. 1967. p. 148.

Part II

Beyond Financial Accounting

Chapter 6

Controllership Redefined

The change from the spelling of the word 'comptroller' to 'controller'
is in some mysterious way related to [a] change in the corporate
status of the controller.

— Jerome Bennett[1]

Strong controllership does not mean trying to run a company by the numbers. Not many companies could succeed doing that. The key is being
able to run a company with the numbers. This means putting a system of
controls in place that protects a company's assets and the integrity of
information. Numbers can help you navigate, but they cannot help you
make operating decisions.

Financial managers play a critical role in running a company, but it is a
supporting one. Their role, it has been said, is similar to brakes on a car.
You need them to keep from going over a cliff, but they can't be in
charge or you will never go anywhere. Robert Townsend, in *Further Up
the Organization*, agrees:

> "When accounting runs the operation (and this happens a lot), the sit-
> uation must be changed. Accountants can be smarter than anyone else
> or more ambitious or both, but essentially they are bean counters —
> their job is to serve the operation. They can't run the ship."[2]

Of course, controllers should not be excluded from management or be
satisfied with just being bean counters. Quite the contrary, from providing information to supporting operating decisions, to ensuring adequate

cash flow, and to identifying cost savings, controllers should be dynamic, proactive forces in their companies.

To be positive forces, two major prerequisites must be met. First, the controller's duties have to be properly defined, particularly the distinction between simply doing accounting and being a controller. Then, the person who fills that job must have the appropriate background, perspective, and attitude. This chapter explores the differences between accountants and controllers, and then redefines the job description for your company's controller.

Controllership or Accounting

As mentioned earlier in Chapter 1, there is a big difference between a controller and an accountant. A large part of a controller's job is, indeed, accounting and most controllers are accountants by background. In many companies, the top accountant is simply referred to as the controller, regardless of the actual job description. To add some confusion, the synonymous, but relatively outmoded, term "comptroller" is sometimes used to describe the same position.

The distinction between an accountant and a controller is more than just education or a title. The two terms imply a different breadth and perspective in financial management:

- Accounting is bean counting. It is little more than recording financial transactions and tallying the results. A controller, on the other hand, can interpret the numbers and provide meaningful feedback.

- An accountant accumulates historical information, while a controller is both historical and forward-looking in perspective.

- An accountant is usually happiest working with figures and may rarely set foot outside of the accounting department. A controller is usually plugged into activity throughout a company and works regularly with managers in all departments.

- Accounting is only concerned with transactions that can be measured in dollars. But, a controller may also be interested in developments that may not be actual financial transactions, such as the impact of potential lawsuits or price changes, as well as nonfinancial measures such as productivity and quality.

- An accountant is overhead — that is, much of the work is routine and dictated by accounting conventions and tax laws, and the less that work costs to perform, the better. A controller will pay for him or herself many times over by finding pockets of potential savings, supporting key decision makers, and anticipating problems. The controller's office can often be a true profit center.

The Traditional Role

Unfortunately, the qualities that make a good accountant don't necessarily make an effective controller. Some of the best controllers don't even have strong accounting backgrounds; others are accountants who can make a transition to looking beyond the numbers and embracing a management perspective. According to *The Journal of Accountancy*, "Controllers whose experience is entirely accounting oriented may lack the expertise to establish appropriate operational and administrative controls."[3]

Perhaps the foremost reason for this lack of expertise is that accountants usually receive most of their formal training in financial accounting and tax, which are certainly important topics. All publicly held companies and many private ones must prepare financial statements that conform with GAAP; all must file tax returns. But, as is discussed below, while these chores make up the bulk of a CPA's work, they are only one part of controllership.

The emphasis on financial reporting can tilt both accountants' skills and their perception of their job toward reporting — and away from operating issues. Without exposure in school to broader management topics or significant on-the-job training, accountants are poorly prepared for or even unaware of the responsibilities of controllership.

When emphasis on financial reporting is the case, accounting reports can become ends in themselves instead of a means to help management. And, not surprisingly, managers often complain that accounting reports contain meaningless information. They observe that financial statements are generally completed well after the end of a period and contain highly aggregated information.

While GAAP statements can and should be useful, one problem is that GAAP principles assume the readers of financial reports are knowledgeable in accounting. Therefore, statements rarely disclose the many conventions and estimates that go into their preparation, making them difficult for the lay reader to properly interpret them. These conventions and estimates are discussed in greater detail in Chapter 3.

Of course, the person best qualified to interpret a statement is an accountant, particularly the preparer. Yet, in many companies, the accountant hands off the completed financial statement to management and returns to day-to-day processing, preparing for the next month's closing. By leaving interpretation to the reader, an accountant leaves managers stranded and increases the communication gap between them. Effective controllers do not lose interest in financial statements once they have been prepared. They recognize that part of the job is interpreting the results and communicating the information to both top management and outsiders.[4]

Personality Traits

The personality traits that attract people to accounting and make them effective are not always desirable traits in a controller. The stereotype of accountants, of course, is that they are humorless, boring, nitpicking types, wearing green eyeshades, spending their workday hunched over ledger books adding up figures. While the green eyeshades have disappeared and computers have replaced ledger books, the role many accountants play in smaller companies remains isolated, narrow, and routine.

Accountants tend to be detail-oriented and very precise. Comedian Bob Newhart, a former accountant who defies this stereotype, describes his view of accounting as a "strange theory of accountancy ... if you got within two or three bucks of it," it was okay. As he says, "This never really caught on."[5]

Accountants need to have an affinity for working with very detailed information. However, a problem arises when they lose the forest for the trees and become overly precise. An intern in a government agency once had a summer job where the first month's assignment was locating a $14 discrepancy in accounts receivable dating back several months. While this example is extreme, many accountants will spend hours, even days, looking for the last dollar needed to balance a reconciliation.[6] In addition, accountants are frequently uncomfortable in providing estimates — or even rounded figures — when asked quantitative questions.

A controller needs to understand when precision is meaningful and when it is simply a number-crunching exercise. Precision can pay off when determining money owed or due — not just shifts between accounts — or where it sheds light on a chronic problem. Precision becomes costly, though, when it chews up valuable time that could be spent better on other tasks.

Because so much of accounting is imprecise, that so much time is spent concentrating on minute details is ironic. Balance sheets will often have items accurate to the dollar next to estimates, such as for bad debt and inventory reserves, that may only be accurate within tens of thousands of dollars. And cost accountants often show unit costs to four or more decimal places when the actual precision is nowhere close to that.

Negative Goals

Accountants are often criticized as plodding, probably because accounting is such a cautious and mechanical field. For example, accounting has the negative goal of avoiding anything that might be misleading, as opposed to the positive goal of being informative. GAAP even has a conservatism convention — as discussed in Chapter 3 — which says when equally acceptable methods exist for valuing a transaction, the one that results in the lowest net income must be used. You might wonder why conservatism, and not accuracy, is a convention?

Accounting leans away from subjective valuations in favor of objective numbers, often conflicting with the information needs of management.[7] Take the example of the balance sheet — discussed in chapters 3 and 5. The values of many assets fluctuate over time and with market conditions. Yet, because GAAP requires objectively measurable valuations, nearly all assets are shown at acquisition costs. This method of valuation works fine when assets turn over frequently, such as with accounts receivable, but introduces great distortion when applied to buildings and land held over many years. These conservative conventions can discourage accountants from thinking creatively about financial values.

Much of accounting is mechanistic. The work is performed by rote, without any real management perspective. So, the wider issues of controllership involve a significant shift. In contrast to preparation of financial statements, management accounting, asset management, planning, and internal controls deal with current operations and may not have any preset rules. The objectivity, precision, and negative goals that apply to GAAP reporting must be set aside.

Management Support

You must support and encourage the impetus of financial staff to take on a broader range of financial issues within your company. If your management style is seat-of-the-pants, you may obstruct this goal. Without a willingness to step back from daily operations to set direction or analyze options, it can be difficult to implement effective planning or management accounting.

A more common problem is that you may view accounting as a necessary evil. You may expect little else from your controller or accountant than producing monthly statements, paying the bills, and filing tax returns. As a result, minimal resources are allocated for the controller's area.

If your financial department is understaffed, broader controllership duties will get passed over. The controller may not have the time to concentrate on issues beyond day-to-day processing. Or, if you own a smaller business and your controller is little more than a bookkeeper, that person may be efficient at handling daily transactions and monthly closings, but be unable to produce very little else.

Substantial resources and effort must be devoted to financial management. In return, a strong, well-rounded controller can provide the controls, analysis, and decision support needed to avoid crises and identify opportunities to boost the bottom line.

What qualifications should your controller have and what should his or her duties be? The remainder of the chapter spells out a job description for the controller. The areas of responsibility discussed here also provide an outline for the material in the remainder of the book.

Beyond the Numbers

The job description of a modern controller demands an individual who is forward-looking and management-oriented. Accounting, particularly GAAP reporting, is just one part of the job. Too often, financial reporting diverts a controller's attention from the things that actually make money or can cause trouble.

Similarly, when hiring a controller, look for someone who can bring a management perspective. Financial reporting is mechanistic and finding someone who can do that task is easy. What is rarer, and more valuable, is someone who can go beyond the numbers. In the job description below, the objectives and areas of responsibility for the ideal controller are listed. Specific tasks for each of the seven main areas of responsibility are explored further immediately following this job description.

Model Job Description for a Controller

Objectives

- Provide relevant and timely information throughout the organization and comply with outside reporting requirements, including financial, tax, and regulatory statements.

- Communicate financial results to investors and creditors and establish internal planning and feedback loops.

- Serve as the guardian of a company's assets and establish a system of internal controls, as well as protect liquidity.

- Manage the accounting staff and perform a number of administrative tasks.

Main Areas of Responsibility

- Financial and tax reporting
- Management accounting and decision support
- Planning and budgeting
- Monitoring
- Asset management
- Internal controls
- Administration

Financial and Tax Reporting

The routine recording of transactions and preparation of financial statements in accordance with GAAP is the most familiar aspect of the controller's job. These tasks include SEC reporting for public companies; preparation for year-end audits; and any special reporting requirements imposed by regulatory agencies, corporate partners, or investors.

While coordinating tax planning and preparation is a responsibility of the controller, he or she does not have to be a tax whiz. This expertise is available from an outside CPA. Tax regulations are complex and change regularly, and the time and cost needed to stay current — beyond maintaining a good working knowledge — is something few smaller company controllers can afford.

As discussed earlier, it is not sufficient to simply prepare a financial statement, hand it off to management, and then return to day-to-day processing. Part of financial reporting is interpreting the results and communicating the information to top management and outsiders. The controller best understands the complexities of GAAP and the assumptions that went into preparing the financial reports, and so, should be involved in analyzing the results.

An effective tool for communicating this information to management and outside investors is a brief letter that accompanies the actual financial statements. This letter can discuss operating trends and variances and highlight key, but nonfinancial, events. Outsiders, in particular, usually appreciate this direct line of communication with the "numbers person." In addition, discussions of financial results are an important part of quarterly and annual reports issued by public companies.

The controller must also choose the proper level of detail and organization for reports. While the minimum requirements may be a consolidated income statement and balance sheet, breakdowns of the information are usually desirable. For example, a company with several divisions probably should have a separate, pro forma income statement for each division. Breakdowns by product line or geography may be desirable. Department managers will demand information for their own activities.

In many cases, satisfying the needs of management will require special and even one-time-only reports. Your controller will need skill in extracting and manipulating detailed information that is captured, but not routinely reported by the accounting system. The controller must ensure sufficient detail is captured and be adept in consolidating and organizing the data into useful reports.

Management Accounting

Financial accounting is only part of the reporting picture. While financial accounting primarily satisfies the needs of outsiders for consistent and objective historical information, management accounting systems are designed to satisfy operating managers' needs for timely and detailed information about internal costs and operations as support for decision making.

Unlike tax and GAAP reporting, management accounting is not required. In addition, the form it takes is entirely up to the discretion of management. While some companies will find the added detail is not worth the expense of collecting the data, others depend on having current cost and operating statistics. And, no matter how strong it is, a financial reporting system is not a substitute for management accounting.

In a manufacturing setting, for example, the management accounting system may be used to determine standard product costs. Operating information can be collected on how actual costs compare, as well as on productivity and machine utilization. In a service setting, information collected might include performance against sales quotas or time needed to complete projects.

Unlike financial reporting, which must conform to GAAP, management accounting is unregulated. Whatever information is required by management, reported as frequently and in as much detail as needed, can be part of a management reporting system. The controller must not only understand the operations of a company, but also be adept at communicating with line managers and be responsive to their needs for information.

Planning and Budgeting

Planning is the process through which companies establish goals, communicate these goals to managers and outsiders, and identify potential problems and opportunities. Plans and budgets are also powerful control tools that set milestones to measure progress against and reward managers for achievement. While seat-of-the-pants operating styles and the pressures of day-to-day operations can deter you and your managers from doing formal planning and control, plans and budgets are key controllership functions.

Plans and budgets should come from you and your top managers and reflect your strategies and objectives. The controller's job is to ensure that these plans exist, coordinate their preparation at all levels, and test them for reasonableness. The controller then monitors actual results against plans, provides feedback, and helps with any needed updates. At least three types of plans should be prepared.

A long-term model covering two to five years. The model should provide pro forma income statements and balance sheets by month for at least one year, by quarter for another year, and annually after two years. This type of plan typically is contained in a company's business plan and should be updated at least once a year.

A line item budget. The line item budget translates the targets in the long-term plan into specific departmental and detailed account budgets. The controller often helps managers prepare their budgets by supplying trend data and other analyses, compiling the figures, and then tracking and reviewing any variances to the plan.

A cash flow forecast. Cash flow forecasts help the controller stay on top of liquidity. Even with budgets and long-term plans, cash flow forecasts are essential because cash flow can fluctuate greatly within accounting periods and may not move in tandem with net income. Ultimately, cash flow — not profit — determines the fortunes, even survival, of a company. The relevant time frame for cash flow forecasts depends on the stability of a company and can be as short as week-by-week or they may be built into the long-term plan.

Monitoring

To be effective, both planning and management accounting must have a monitoring function. The setting of goals and standards is not fully meaningful without evaluating progress made and using that information to improve operations. Just collecting data and issuing reports is insufficient. Active review and analysis, followed by action, provide meaningful feedback.

The controller is the logical choice to perform the review and analysis because this person is most familiar with how the numbers were prepared, and probably is the most number-oriented staff person. Analysis can be a time-consuming task and, just as day-to-day concerns can push planning aside, the monitoring process can get shortchanged.

In analyzing results, the controller's focus should be forward-looking. The goal is not simply to provide a scorecard, but to identify problem areas and suggest improvements. Correcting a variance or having an early warning of a potential cash crunch are more important than measuring the amount of a shortfall.

Asset Management

The controller is the guardian of a company's assets. From cash disbursements to credit policy, inventory control to capital expenditures, the controller is involved in managing the movement and integrity of company assets. Often, asset management is where the controller makes the most direct impact on the bottom line.

Both physically and figuratively, the controller controls the checkbook. Ensuring proper authorization for all cash disbursements, plus managing cash flow — the timing of both expenditures and receipts — are jobs of the controller. A controller also works hard to squeeze cash out of assets, such as receivables and inventory, while stretching payments to the greatest degree possible.

Accounts receivable can tie up large amounts of cash and expose a company to bad debt losses. By establishing and enforcing a credit and collections policy, a controller can achieve timely collections and reduce potential write-offs.

Inventory, for companies that carry it, usually is the greatest control risk. Not only is it expensive to carry, but any on-hand stock is subject to obsolescence, theft, and damage. Through physical controls, reporting systems, and sharp analysis, a controller can work to improve turnover, while ensuring a proper mix of materials and finished goods.

Internal Controls

The accuracy and integrity of financial systems and data depend on having a system of internal checks and balances. The controller must be familiar with basic controls and implement them.

While fraud is one target of controls, the actual incidence of fraud is quite slight. For example, restricting physical access to assets, plus ensuring that at least two different people must authorize any transaction that expends an asset are simple, but often sufficient, controls against fraud.

Two more important targets of controls are reducing errors and ensuring proper accountability for transactions. Many companies suffer from redundant processing, costly errors and omissions, or double-checks that could be avoided with an orderly system of checks and balances.

A controller will often find resistance to the work that goes with enforcing controls. When pressure rises to push work out, shortcuts that bypass the control process often slip in. The controller must be able to explain the need for controls and enforce adherence. Support by top management is especially important in this area.

Administration

A controller in most companies is asked to handle a wide range of administrative tasks. The exact mix will vary from company to company, but some common areas include:

- Benefits
- Computer and office equipment selection and upkeep
- Insurance
- Legal and contract issues
- Office management
- Payroll
- Personnel
- Records management

The size of a company and whether it has additional managers for personnel and treasury will determine the breadth of the controller's job. But even if the controller doesn't have primary responsibility, his or her input will typically be sought on these matters.

Controller as Ombudsman

In addition to these seven main areas of responsibility discussed above, your controller should be available to act as your company's ombudsman. The controller is most likely the person with the greatest overlap into the various functions within your company and often knows more about your company's operation than anyone except yourself. Because so much information flows through the controller's department, and from nearly all areas of a company, the controller often has a better overview of the total operation than anyone else on the management team.

Show all business proposals to your controller to ensure they make economic sense. Your controller must be prepared to ask questions about how projects will be funded, raise legal questions, or ensure that proper milestones are established. Within limits, the controller's job is to be a cynic. Not to unnecessarily beat on managers or be a pessimist, your controller's job is to make sure the tough questions get asked and the numbers get run about planned projects or past performance.

Working Together

Clearly, the traditional bean counter role for a controller is inadequate. The job calls for a dynamic, management-oriented person who can play a key role in setting and achieving the goals of your company.

The job may also require an additional investment in staffing the accounting department. The controller's slot demands a highly skilled and experienced manager, a harder person to find than a technically skilled accountant. And because the duties are also expanded, additional support staff may be required. However, this investment in the controllership function will pay off.

To repeat, no matter how skilled the controller or large the support staff, their job is to support you and your management, not run the company. To return to the airplane analogy, the controller provides the instrument panel, but is not the pilot. The controller's job is to provide accurate, timely, and relevant information. He or she can flash warnings, suggest action, and even make some minor corrections directly. But the ultimate decision making rests with you.

For managers and the controller to understand these roles and work closely together is crucial. Both you and your top managers need useful information, as well as assurance that day-to-day transactions are accurate and complete. Conversely, the controller needs feedback from you on what information is needed, plus your support to enforce compliance with policies and procedures.

Just as the notion of the controller as bean counter is obsolete, so is the idea that an effective controller can work in the isolation of the accounting department. The controller must get into the trenches and work with you and your managers throughout a company. The term "shirt-sleeve controller" is often used and appropriately connotes someone who works hands-on and who is able to communicate through informal, as well as formal channels.

Desired Background

An effective controller in a smaller company should not just be adept at figures. He or she must have management savvy and the forcefulness to get things done throughout an organization. Prior small company experience is essential; the orientation of larger companies is very different and the transition from a larger to a smaller company more difficult than it appears.

Should the controller be a CPA? It doesn't hurt, but it should not be a prerequisite. The CPA designation means someone has proven expertise in financial accounting, audit, and tax. But, the CPA designation says nothing about management experience and, therefore, is greatly overrated as a qualification for company controller candidates. In fact, a certified management accountant (CMA) is often a better prospect.

In addition, many highly skilled accountants choose to bypass the certification process or have passed the CPA exam, but simply lack the public accounting work experience or continuing education necessary for the CPA designation.

A controller could even be a nonaccountant. Technical accounting skills should take a back seat to management skills and hands-on experience.

Controlling the Controller

Simply redefining the controller's job description is not enough. You must take an active role in accounting issues and, in short, control the controller. Just as the controller must have management savvy, you should have a working knowledge of accounting.

The remainder of the book explores further several of the areas of controllership described above. By understanding the objectives and practices in each area, you can ask better questions of your financial managers and work more effectively with them. The next chapter focuses on how to have your internal needs for information satisfied.

Endnotes

1. Bennett, Jerome V. *Administering the Company Accounting Function*. Englewood Cliffs, New Jersey: Prentice Hall, second ed. 1981. p. 38.

2. Townsend, Robert. *Further up the Organization*. New York: Alfred A. Knopf, 1984. p. 2.

3. Kuttner, Monroe S. "Putting the Controller in Control." JOURNAL OF ACCOUNTANCY May 1993: 89.

4. Ross, *The Elusive Art of Accounting*, p. 14.

5. Newhart, Bob. "Retirement Party." *The Best of Bob Newhart*. Warner Brothers Records.

6. There is an element of validity here. Even though a reconciliation may only be out of balance by a dollar or two, there is no guarantee that the difference is trivial. The error could consist of two large transactions, one a plus and one a minus. In addition, tracking down a $50 difference in some accounts may uncover a billing or payment error that translates into cash for a company. In these situations, the cost of the time needed to reconcile and the potential benefit should be compared.

7. Ross, p. 12.

Chapter 7

What Is Management Accounting?

If you can't measure it, you can't manage it.

— Anonymous[1]

Tell me how you measure me and I'll tell you how I will perform.

— Eli Goldratt[2]

Sports is a common metaphor for business and, in the case of how information is used, a direct correlation exists between the needs of business and baseball managers. In baseball, a handful of accepted measures of performance are used: batting averages, earned run averages, saves, and runs batted in, to name a few. Specific rules about how each is calculated limit the use of individual judgment. Having these rules assures that games in different cities are accounted for the same, making statistical comparisons valid across the league and across seasons. Knowledgeable fans are also aware of how the accounting is done and can interpret a box score or an individual player's statistics.

The baseball manager, however, quickly finds these popular measures insufficient. Information may be needed on how a batter does against a particular pitcher, or in "clutch" situations. Does the manager "play the percentages" and change pitchers? Order a bunt? How should fielders be positioned for a hitter? The manager needs statistics tailored to these decision making needs.

The manager also needs certain information almost as fast as it is available. By the time the box score is published the next morning, the statistics are too late to help. Watch any baseball telecast and the availability and proliferation of statistics is evident, attesting to the desire for information beyond that supplied by traditional performance measures.

Financial Versus Management Accounting

Information needs in business directly parallel the needs in baseball. Financial accounting is akin to traditional baseball statistics, providing a consistent and fair method of keeping score, while primarily intending to serve the needs of outsiders. But often, this traditional information isn't enough and you need additional information that is tailored to support decision making and provide meaningful feedback. Often, the information must be more detailed, timely, and focused on internal operations than GAAP reporting. Management accounting — also known as cost accounting — is a separate discipline designed to meet this need for internal, operating information.

The major differences between financial and management accounting can be summarized as follows:

Financial Accounting	**Management Accounting**
Financial accounting is required.	Management accounting is optional.
Financial accounting is governed by GAAP.	Management accounting is unregulated.
Financial accounting only reports on monetary measures.	Management accounting will report on nonmonetary measures.
Financial accounting only reports on the past.	Management accounting can report on the present and take future events into consideration.
Financial accounting often aggregates figures.	Management accounting is detail-oriented and more likely to focus on segments of a business.
Financial accounting uses defined fiscal periods.	Management accounting can report over any time period deemed relevant.

Management accounting is often referred to as a fairly recent development. At least two influential writers, Robert Kaplan of Harvard Business School and H. Thomas Johnson of Portland State University, convincingly argue that management accounting practices flourished in 19th and early 20th century businesses.[3] Unencumbered by the need to report to outsiders, business owners kept tabs on key operating factors, secure in the knowledge that if these were in order, profits would take care of themselves. According to Kaplan and Johnson, the increasing use of outside financing in the early 1900s led to the dominance of financial reporting and squeezed management reporting out of many companies.

Management accounting can address your information needs about internal operations that are unmet by financial reporting. The information you receive should provide detailed and timely feedback on the efficiency of your operations, plus provide a measure of your product costs. This chapter covers the basic issues of management accounting that arise in practice.

Topics covered include:

- Uses of management information;

- Terminology, such as variances and standard, fixed, and direct costs; and

- Problems in implementing management accounting, including joint products costs and allocating overhead.

Interestingly enough, management accounting is not just for large companies. If you are a smaller business owner, you will find management accounting to be an important and useful tool, as well.

Management Uses

For many companies, management accounting is introduced to establish the value of inventory. As discussed in Chapter 9, inventory valuation is probably the most complex issue in accounting and some systematic method is needed to give you accurate information to work with. A manufacturer, for example, must total the cost of materials that make up a product; determine the cost of the labor that went into manufacturing it; and allocate an appropriate portion of overhead expenses, when valuing his or her inventory.

Management accounting, whether used for valuing either products or services, will usually require reporting, and perhaps even an entire system, separate from the basic accounting system you use for financial reporting. This is partly because management accounting classifies information differently and requires complex calculations that financial accounting systems are not designed to provide. However, the main reason is that financial accounting usually reports highly aggregated numbers, while management accounting is intended to report highly detailed information.

For example, GAAP reporting only requires that aggregate inventory costs be correct. Within reasonable limits, how costs are spread among products does not matter as long as the total inventory value is accurate. Consider a company that produces five products and incurs $500,000 in materials, manufacturing labor, and overhead expense. For financial reporting, any reasonable allocation of the production costs is allowed as long as the entire $500,000 is included in cost of sales or inventory.

For internal decision making, however, accurate information on the unit costs of individual products is needed. You can use this information to properly set prices, decide whether to make or buy components, or analyze the profitability of products and product lines. Not only is it not enough to have aggregate costs, but knowing the relationship of the $500,000 of manufacturing costs to each of the five products is valuable, strategic information.

Management accounting is often thought of as an inventory valuation tool, but the concept can be applied across a broad range of organizations and activities. The key is getting timely and useful information, in any format you desire, unencumbered by the conventions of financial accounting. To effectively operate your business, you want whatever it takes to get a handle on key indicators of success, whether it is the true contribution to profits of various products and activities, or an alert to possible problems. Some examples of other ways to use management accounting information are described in this section.

Nonfinancial Information

Financial accounting only reports on transactions that can be measured in monetary terms. Yet, some of the most important feedback management can get is nonfinancial. Of course, these factors do have a long-term financial impact. Important nonfinancial feedback you may receive includes the following types of information:

- Quality might be measured by parts rejected, customer returns or complaints, scrap, or a teacher-to-student ratio.

- Productivity is indicated by units produced, sales per salesperson, and transactions processed. The information could be used in manufacturing, sales, and general and administrative departments (G&A), respectively.

- Capacity utilization is very important for industries with a fixed capital plant. Hotels measure vacancy rates; airlines watch the percent of capacity; and manufacturers track plant and machine utilization.

- Efficiency can measure how quickly assets turn over. Grocers track stockouts and spoilage; credit managers watch average days receivable. Inventory turns are often key indicators.

- Absenteeism and turnover rates may give insights into morale problems.

- Overtime hours may indicate activity or how smoothly work is scheduled.

- The number of new leads generated and percentage of sales closed may be key for a sales organization.

Key Indicators

Formal management accounting systems may be beyond the reach of many smaller businesses. The cost of collecting and summarizing the information may outweigh the benefits. However, even the smallest businesses can benefit by identifying and tracking key indicators.

Key indicators will vary from organization to organization. Some managers like to focus on their top line products. High-tech manufacturers often track bookings, backlog, and billings. Other managers may want to simply know total cash in and out. Most of the nonfinancial measures mentioned earlier, such as those that measure quality, productivity, efficiency, and capacity utilization, could qualify as key indicators.

You may find it useful to ask your controllers or bookkeepers to develop daily or weekly flash reports that track these kinds of vital numbers.

Most of the information is easy to gather and, therefore, can be available on a timely basis. And best of all, the format can be simple to read and understand. Rather than dig through printouts, a one-page report can keep you on top of business trends.

Often, measurements of key indicators take the form of ratios. Gross margin, sales per salesperson, sales per square foot, and billable versus payroll hours are typical measurement ratios.

Operating Ratios

Ratios, by themselves, may not have much meaning. They are more useful when compared to other companies in the same industry or with similar growth patterns. Trade associations can be a good source of standard ratios for your industry. You can also compare your ratios with other companies of similar age or capital structure. A company that invests heavily in automated equipment may have a higher sales per employee ratio than a company that is labor intensive. Young, emerging companies may operate quite differently than more mature competitors.

The actual value of a ratio is often less important than the change over time. You will want to investigate any changes in your ratios. For example:

✓ One company growing slower than expected noticed that sales per salesperson were decreasing. The cause turned out to be that older salespeople had to spend much of their time training new ones, which kept them from calling on customers. The company, which had to make long-term advance commitments for capital equipment and, therefore, needed accurate sales forecasts to avoid unnecessary spending, was able to adjust their sales expectations and bring their expenditures in line.

Designing flash reports, tracking nonfinancial measures, and developing key ratios, like sales per salesperson, are simple, yet effective techniques. They can track operating performance in ways not measured by financial accounting and on a much more timely basis. While basic, these techniques are an important element of management accounting that can be implemented even if more elaborate systems are impractical.

Management System Primer

The key to management reporting is that it is, indeed, for managers. Management accounting is not just for inventory, can be as often as needed, can report on nonfinancial measures, and can be defined in whatever manner is useful. Management accounting can be integrated with or function totally independently of financial accounting.

Of course, traditional management accounting systems are designed for manufacturing companies and the costing of inventory. However, these systems can apply to other types of businesses. The remainder of this chapter discusses these systems, giving an overview of terminology, practices, and methods of management accounting.

Terminology

Usually, management accounting systems are concerned with determining what products or services should cost, tracking actual costs, and examining the difference between them. Listed below are some of the terms accountants use to describe these processes.

Standard cost. Probably the most familiar management accounting term is standard cost. The standard cost is the predetermined estimate of what should be achieved, a target or average cost against which performance can be gauged. Standard cost usually refers to a unit cost.

Variances. Another familiar management accounting term is variances. Variances are the difference between actual and standard cost. Where performance is better than standard, such as lower costs or higher margins, a favorable variance results; if performance is worse, the variance is unfavorable. Variances can usually be broken down to isolate the impact of changes in labor hours, labor rates, the price of purchased components, volume, and total overhead costs. Therefore, accountants will talk about the pieces of the total variance, such as a purchase price or labor rate variance.

Variable or direct costs. The costs that go into a product can be classified as variable, fixed, or semi-variable costs. Variable costs, or sometimes termed direct costs, are those expenditures that change with each unit produced. The material that goes into making and packaging a product, plus the labor used to assemble and transport it, are all variable costs. Adding one additional unit of production or service is assumed to increase direct costs proportionately.

Fixed costs. Fixed costs are those expenses that are assumed to be constant, or at least constant over a certain time period. Fixed costs may also be referred to as overhead, burden, or indirect costs. Heat, rent, and equipment depreciation are examples of fixed costs. Adding one additional unit of output would not change the expenditure on these items. Of course, no costs are totally fixed — given a large enough change in volume or passage of time, all costs are subject to change.

Semi-variable costs. Some costs vary in discreet steps. Producing one additional unit would not change costs, but adding 100 units might. These costs, which could include supervisory labor, machine repairs, or trucking costs, are called semi-variable. Sometimes, semi-variable costs are treated as a separate category. More frequently, companies only distinguish between fixed and variable costs, forcing a decision on which group these costs belong to.

Joint-product costs. Many manufacturing processes contribute to multiple products simultaneously. The costs incurred in shared processes are called joint-product costs. These costs pose a particularly difficult accounting problem — though they may vary directly with total volume, they cannot be traced directly to a single product.

Allocation of costs. Allocation is the apportionment of expenses or revenues, based on an estimate rather than direct measurement. Financial accounting requires that all costs of manufacturing be included in valuing inventory and cost of sales. If the cost system is being used to value inventory for financial reporting, some allocation of overhead must be made to individual products. This allocation can be done based on units produced or inputs, such as labor or machine hours. However, as is discussed in detail below, allocations that are acceptable for GAAP accounting may have little relevance for internal reporting and decision making.

Full cost. A product's full cost — or fully absorbed cost — is the sum of all the costs of production: direct costs plus an allocated portion of indirect costs.

Gross margin. The difference between a product's selling price and full cost is called the gross margin.

Direct or contribution margin. The difference between selling price and direct cost is termed the direct or contribution margin.

Process costing. Process costing tracks production costs by department or procedure and then allocates costs to units produced.

Job costing. Job costing tracks costs by project or by individual unit of product.

Process or Job Costing?

You can use two contrasting methods of accumulating product costs — process or job costing. Where large numbers of units are produced and it is easier to deal with an average cost per unit, use process costing. But if the number of units produced is fairly small and costs can be applied to specific physical units or lots of production, use a job costing system.

Process costing is found in assembly line types of operations where work proceeds through a series of standard production operations. Process costing can apply to high-volume manufacturing, such as semiconductors or plastics, as well as service industries, such as check clearinghouses or telemarketing. Costs are tallied for a given department over a period of time and then divided by the units of output to arrive at an average unit cost.

Job costing is useful when costs can be directly measured for specific units of production. Job costing could include manufacturing of custom furniture or large computers, or service businesses, such as hospital care or heating, ventilation, and air conditioning (HVAC) installation. As materials are consumed or hours spent, they are recorded and assigned to a specific job.

In many processes, no clear line can be drawn between process and job costing. Again, since management accounting has no rules, many hybrid systems are found.

Setting Standards

Standard costs are the basic measures of management accounting. They provide not only a basis for valuing products and services, but they also provide targets against which performance by your company and your employees can be measured. Because feedback is often provided in comparison to a standard, you must decide how easy or difficult standards should be to achieve. You have three basic choices for setting standards:

Historical performance standards. Standards based on historical performance have the advantage of being objectively measurable and will highlight trends in operating performance. However, this method has the weakness of ignoring changes in production processes, volumes, and product design. Past inefficiencies are also built into current targets.

Ideal or engineered standards. Standards set by ideals represent costs under perfect conditions. Even though ideal operations are rare, you may feel that lofty targets provide the proper incentive.

Attainable standards. Setting attainable standards is a popular technique that allows for a certain amount of inefficiency, such as down time, machine breakdown, and rework; however, these standards are set tough enough to provide meaningful targets.

Which method you choose will depend on your use of the standards. A mix may be appropriate, as can be seen from the following example:

✓ One company that produced disposable medical devices, which were packaged into kits, used a very effective mix of standards. Historical standards were applied to machine time used in molding and extruding high volumes of cups, syringes, and tubing. This provided times that were realistic — since no machine upgrades were planned — and easily measured. Since little labor was involved, the lack of an incentive to boost output was immaterial.

Engineered standards were used for component and packaging materials, where product specifications were tight with little tolerance for variances. Attainable standards were an integral part of the labor standards for packaging. Employee compensation included individual incentive pay for meeting and beating standards. Standards that were unattainable led workers to give up or leave the company due to low pay. Unattainable standards also understated a product's cost — since standard labor hours were too low. Standards that were too easy were costly to the company. Once the company revised its standards to a rate slightly below what the very best workers could do and adjusted further for normal down time, productivity rose and standard costs better reflected actual production costs.

Labor Costs

A basic, and sometimes tricky, management accounting calculation is determining your cost of labor. This is vital information, whether you need to know labor costs to price a service or to compute the value of labor used in production.

The first concern is to account for all of your payroll-related costs. On top of wages paid to employees, payroll taxes and benefits often add 30–40% or more to the hourly cost. Examine the direct labor costs as added up for a manufacturing company, shown below.

Payroll Cost Calculations

Average hourly wage rate		$10.70
Paid days/year		260
Hours per day		8
Annual pay		$22,256
Plus: Christmas bonus of 5%		$1,113
Subtotal		$23,369
FICA (employer share)	7.65%	$1,788
Workers' compensation	11.00%	$2,571
Federal unemployment (FUTA)	0.8% on first $7,000	$56
State unemployment	3.50% on first $10,800	$378
Life/disability insurance	2.10%	$491
Average health insurance		$3,682
Total average annual wage & benefit cost per employee		$32,335
Paid days		260
Less: vacation days (average)		12
Less: holidays		10
Total work days		238
Total work hours		1,904
Average total cost per day per employee		$135.84
Hourly wage rate, including benefits		$16.98
Premium over base rate		58.7%

Many companies record payroll taxes and insurance costs as overhead expenses. This makes it easy to:

■ Overlook that these are costs directly associated with every hour worked; and

■ Understate the cost of labor.

Another factor in the cost of labor is down time. No matter how hard employees work, there is always unproductive time during the workday.

Causes include set-up time, breaks, meetings, and assignment to nonproduction tasks, such as cleaning or administration. You can factor down time into the cost of labor per product or service in at least two ways:

- You can compute the hourly cost as shown in the sample calculations, but include in labor hours the elapsed time to complete a job. Down time is captured by including all hours, whether productive or not, from the start of a job to its completion — and the start of another task.

- You can count only hours actually spent on the product or service but factor down time into the hourly rate.

At the company above, a down time factor of 33% — two out of every eight paid hours — was used, bringing hourly wage costs to $22.63. This calculation was instrumental in deciding to raise the charge for their occasional repair jobs from $25 per hour to $45.

Allocating Costs

Allocation of overhead and other indirect costs is a necessary evil of financial accounting. For decision making purposes, though, allocated costs are often irrelevant. For example, an order for ten more units of product or five hours of service time won't require an increase in a company's rent or salary expense. Within a narrow range of activity or time, the cost of your product or service is the sum of your direct costs, such as materials used or travel to and from the job. Your overhead expenses do not change.

This is not to say that individual products or services do not consume or require overhead resources or that overhead expenses can be ignored. Rather, the relationship between output and overhead may be changeable or not lend itself to simple allocation schemes. Any allocations could be misleading or, worse, distort decision making, as seen in the continuation of the medical device company example.

✓ The medical device company's management accounting system showed that it was losing money on every unit on three of its top-ten selling products. Over the protests of the sales manager, the company tried raising prices only to see volume sink in the highly competitive market. After restoring their prices, management took a closer look at the standard costs. They discovered that overhead was allocated based on inputs, such as standard machine and labor hours. Standard cost per unit was the same whether 1,000 units of product were made or just one unit. This application of standard costs ignored efficiencies that large production runs of these popular products generated, such as reduced setup and handling time. As a result, the best-selling products were being assigned a disproportionately high amount of overhead expenses. So, the top-ten products were actually profitable.

Allocating overhead to individual products serves two legitimate purposes.

- First, as a requirement of financial accounting, you will need to develop a satisfactory allocation scheme to satisfy GAAP requirements — but there is no obligation to use that allocation for management accounting. Nor is there is a requirement to reconcile between the cost figures used for management accounting and the inventory figure on the balance sheet.

- Second, while decisions about individual or incremental orders may hinge only on direct costs, overhead expenses are real and your overall price structure must provide an adequate return to cover both direct and overhead expenses. To see the average full cost of a product is generally useful, but pricing decisions should not be made on this information alone or without fully understanding all the cost elements.

With that caveat in mind, how should your company approach the allocation of overhead? Typically, a company will incur expenses for its:

Allocation Schemes

- Building — rent, property tax, and heat;

- Power; and

- Indirect labor — supervisors, inspectors, and receiving.

Basically, the allocation process is a search for a reasonable relationship between the costs incurred and the products that used those resources.

There is no single way to allocate costs, but some relationships will stand out as logical. For example, power can be tied to the number of machine hours a product requires. Expenses for the building can be allocated first to departments based on square footage and then to any products produced in that department.

Many allocations proceed in a step-down manner. For example, some portion of building costs may be allocated to a quality assurance department. These costs, added to wages in the department, are then allocated to several different assembly and packaging departments. Next, total costs for these areas are allocated to products.

This last step, allocating department costs to units of production, is the stickiest issue. At the medical device company, some packaging operations were manual, while some were machine-based. Each operation had a different number of required workers. Should expenses be allocated based on total units produced? The value of the units produced? Total machine hours? Total labor hours? Average labor hours? Dollars of direct labor? The space occupied by each operation?

In many companies, labor hours are the basis of allocation. This scheme makes sense when production is labor intensive; however, as processes have gotten increasingly automated, many such allocations have become outdated. The best allocation scheme is one that traces costs as closely as possible to their source. If a staff of mechanics is on hand, the cost could be allocated based on machine hours, although it probably is even better to know what products require extra setup or put strain on the equipment. Inspectors' wages can be allocated based on units produced, but knowing which products are hardest to test or generate the most rejects, allows you to assign costs more closely.

Allocation issues are generally easier for job cost situations. Since you are dealing with longer periods of time and fewer units, it may make sense to track certain indirect expenses, such as supervisory wages and machine set-up time directly to a job. Entire work areas or machines may be dedicated to one job instead of many, or supplies may be issued to specific jobs, rather than departments.

When you are setting up allocations, check if you are allocating all of your costs. Do this by comparing budgeted overhead expenses to budgeted activity — whether expressed as labor hours, machine hours, or units — multiplied by the standard overhead rate. Then, at the end of the period, do the same comparison except using actual expenses and activity. For more information about budgeting, refer to Chapter 14.

Activity-Based Costing

One of the most recent developments in management accounting is the field of activity-based costing (ABC). ABC is a management accounting approach that traces all indirect costs, including administrative costs, back to the products that generated them. This practice recognizes the problems traditional cost systems have with allocating overhead and with ignoring selling and administrative expenses, even though these may vary with sales or production volume.

Financial accounting requires that all the costs of acquiring and converting inventory be capitalized, but that R&D, selling, and administrative outlays be expensed immediately. Even many cost systems only track purchases and production costs and ignore the other overhead expenses. Yet, many nonproduction expenses are directly related to product and service sales. Buying raw materials or finished goods may involve a purchasing agent. Commissions or royalties may be due on every sale. Product development or ad campaigns may be devoted to individual products. A cost system can and should recognize these expenses.

You do not need to be a manufacturer to make full use of a cost accounting system. Though traditional cost systems focus on production expenses, this may be a limitation carried over from financial accounting. Expanding the definition of relevant product costs opens up the field of cost accounting to service, retail, and distribution companies.

Last Dollar Pricing

A corollary to the discussion of overhead allocation is the concept of last dollar pricing. This concept expresses the idea, touched on above, that in setting prices for incremental orders or products, you should only consider the variable costs involved. Many orders that may appear to produce a loss if an average overhead factor is tacked on, may actually be profitable as long as direct costs are covered.

This is a very simple, yet powerful, idea. A company with excess capacity can ill-afford to turn away sales that generate cash just because the margin doesn't cover a somewhat arbitrary fair share of the overhead. A truly enlightened approach is to ignore sunk costs — unrecoverable prior expenditures — and concentrate on the added benefit a job can bring.

However, you can very easily go overboard with this approach. Rarely are overhead costs truly fixed. Rather, they simply tend to move in discreet steps. Utilities and supplies, for example, often increase on a unit-to-unit basis, but not always proportionately. The changes may also be impractical to measure. And while it is fine to accept the incremental order that only covers its direct cost, somewhere along the line, a company's pricing must be set to cover overhead as well.

A commonly heard expression is that incremental sales help absorb overhead. This term seems to downplay two important facts:

- First, in aggregate, for a product's price to simply exceed direct costs is insufficient. The product must be profitable after all costs are considered. The price must not just absorb overhead but cover it.

- Second, the phrase implies that overhead is fixed and somehow beyond control, and that any profit must be derived from increasing direct margins. In truth, overhead expenses are often as controllable as direct costs.

The bottom line is that if an order is truly incremental business, then you are correct to consider only incremental costs — which may include direct and semi-variable costs. Long-term decisions must take overhead into account. After all, in the long run, all costs are variable. In addition, if accepting one piece of business affects your company's ability to take on other business, the lost profit is part of the incremental costs.

Learning Curves

An innovative approach to pricing, made popular by Texas Instruments for products such as digital watches and calculators, is to take advantage of learning curves. Empirical evidence points out that for new products or processes, costs decline as experience increases. At least one study has shown that cost reductions are from 20–30% for each doubling of cumulative production — machine intensive operations show lesser, but still significant, reductions.[4] This approach suggests that it may be profitable to drop prices below current costs if dropping the prices buys sufficient market share to increase volume and move down the learning curve to lower costs.

Not every business should rush to cut prices and pump up volume. But, you should realize that costs are not static and that pricing decisions require an understanding of business dynamics.

Decision Support

Many companies implement management accounting to help value inventory, however, its true benefit is in supporting decision making. Unencumbered by GAAP requirements, you can use management accounting in any way that helps you control and guide your company. Though the emphasis in practice is on manufacturing cost, the techniques can be applied to service businesses and staff functions as well.

This chapter has discussed the basic, textbook terminology and methods of management accounting. However, you need to recognize that management accounting is an art, not a science. Management accounting is individualized, according to the needs of you and your company and, therefore, you must take an active role in designing the systems. Even very small companies that are not candidates for traditional, large-scale management accounting systems can benefit by identifying and staying on top of key financial and nonfinancial measures.

As with financial reporting, you must also understand all of the underlying assumptions before you can properly interpret the results. Faulty cost systems can lead you astray. As the next chapter explores, weak accounting practices may be responsible for management practices that weaken the competitive position of many companies.

Endnotes

1. Anonymous, quoted in *The Manager's Book of Quotations*, p. 394.

2. Quoted in the newsletter of the Boston Chapter of Institute of Management Accountants, October 1993.

3. Kaplan, Robert S. and H. Thomas Johnson. *Relevance Lost*. Boston: Harvard Business School Press, 1987. p. xii.

4. "Note on the Use of Experience Curves in Competitive Decision Making." Boston: Harvard Business School, 1975.

Chapter 8

Applying Management Accounting

A good part of the problem (poor productivity) . . . lies with the current accounting system which sort of makes overhead disappear — it simply gets added into the cost of a product like a tax.

— Paul Strassmann[1]

With the renewed interest in management accounting systems, many managers started to believe that companies could be run by the numbers. Just as calling accounting "the language of business" raises it to a too lofty status, this belief exaggerates the value of accounting. Accounting is often better at supplying the questions than the answers. A better credo is "always run the numbers — but don't try to run anything by the numbers."

This approach is especially practical when the numbers are misleading, irrelevant, or outright wrong. Many pitfalls can occur in the preparation and interpretation of meaningful performance measures. Relying blindly on the numbers can lead to inappropriate decisions. But the consequences of failing to run the numbers at all are almost sure to be worse. In the words of one bank president, "It bugs us when there is no real ambition to translate thoughts into numbers. A company must run the numbers on a proposal to see if they work."[2]

Why Run the Numbers?

Nearly every company already has a basic financial accounting, or cash basis system. These systems provide basic tracking of transactions and a regular scorecard of financial performance. What objectives can a management accounting system help meet? Is a separate system really needed?

As mentioned in Chapter 7, many companies initiate management or cost accounting to value inventory. Their financial accounting systems, if they can handle the task at all, only provide data on the aggregate value. The detailed information needed to support pricing decisions or determine individual product margins has to come from a cost system.

> "Without a good cost accounting system," says one manager, "It's management by anecdote. Salespeople regularly make passionate pleas for price relief on specific orders. When I press them, they say 'threat of competitive entry.' What choice do you have in the absence of cost data except to go by your judgment of the salesperson's credibility?"[3]

In addition to inventory valuation, management accounting systems provide the benchmarks for measuring progress and performance. If it is true that "If you can't measure it, you can't manage it," and "What gets measured, gets done," then management accounting is a necessary tool for setting and achieving detailed goals.

Management accounting also provides the tools for evaluating the performance of individual managers. Whether you use it to set specific performance goals or tie compensation to departmental achievement, management accounting provides the information at the departmental, or even individual, level. Unlike financial accounting systems, the information used can be nonfinancial, such as rewarding managers for improved quality or reduced scrap rates.

Tracking performance on a particular project or providing information to give quotes on jobs are also made possible by a management accounting system. While financial reporting may only record total wages or purchases, a project cost system can trace actual hours and materials to individual jobs.

Management accounting information can project future performance, making it essential for decision making. A company deciding between outsourcing an operation or bringing it in-house needs the detail the management accounting system provides to compare the two alternatives. Similarly, a company can use information to identify new opportunities. By projecting cost reductions from improved operations or economies of scale, a company can recognize opportunities that financial accounting numbers, which provide only a historical perspective, will miss.

These types of forward-looking decisions are very similar to the notion in economic theory that companies are most profitable where marginal revenue equals marginal cost. Marginal cost is the term used to describe the cost of producing one more unit of product. Knowing your marginal cost requires an understanding of the cost of each unit sold, information the cost system is intended to supply.

Management accounting can transcend the rigid fiscal periods used in financial accounting, so data can be reported in the most timely and meaningful fashion. If production managers need daily or even hourly feedback, the management accounting system can respond. On the other hand, a construction company may set milestones several months apart. Monthly statements on buildings in progress may be irrelevant, so that a report covering the life of the project is needed.

Management reporting can be designed to support the long-term goals of a company. American managers are often accused of focusing almost exclusively on short-term profits at the expense of long-term investment and strategy — partly a consequence of financial accounting, which imposes a short-term profit measure. If companies use their management accounting systems to reinforce long-term strategies, including nonfinancial goals such as quality and on-time delivery, they can enhance their compctitiveness.

Individualization

By now it should be clear that management accounting is a distinct discipline and is not a byproduct or branch of financial accounting. Management accounting supports internal decision makers and helps them to evaluate and control operations — a very different function than the periodic, objective scorekeeping of financial accounting.

Since managers are the users of the system, you should be actively involved in the design of your system. Accountants are needed to develop and implement data collection systems and calculations, but designing the system should not be their task alone. As one expert says, "The task is simply too important to be left to accountants."[4]

Finally, a cookie cutter approach will not work. While having one set of rules is important for financial accounting, where objectivity is essential and comparisons must be made across companies, management accounting must be individualized. A computer chip maker is different from a shoe manufacturer, which is unlike a department store or construction company. Each management team, even within an industry, looks at information in a different way. Standard definitions and systems can provide a framework or starting point, but should not limit the design of a management accounting system.

Common Pitfalls

No blueprint exists for the design of a management accounting system. Not only is the field evolving, but current practices are coming under intense criticism. Less can be said about the right way to design a system than caveats can be made about mistakes to avoid. The good news is that increasing attention is being paid to management accounting and technology is bringing the ability to collect and use detailed information within the reach of smaller companies.

Companies that learn to exploit management accounting, and run the numbers, have the chance to develop a true competitive edge.

What follows, then, is a discussion of the do's and don'ts of management accounting systems.

Don't Tie into GAAP

As has been discussed, management accounting and financial accounting serve two distinct purposes, even though the two functions overlap. A management accounting system is often used to value inventory for the financial statements. At the same time, the accounting systems that are put in place for financial reporting can simultaneously capture all, or most, of the data needed by the cost system.

Management and financial accounting should coexist, one geared toward internal decision making, the other done in accordance with GAAP and intended for outsiders. Where many companies get in trouble is forcing cost figures and reporting to tie into financial reporting.

The conventions, definitions, and timing of financial reporting are simply inappropriate for management reporting. Management accounting is not simply a subset or rearrangement of financial accounting data; it is a separate discipline, requiring a different approach and mindset.

For manufacturers, GAAP sharply divides expenses related to production from R&D, selling, and administrative costs. Manufacturing expenses are allocated 100% to inventory and cost of sales, while all other expenses are excluded, meaning that many indirect costs of production are allocated to product costs. At the same time, selling and administrative costs, even if directly associated with acquisition and sale of a product, are excluded.

If, for example, you are trying to determine the expenditure needed to expand a product line, you need to look beyond the manufacturing expenses. Information is needed, for example, on sales commissions or the cost of added volume in purchasing and accounting. At the same time, if product costs include a certain amount of unrelated overhead, these allocated figures must be pulled out. When the analysis is completed, those costs you feel are relevant, are likely to be organized much differently than under GAAP accounting.

Ignore Sunk Costs

In management decision making, sunk costs are usually irrelevant. Past expenditures for equipment, advertising, or goodwill cannot be altered, so you must focus on making best use of your current resources. At the same time, you will realize that some current and future expenditures will provide a long-term benefit while others provide only an immediate return.

Remember that GAAP rules do not always align with these decision making criteria. Many sunk costs, such as equipment purchases, goodwill, and pension benefits for prior service, must be spread over future periods. At the same time, other expenditures with possible future benefit, such as R&D and advertising, are expensed immediately.

GAAP also requires reporting for uniform fiscal periods, usually months, quarters, or years. Most reports are also prepared well after the close of the period. While having financial statements completed within 15 days of month-end may be acceptable for financial statements, you and your operating managers may need information weekly, daily, or even hourly. Your needs are continuous and don't usually fit within typical accounting periods. Your cost system should be prepared to issue information as needed. It should not be made a slave to the reporting cycle of financial accounting.

Financial reporting is also geared to a monthly, or longer, reporting cycle. To impose this type of schedule on the management accounting system is arbitrary and inappropriate. A monthly P&L for a team developing a new computer is meaningless; monthly feedback to the production manager of an assembly line is ancient history. Yet, many companies' management reporting systems function this way.

To make decisions, you need information on a timely basis. The definition of timely will differ according to what is being managed. A highly automated, large volume operation, such as a paper mill may require reports every few hours to highlight any equipment problems that slow operations or waste resources. An assembly operation will likely require daily feedback on jobs in progress to do scheduling and review productivity. A large-scale project, such as a construction project or R&D, may only require feedback every few weeks or as milestones are passed.

As discussed in Chapter 7, most companies have a large pool of expenses that do not appear directly related to the level of production or sales. In many companies, this may even be the vast majority of expenses, including manufacturing overhead, such as wages for supervisors and inspectors, power, maintenance, insurance, and rent. All selling, administrative, and interest expenses are also in this group.

In GAAP accounting, any manufacturing expenses are allocated to inventory and cost of sales. Selling and administrative expenses are lumped together below the gross margin line on the financial statements. Since the reporting is for companies in aggregate, and not item-by-item detail, this approach suffices for financial accounting.

For you, however, the message should be loud and clear: ignore these so-called overhead expenses and their relationship to products and services at your own risk. For one thing, they often represent 60%, 80%, even 95%, of a company's expenditures. They also are not as fixed as is often assumed. Although one additional unit of output won't change what is spent in the short term on rent, insurance, or supervisors, these expenses can change and do bear a relationship to activities. Three months, a year, or five years may pass, but all expenses become variable at some point. Since most management decisions involve some long-term commitment of resources — space, people, marketing — the impact on "fixed" costs becomes very relevant.

While the relationships may be hard to spot, most overhead costs are, indeed, driven by specific products and activities. The number of accounting clerks, purchasing agents, or warehouse personnel is often related to volume. If a company employs inspectors, which products have high rework or reject rates? To the extent possible, the management accounting system should tie products, services, and projects, to the full range of costs that they drive. Refer to the section in Chapter 7 about activity-based costing. Avoid simplistic allocations. At best, they are accounting exercises. At their worst, they distort reported costs and mislead management.

Don't Overburden Labor

If all your management accounting system is doing is taking the pool of overhead expenses and assigning it to units of output, little is accomplished. For example, overhead is often allocated based on direct labor hours. This is convenient, but does it reflect the actual relationship between activity and expenses? For companies with multiple services or products, different processes will lead to different relationships between labor and overhead. And what about other factors such as machine time, volume (short or long runs), or materials? Without the effort to uncover the true relationship between activity and cost, the time spent devising allocation formulas will succeed in spreading overhead costs, but will say nothing about what actually causes them or how you can control them.

Even worse, you may rely on these faulty costs to make critical decisions. The use of direct labor to allocate overhead is a prime, and common, example. While this may have been a reasonable basis 20 or 30 years ago, many companies have become increasingly automated over time. Automation reduces the labor pool over which to spread overhead expenses and makes labor seem increasingly expensive. Automation also makes departments that are labor intensive seem increasingly expensive by comparison.

The results can be appalling. Companies, seeing their fully burdened labor cost rise, have been led to outsource work in search of less expensive labor only to find they have been led astray by the accounting system. Although labor costs may seem to decline, outsourcing adds a very large overhead expense in purchasing, shipping, inspection, accounting, and top management time and money. And if the accounting system ignores or fails to properly allocate these expenses, the outsourcing option will continue to look good. Even worse, since the internal labor pool has shrunk further, burden rates become even higher making in-house production look even less attractive.

For information about determining labor costs and allocating indirect labor, refer to Chapter 7.

Watch Other Allocation Issues

Similar distortions can occur in decisions to shift work among departments within a company. Any system that does not reflect true cost relationships will result in cross-subsidies between products. Profitable products assigned excessive overhead costs can end up being eliminated or priced out of the market. Allocating on a basis other than labor may not solve the problem since the issue often is the decision to allocate costs in the first place. In *Relevance Lost*, authors Robert Kaplan and Thomas Johnson present an example of a company that made this mistake.[5]

✓ The company had incurred a large expense for prior service pension costs. Under GAAP accounting, these costs are capitalized and amortized over time. The company, quite logically, allocated the expense to different plants based on years of service of the workers. This allocated most of the expense to the plant with the older workforce. Even though this plant was actually more efficient than newer plants with younger workforces, the numbers made it seem more expensive to operate, and it was shut down as a result. The problem, as explained earlier, is that these pension costs were sunk costs; they had nothing to do with current operations, yet were accounted for as if they did.

The costs of high-volume, mature products can be distorted when setup and down time are not factored into the total hours on which an allocation is based. Whether labor or machine hours are used, a system that ignores down time can make one run of 100 hours look as costly as 100 runs of one hour each.

Renowned management consultant and writer Peter Drucker asserts that actual costs are in proportion to the number of transactions an operation generates; however, accounting assigns costs based on the volume of production.[6] Until accounting reflects this reality, reported costs will be distorted.

A related problem is caused by the wide range of product options customers increasingly have come to expect. Gone are the days where consumers are offered "any color, so long as it is black." As management offers a wide range of "flavors," they introduce what Drucker terms as product clutter.[7] According to Drucker, this can be very costly, because in most companies, a 90-10 rule exists where 90% of the profits come from 10% of the products. The accounting system must be able to distinguish the very real cost differences that arise from the longer runs, higher turnover, and learning curve efficiencies enjoyed by mature or popular products.

Beware of Disappearing Overhead

Direct labor is not only a popular basis for allocating overhead costs, but also is a favorite target of managers. Some are constantly looking for ways to boost productivity or motivate workers. These are worthwhile goals, but even dramatic improvements may have only modest impacts on the bottom line, because direct labor expenses are often substantially smaller than either materials or overhead. In many manufacturing companies, direct labor expenses are just 5–10% of sales while overhead runs between twice or four times that.

While minute detail is collected on labor hours, overhead expenses may escape scrutiny. And accounting systems may be partially to blame for several reasons.

- First, allocations of overhead expense may make direct labor seem more costly than it really is. These allocations also make overhead seem as if it is really a function of labor hours.

- Secondly, the tendency to aggregate overhead expenses rather than break them down by department may deter any effort to determine which operations gave rise to the expenses. For control purposes, overhead just seems to vanish in many companies.

- Finally, because managers are allocated a portion of overhead, much of which arises in other departments and is considered beyond the line managers' control, no one is held accountable for overhead. Managers have an incentive to reduce their direct costs on which overhead expense is allocated, but no incentive to reduce overhead itself.

Overhead is indeed controllable and your accounting system must reflect this. As mentioned earlier, if overhead expenses can be traced to the products or services that give rise to them, they should be. If not, recognize that not all expenses need to be allocated. If there is really no relationship between a product or service and an overhead expense, an allocation serves little purpose.

To budget and control these expenses separately is a better option, rather than create the illusion that volume or production efficiencies can change them. If the cost of the human resource department is independent of or too costly to trace to individual products, you are better off establishing an operating budget and holding the department manager responsible for it. Perhaps, you can develop measures such as cost per applicant to measure efficiency. If costs change, the results are reported for just the department; the difference does not have to be absorbed by other departments or individual products.

The same holds true for companies that like to allocate a portion of all corporate expenses to divisions or product lines to create pro forma P&Ls. Although the allocation may ensure that all the costs of business are reported, it ends up assigning the costs to departments that have no control over them and the allocation is unrelated to the source of the expense.

The important thing is to not ignore the expenses or the line managers held responsible for them. Overhead is too large to simply vanish in a series of allocations. The accounting system must ensure accountability for the level of overhead, and it must be aligned with what your managers can actually control.

Encourage Feedback and Motivation

Management reporting systems not only report on performance but, because they provide feedback and incentive, they also influence behavior as well. The key issue is that your accounting system must be in line with the strategic goals of your company. These goals can be both financial and nonfinancial.

In financial accounting, success is generally measured by profits — or a related criterion, such as ROI. One problem with this standard is that profit is basically a short-term yardstick. Unfortunately, short-term profits can rise while the long-term health of a company declines. Slashing expenses, such as advertising or R&D, boosts profits but sacrifices future returns; a sharp increase in inventory hurts cash flow, but has no impact on profit.

One of the most difficult tasks facing top executives as an organization grows is keeping managers focused on long-term, strategic goals. Management accounting opens the door to measures that report on progress against these long-term goals, not just short-term profit. Management accounting provides a chance to report on the health of operations, not just the balance sheet.

Finally, the accounting system must provide your managers with a motivation to reduce costs. One Japanese manager has argued that American cost accounting is too concerned with calculating precisely what demands each product makes on corporate resources, and therefore plays only an "informing" role. Japanese systems, he argues, play an "influencing" role by emphasizing how overhead allocation can shape the cost reduction activities of production employees.[8] In other words, the accounting system should move from being a scorekeeper to being a coach.[9] Information needs to be timely to support decision making. However, collecting and presenting the financial scorecard follows after.

On a day-to-day basis, line managers depend on the management accounting system for timely and accurate feedback. The feedback must be both timely and appropriate, or managers will either ignore the system or develop personal systems to get the information they need. In the latter case, this creates duplication of effort that needs to be eliminated. Consider the illustrations below.

✓ At one manufacturer, inaccurate bills of material (BOMs) and failure to account for leftover scrap caused inventory to be consistently misstated. To adjust for this, the purchasing manager sometimes took a physical inventory of items to determine how much to buy or routinely added 10% to whatever reorder quantity the system recommended.

✓ At another company, the BOMs were so inaccurate, they ceased putting inventory transactions through at all. All purchasing was based on walking out to the stockroom to see what was short.

Determine How Much Detail

Clearly the benefits of management accounting information must be weighed against the cost of collecting and compiling the information. Since management accounting is very detailed, the amount of information collected and reported can be substantial. How much data is too much?

Lack of technology is one constraint that is rapidly disappearing. Early management accounting systems in many companies probably died because the necessary hardware and software either was not available or was too expensive. The dramatic advances in computer performance and the accompanying reductions in cost put management accounting systems within reach of even smaller companies.

Just because the data can be collected, does not mean you should collect it all. Accountants are very comfortable with detailed, precise information and, left to their own devices, may design an overly elaborate system. You will want to take an active role in defining what information is important, so the system provides the most benefit.

The overall precision of the system depends on how accurate each component is. In determining the cost of a manufactured product, if labor costs can be precisely tracked but material costs cannot, total cost will not be accurate. Therefore, the efforts in capturing labor costs may be wasted.

An unfortunate feature of management accounting systems is that they tend to be very precise — or at least appear that way. A product's cost may be broken down to its minutest components or carried out to four decimal places.

The latter occurs because components are bought in bulk and labor or machine output is often tabulated in units per day or hour. If you buy 20,000 screws at a time for $75 and use 2 per unit, your cost is $0.0075 per unit.

If one person making $12 per hour can process 130 pieces per hour, the labor cost for that operation is $12 divided by 130 or $0.0923 each. The use of four decimal places results from the arithmetic used and does not necessarily mean that you should have confidence down to one-hundredth of a penny.

In fact, that very precision often masks a high degree of uncertainty. How many managers, looking at a cost carried out to four decimal places, would suspect that the numbers before the decimal could be wrong? What if production in the example above ranged from 100–150 pieces per hour and there were 100 such operations per finished product.

Total labor costs could be as high as $12 or as low as $8. A unit cost carried out to four decimal places would give no hint of the wide variation in cost.

Even where a high degree of precision is possible, it is usually best not to sweat the small stuff, as the example below illustrates.

✓ At a circuit board assembly company, the person preparing kits for production always counted out the ten nuts and screws that went into each product. This practice lasted until the owner walked by and recognized the inefficiency. The owner reached over, grabbed a handful of nuts and screws, tossed them in the kit, and said, "That's ten."

What if your company establishes expense targets based on $100,000 of sales per month and actual volume is $120,000 or $200,000? Some expenses, such as rent, will be unaffected by the increase in volume, but will decline on a percent of sales or per unit basis. Many other costs will increase with volume and, perhaps, exceed originally budgeted levels. If sales fell to $80,000, the reverse would be true. How valid can standard costs and budgets be if sales volumes fluctuate from projected levels?

Using Flexible Budgeting

If you understand the relationship between your expenses and volume, then using standards and budgets remains sound. One common tool for capturing these relationships is the flexible budget. Rather than pegging budgeted expenditures at fixed levels, the budget for each variable expense is expressed as a function of the activity that drives it. These activities that drive expenditures may be sales volume, units produced, sales calls made, or number of clients seen.

Once these relationships are determined, the flexible budget can adapt to any level of activity. More information about flexible budgets is provided in Chapter 14.

For managers trying to stay within budget, a flexible budget means having the freedom to hire more people as volume increases or having pressure to cut costs if activity declines. And rather than going through the roof when travel expenses exceed budget, top managers will relate the costs to the number of sales calls made. In fact, some of the most valuable and quick tests you can make are ratios between costs and total activity. These ratios might include sales per salesperson or employee, sales per square foot, and direct labor cost per unit produced.

Some expenses, of course, may not change with volume. For these, the budget would remain fixed and variances would be unaffected by activity. However, remember that in the long term no expense — even rent, equipment, and administrative salaries — is really fixed. When establishing long-range plans or evaluating performance over several periods, these expenses should also be required to meet expense to activity target ratios.

In addition to trying to more accurately record both product costs and the relationship of activity to overall expenses, as described in Chapter 7, activity-based costing (ABC) looks at seemingly fixed costs as resources and examines how efficiently they are used.

Using Activity-Based Costing

If a purchasing manager can process 2,000 transactions a month, but only handles 1,500 this month, there is excess capacity of 500 transactions. ABC can show department managers how they are using the purchasing manager, the economics of having excess capacity, and what would happen if the number of transactions increased. And, since in the long run the amount spent on purchasing managers and other overhead departments will adjust to volume, the future impact on these costs can be determined.

While ABC improves the quality of management accounting information, it still uses the same accounting information as traditional systems. The underlying data must be sound, or ABC will just be a rehashing of those figures.

More importantly, ABC also only takes quantitative measures into consideration. Critics argue that accounting based systems cannot tell you about quality, customer satisfaction, and other nonquantitative concerns. To the extent that these are critical success factors, even the most sophisticated accounting system will come up short.

The Control Panel

Much of this chapter has discussed common flaws found in management accounting systems and given warnings of things not to do. But, don't be discouraged from implementing management accounting systems; management accounting is critical for internal decision making and control over your organization. If managers are indeed like navigators of a ship or plane, management accounting systems are the control panel, the instruments they rely on.

That is why it is critical that your cost system be more than just an extension of the financial accounting system or an attempt to allocate expenses to activities. Financial and cost systems serve different purposes, and while they may share much data, they must operate independently.

The numbers produced by management accounting will be no substitute for judgment, but will certainly assist you in decision making and control. By translating operating objectives to quantifiable goals, operating performance can be guided and evaluated. And by understanding the relationship between activities and costs, you can react to variances and properly allocate resources.

On a global scale, current management accounting systems have taken much of the blame for American managers' focus on short-term results and for causing misallocation of resources. Internal use of traditional measures, such as ROI and quarterly profits, which are based on financial accounting figures, also should be challenged. To say that a transition is essential to the competitiveness of individual companies and American companies in general is no exaggeration.

Efforts toward transition must involve both you and your controller. The issue that must be addressed is the information that you need, not simply how to rearrange the numbers your accounting system already has. Not only are these the concerns you are most familiar with, but they are well beyond the standard GAAP accounting treatments most accountants know best. Like so much of controllership, the task is too important to be left to accountants. But working together you, as a manager, and your controller can forge the system you need to steer your company.

Endnotes

1. Paul Strassmann, quoted in the *The Manager's Book of Quotations*, p. 9.

2. James Lientz, quoted in *The Manager's Book of Quotations*, p. 6.

3. Shapiro, Benson P., V. Kasturi Rangan, Rowland T. Moriarty, and Elliot B. Ross. "Manage Customers for Profits (Not Just Sales)." HARVARD BUSINESS REVIEW Sept.–Oct. 1987: 106.

4. Kaplan, *Relevance Lost.* p. 262.

5. Ibid. pp. 199–200.

6. Ibid. p. 241.

7. Ibid. p. 241.

8. Hiromoto, Toshiro. "Another Hidden Edge – Japanese Management Accounting." HARVARD BUSINESS REVIEW July–Aug. 1988: 22.

9. McNair, C.J., Richard L. Lynch, and Kelvin F. Cross. "Do Financial and Nonfinancial Performance Measures Have to Agree?" MANAGEMENT ACCOUNTING Nov. 1990: 34–35.

Notes

Part III

Managing Your Assets

Chapter 9

Inventory Tracking and Valuation

It is misuse of cost accounting to derive from it figures for a particular product's share of the total business cost .... Figures that allocate the great bulk of the costs are useless.

— Peter Drucker[1]

A corporate controller at a Fortune 1000 manufacturing company used to ask this question of prospective employees: "What asset should a financial manager devote the most effort to controlling?"

The right answer was inventory. Cash is certainly precious, but it is easy to protect and account for with basic internal controls — such as bank reconciliations. Receivables tie up great amounts of capital, but the only risk is whether they are collectible. Fixed assets are stable and, though they can get damaged, are hard to steal without detection. Inventory is, by far, the asset that is the most difficult to control and value.

Control of inventory involves multiple, difficult issues a controller must deal with, including:

- Preventing physical losses such as theft, damage, and obsolescence;
- Valuing inventory, both in aggregate for financial statements and on a unit basis for pricing decisions and other analysis;
- Freeing up cash by keeping inventory from sitting on the shelf; and
- Maintaining accurate records of stock on hand to ensure smooth production and improve purchasing decisions.

Excess, overvalued, or uncontrolled inventory can weigh a company down and throw management off balance. The solutions are rarely simple or straightforward, whether inventory is manufactured or purchased.

The previous two chapters discussed management accounting, including the methods used to determine the unit cost of manufactured products. This chapter examines the accounting issues surrounding inventory tracking and valuation for financial statement purposes.

As discussed in Chapter 5, most accounting practices will not give you accurate information for inventory control purposes. Knowing how your inventory is valued and kept track of and what kinds of measures you need to take to obtain more accurate figures, will help you determine how to better manage and control your inventory. Chapter 10 deals with inventory control and management.

Shrinkage

Why should you be so concerned with how inventory is valued when it is just one of many components of the financial statements? Because, for companies with inventory, accurate valuation is usually the greatest single variable in preparing financial statements. How you choose to value inventory and differences between what is shown on the books and what shows up in a physical count can dramatically alter your financial statements and the perceived health of your company.

Inventory shrinkage is the term used to describe the difference between actual inventory on hand and the higher figure shown on the general ledger. Even though differences between book and actual inventory may build slowly over time, many companies only uncover the true differences at year-end when the books are fully adjusted and a physical inventory, perhaps the only one all year, is taken. A large discrepancy can turn a profit to a loss, or at the least, provide a nasty surprise. As one small business owner described it:

> "I thought we were doing really great. Then, at year-end, I was shocked by a write-down of $66,000 in inventory that offset about a quarter of our pretax profits. I felt like I'd been kicked in the stomach. My illusion of having established control was shattered."[2]

The big question for both managers and controllers is, "Is inventory, as reported on our statements, really all there?" In one study, over 95% of the companies surveyed reported inventory discrepancies. For smaller companies, these differences averaged between 2.5% to 4.5% ($60,000–100,000) of inventory on hand. Both gains and losses against book were reported, although losses were roughly two and one-half times more common.[3]

The study also strongly indicated that accounting weaknesses are to blame. Only 1% of the discrepancies were blamed on theft. Errors, such as unreported scrap, inaccurate standards, or misreported production counts, accounted for over 80% of the variances.[4]

How do you avoid a year-end inventory surprise? A partial list of suggestions includes:

Controlling Shrinkage

- Record scrap as it occurs or create adequate reserves. This is particularly important if the only way on-hand inventory is reduced is when an item gets shipped. You need a procedure for subtracting items that are damaged, rejected, or thrown out, or the accounting system will continue to report them as on-hand.

- Check incoming shipments and invoices for price and quantity discrepancies — the number of errors is often surprising. You will save money on under-shipments, as well as improve the accuracy of your records.

- Deter theft by physically restricting access.

- Physically control component parts so that employees must report requisitions for repairs or assembly. A major source of shrinkage is caused by employees simply pulling parts they need off the shelf without completing any paperwork.

- Invoice all shipments.

- Check coding of invoices in accounting so that nonmanufacturing expenses aren't charged to inventory. Since GAAP requires that all costs of production be allocated to inventory, inflated manufacturing expenses will inflate the book value of inventory. So, make sure the nonmanufacturing expenses can be sorted out for your management accounting purposes.

- Have accurate bills of material (BOMs) — listings of component parts and quantities needed for higher level assembly — so that inventory is properly relieved for production and shipments. At one company, a shortage of one part forced them to use a substitute item in assembling several products. However, the BOMs were never updated, leading to negative quantities of the first item (which, to compound the problem, were usually adjusted back to zero) and overstated amounts of the substitute.

- Watch reported production, especially for employees on incentive programs. Make sure that rework is not double-counted.

- Check for parts with similar descriptions or prices being confused in billing and receiving.

- Perform cycle counts — periodic test counts of inventory — to catch discrepancies during the year, not just at year-end.

- Book adequate reserves during the year to avoid a year-end hit if specific losses cannot be tracked.

Take time to implement the suggestions listed above as part of your company's standard operating procedures. Once you have addressed controlling your shrinkage, the next step for control is choosing the most appropriate method to keep track of your inventory.

Tracking Inventory Costs

Inventory is generally accounted for in one of two ways, the perpetual or the periodic method. The system you choose depends on your type of business and your particular needs.

Perpetual Method

Under the perpetual method, all ins and outs of individual items are recorded as they occur so that the system always has a detailed record of what goods are on hand. Cost of goods sold is calculated directly as goods are taken out of stock, and any inventory losses are captured as they occur.

The perpetual method works best where inventory can easily be measured and tracked in discreet units, and accurate information about on-hand quantities is important. Typically, retailers, distributors, or assembly operations use the perpetual method. Most companies with perpetual inventory systems still take physical inventories to verify the accuracy of the book figure, however, this can be accomplished with cycle counting rather than a 100% physical inventory.

Periodic Method

The periodic method does not track movement of the components of inventory, relying instead on period-end physical counts to determine stock on hand. Cost of sales is determined via the familiar equation:

Cost of Sales Equation

Cost of sales = Beginning inventory + Purchases – Ending inventory

The periodic method is easier to implement than a perpetual system. Instead of recording each purchase and sale on an item-by-item basis, purchases are recorded in aggregate and the number representing the cost of goods is derived based on ending inventory.

The major weakness of the periodic method is that it leaves you exposed to a year-end surprise if the physical inventory reveals an unexpected shortfall. Similarly, without occasional physical inventories during the year, interim financial statements may be unreliable. The periodic method assumes that any inventory not accounted for at year-end must have been sold. If significant scrap, theft, and other losses have occurred, they will not be detected without a physical. Not only is a major physical inventory too late for interim statements, but determining the cause of the shortages becomes difficult.

Nonetheless, even where the costs of tracking inventory are high or with little benefit, and the risks of losses from shrinkage low, the perpetual system can make sense. You can beef up your system by specifically tracking events, such as scrap and damaged goods. You can also track units on hand with a perpetual system, but account for costs using the periodic method.

From a financial accounting standpoint, either method is acceptable. Your choice should be governed by the costs and benefits of each system, especially the need for accurate interim statements and information about on-hand quantities.

Valuation

Once inventory quantities are known, whether by perpetual tracking or a physical inventory, the next question is, "What is it worth?" Under GAAP, the basic answer is that inventory is valued at whatever you paid for it.

What seems like a simple answer, however, quickly gets complicated by some of the following issues:

- What is the flow of goods? If you buy goods every month and prices fluctuate, how do you figure out when you bought the units that are still on the shelf and what you paid for them?

- If you add value, such as in manufacturing, what costs do you add in?

- If the market value of the goods changes while they sit on your shelf, should you make adjustments?

To understand some of the many possible complications, consider this example.

✓ The local stationery store carries a stock of printer ribbons. In November, the store buys 1,000 at $1.00 apiece. Sales are good and when the stock on hand drops to 500 pieces at the end of the month, the store reorders another 500. However, there has been a general 10% price increase; in addition, it is $0.10 more expensive to buy a smaller quantity. The new price is now $1.20 each. The store sells another 300 in December. At year-end, the store's accountant must compile a balance sheet. What is the value of the 700 ribbons still in stock?

Of course, the problem is an accounting, not an operating, question. From your management standpoint, the main question is what the ribbons can be sold for and, perhaps, what you will have to pay when you reorder. Only accountants are concerned with historic cost.

Based on differing assumptions and methods, five correct answers to the question about the value of the 700 ribbons are possible. The accountant starts by asking how much was paid for the inventory. Immediately, an assumption must be made about the flow of goods. Did the store sell the oldest goods first — in which case they still have all 500 of the ribbons bought at $1.20 and 200 of the original ribbons — or have some of the newer ribbons also been sold? Maybe the accountant could tell by looking at the boxes themselves, but with thousands of different items in stock this hardly makes sense. A shortcut is needed.

LIFO and FIFO

What if the accountant assumes that the newer ribbons were sold first? Called last-in, first-out (LIFO) accounting, in this case, only 200 ribbons purchased at $1.20 would remain, plus 500 bought for $1.00, yielding an inventory value of $740.

Another possible assumption is that the oldest goods are always sold first, since this is in keeping with good inventory management. Known as the first-in, first-out (FIFO) method, the accountant assumes that the 700 units on hand consist of all 500 bought at $1.20 and 200 bought at $1.00, for a value of $800.

Forced to make a choice, suppose the accountant decides that FIFO better reflects the condition of the inventory and makes the appropriate entries. From a profit and loss standpoint, the assumption that the flow of goods is FIFO ends up with a higher markup of the goods and increased profits. In using FIFO and assuming that the store only sold older ribbons costing $1.00 each, the markup, if the ribbons are sold at $2.00 each, is $1.00, yielding a net profit of $300. Yet the cost of each ribbon purchased in December was $1.20, and had that been used as the unit cost, as would happen under LIFO, the cost of sales would be $360 (300 ribbons times $1.20 cost) and profit $240 (300 ribbons times $0.80 markup).

If the flow of goods is deemed to be LIFO — where the most recently purchased goods are assumed sold first — because this better matches current revenues and expenses, then another problem is encountered. How can you still carry 500 ribbons at $1.00 each when the same ribbons today would cost at least 10% more? When ribbon prices rose, didn't the value of the ribbons sitting on the shelf increase? By buying smart, in large quantity and before the price increase, didn't the store profit?

According to GAAP, you don't earn a profit until you have actually sold something. Just because prices went up on something you own, doesn't mean you actually made money. The same is true if you buy in a large enough quantity to qualify for a price break — you have not made an accounting profit until you have sold the products.

Weighted Average

LIFO and FIFO are not the only choices. A weighted average can also be used. In the example above, the 1,500 ribbons cost a total of $1,600 and both cost of sales and finished inventory could be calculated to yield a cost of $1.067 each.

Standard Cost

Another method is to develop a standard cost, which is an estimate of what purchased or manufactured inventory should cost. Both inventory and cost of sales are computed using the standard cost. Any variances, actual costs that differ from standard, are included directly in that period's cost of sales. In the example, the store might establish a standard of $1.00 per ribbon. The $0.20 per ribbon ($100) extra paid in December would be expensed as a purchase price variance and the remaining stock of 700 ribbons carried at $700.

Actual Cost

For big-ticket items, where each unit of inventory can be tracked separately — perhaps by serial number — you may be able to use the actual cost of each unit, eliminating the need for any flow assumption. Unfortunately, this method does not apply to the low-cost, high-volume items carried by the stationery store.

Choosing a Method

The final decision about which method to use is basically a win or lose trade-off between the balance sheet and the income statement. All of these methods are valid and in use. Under LIFO, in inflationary times, your income statement will better approximate current costs and will result in lower income — and therefore, taxes. The balance sheet, though, will show inventory at lower than current costs and you have to track "layers" of inventory — such as $X of inventory at 1993 prices, $Y of inventory at 1994 prices and so on. FIFO brings the balance sheet closer to current costs and may better approximate the way goods actually flow. But you will have higher income, and therefore, higher taxes, when prices are rising. The average cost method is somewhere in the middle, between LIFO and FIFO. Standard costs are less commonly used for financial statements — they are largely an internal, management accounting measure — but would make sense if your computer system can't track purchase history

Reserves and Write-Offs

Another consideration in valuing your inventory is what you pay for goods, of course, is not necessarily what they are worth. Many things can affect an item's value as it sits on the shelf, such as obsolescence, shifts in market prices, or damage. How are these events recorded?

Accounting rules require that inventory be carried at lower of cost or market value. As was discussed in Chapter 5, if an item's value rises, the company cannot book a gain; but if the value for which it can be sold — the realizable value — drops below cost, the value must be written down.

Since this rule can be applied in aggregate instead of an item-by-item basis, normal price shifts, in which some prices rise and others fall, shouldn't require an adjustment. But if an item, or group of items, suffers a significant loss in value, this loss should be reflected on the books.

A write-off is made when inventory is determined to have no value, such as in the case of damaged, stolen, or obsolete goods. Usually, though, inventory on hand retains at least some value. Perhaps, it can be repaired or sold at liquidation prices. Instead of writing off the entire balance, an estimate is made of the realizable value and book value adjusted down to it. This is called a reserve.

For tax purposes, inventory adjustments and write-offs can only be deducted if the inventory is actually disposed of. For financial accounting, a reserve or write-off can be recorded without physically disposing of the inventory.

Since carrying inventory always includes the risk that some losses will occur, many companies prefer to book reserves on an ongoing basis, rather than wait to identify specific losses. For example:

✓ An apparel manufacturer that was affected by changes in styles from season to season booked a monthly reserve for cloth. They knew that as the product line changed some unsalable material would be left over. At year-end, this amount would be computed and the actual estimated write-down booked. By booking the reserve over time, the hit had already been spread out and a year-end surprise avoided.

Some typical events companies choose to reserve for include expected, but as yet unrealized, losses for shrinkage, obsolescence, and damage. Booking reserves is conservative, helps prevent future negative surprises, and often reflects a realistic expectation of losses. However, they tell you nothing about the source of the losses.

Inventory reserve entries require a great deal of judgment. Predictions of what a fair reserve for scrap is or what goods will become obsolete may be impossible. In the end, you have a wide range of possible figures. Since the choice will impact the income statement, the reserve entry can give you great influence over reported profit.

Determining Cost

When valuing inventory, companies with value added — through labor, machining, or other operations, the goods become more valuable — have the additional problem of deciding what internal costs should be added to the purchase price of materials. Once the costs are determined, how are they traced or allocated to specific products?

Full Absorption Versus Direct Costing

As was discussed in the chapters on management accounting, the costs of a product can be roughly divided into two categories: direct costs and indirect costs. The term direct costs refers to expenditures, such as labor and materials, that vary in direct proportion to units sold or produced. The term indirect costs is used to refer to any of your fixed or continuing costs, such as rent and utilities, commonly called overhead. If you are trying to calculate what it costs to produce an incremental unit, then the answer is the sum of the direct costs. Adding overhead to direct costs results in what is termed a full absorption cost or simply, full cost.

Significant management implications arise in determining whether to use direct or full costs for analysis. Direct costs are generally more relevant when analyzing the incremental impact of pricing or production decisions. However, a company cannot ignore overhead, particularly in long-range decisions, such as setting prices and revenue objectives. Using full cost helps ensure that overhead expenses are not simply ignored in management decisions.

What Is Included?

For financial reporting, you have no choice of which method to use because GAAP and tax reporting require use of the full absorption method. For your own internal information needs, if you require direct costs for analysis, make sure you get those numbers from your controller or accountant.

For financial statements, how overhead is allocated to individual items is unimportant as long as the method is reasonable. GAAP only requires that the aggregate cost of inventory be correct.

Virtually all costs of acquiring or converting materials into finished, salable product are part of the full cost. For purchased items, whether for resale or as an input to an assembly or manufacturing process, all costs of getting the goods in the door, such as freight and insurance charges, plus the costs of handling and inspecting the goods, are included. Cash discounts for paying early are usually netted in as well.

For manufacturing companies, all costs in the production area are included. The determining factor for GAAP is in what department expenditures occur, not how directly the expenditures vary with production. Operating expenses can cover a broad range, such as tools, packaging materials, rent, and utilities. For some expenses, such as heat and rent, an allocation might be made between production and administrative functions. Labor cost would include assemblers, machine operators, inspectors, and, perhaps, the purchasing agent and the vice-president of manufacturing.

The wages of people in other departments, such as R&D and G&A, are excluded even if their work supports production. For example, accounting salaries, even for people who process production paperwork, are not added into the cost of inventory.

As was discussed in Chapter 8, this sort of allocation provides an objective basis for valuing inventory, but may have little to do with how costs are actually driven. Again, the goals of financial and management accounting are quite different and GAAP rules should not determine internal cost reporting.

Inflated Costs

What if your production costs ballooned unexpectedly one month? Perhaps a flaw in a purchased component forced you to do a lot of rework or an accident occurred causing disruptions and repair costs. From an operating perspective, you may resign yourself to having a bad month and moving on. But for financial reporting, depending on your choice of accounting methods, the bad news could get delayed.

This will not be the case for most companies. The most common accounting methods expense variances as they occur. Some companies, though, choose to treat monthly variances as part of the cost of acquiring inventory. They add the variances to the value of their inventory and do not expense them until later months when the inventory is sold. This is a valid accounting treatment that fits within the FIFO cost flow. But it means that unfavorable variances will not be included in your costs of sales until several months after they occur.

Variances can also build up if your costs of sales are booked at standard costs that are higher or lower than actual costs. If inconsistencies are not caught and adjusted for, you can end up with a year-end inventory surprise, as discussed at the beginning of this chapter. To avoid this, regularly compare actual expenditures for labor, materials, and overhead with what is being expensed at standard cost.

Beyond Valuation

If you have ever applied for a line of credit, you will have discovered that banks are reluctant to lend against inventory. At best, you may find that you can borrow 50% of book value and with a fairly tight cap. Yet, the same bank may be willing to lend up to 80% of accounts receivables.

The bottom line is that book value is not a reliable indicator about what inventory is worth, particularly to a lender. Part of this has to do with what the inventory would be worth if the bank had to seize it. Without an on-going business, the parts and finished goods may be worth a fraction of their cost.

The risk of damage, obsolescence, and other losses also cause lenders to depreciate inventory value. And, finally, the vagaries of accounting play a role. Bankers realize that what it costs to acquire or make a product may not be what you can sell it for.

Inventory, of course, also ties up cash. Although inventory is classified as a current asset on the balance sheet, it can be highly illiquid — not readily convertible to cash. A company with many current liabilities and a high portion of its current assets tied up in inventory, could find itself in a cash crunch.

If you are analyzing financial statements, either your own or someone else's, spend time evaluating inventory. Can you determine whether there is excess inventory, in which case an asset could quickly turn into a write-off and a profit turn into a loss? No matter how healthy the current ratio, is the company liquid? If the company had to be liquidated, how much of the inventory value could be recovered? And, as discussed in the next chapter, high inventory can be a sign of inefficiency. Looking beyond the book number is likely to reveal insights into the company's true health.

Issues in valuing inventory have been discussed extensively in several chapters. But as important and challenging as tracking and valuing inventory can be, controlling the amount of inventory is even more vital. Excess inventory ties up cash and risks loss or damage from a range of sources. Too little inventory risks stockouts that can slow production and hold up deliveries to customers.

Perhaps the controller's most essential tasks are to meet and balance these demands for effective inventory management. How to accomplish these tasks is the topic for the next chapter.

Endnotes

1. Drucker, Peter. *Understanding the Business.* New York: Harper & Row, 1964. pp. 28–29.

2. Bodenstab, Charles J. "Surprise! Surprise!" INC. Sept. 1988: 135.

3. Kim, Il-Woon and Arjan T. Sadhwani. "Is Your Inventory Really All There?" MANAGEMENT ACCOUNTING July 1991: 37–38.

4. Ibid. p. 39.

Notes

Chapter 10

Inventory Control and Management

FISH – First In, Still Here.

— Popular acronym

OSWO – Oh Shit, We're Out.

— Acronym attributed to Oliver W. Wright[1]

== **A Sign of Trouble**

No matter how you choose to value inventory, the bottom line is that just having items on the shelf is costly. Not only does inventory tie up cash, but resources are needed to store it, move it, and count it. You are also exposed to losses such as spoilage, shrinkage, theft, obsolescence, and damage. Because inventory can be a large portion of your company's assets, gaining control of your inventory is an important step to sound management.

The answer is not as simple as stripping the shelves of inventory or changing buying habits. Excess inventory can be a sign of deeper, structural problems that must be resolved as a prerequisite to reducing inventory levels.

This insight is illustrated in the drawing on the next page. Stocking excess inventory provides a buffer against, and can hide, a multitude of problems. Put another way, system weaknesses force managers to keep excess inventory on hand to compensate. Since many of these issues and their solutions are in accounting and control systems, a controller and all levels of management must work together to correct them. The first step to controlling your inventory is to evaluate your company's inventory management practices.

Excess Inventory Covers Up Problems

The Walkthrough

The quickest way to gain insight into the quality of inventory management is to walk through a plant or warehouse. A tour usually provides a number of visual clues about the amount and quality of inventory, which in turn, signal operating problems and potential cash drains. Consider the following examples:

✓ A medical products manufacturer's warehouse was filled to near capacity. Forklifts were busy shuffling boxes around to make space for new production. Though most of the inventory was current, some locations contained stacks of boxes covered with dust, damaged by forklifts, and crushed under the weight of other boxes. It was quickly apparent high stocking levels were creating costs from obsolescence, damage, and simply having to store product.

✓ A heating, ventilation, and air conditioning repair and installation business had replacement parts and duct components stored in all corners of its shop. This provided a clear sign that there were no controls over the amount or movement of materials.

✓ A jewelry company that generally made items to order had a roomful of unsalable finished goods. These items were production overruns from shipped orders and customers did not accept excess goods. Further investigation revealed that they resulted from increasing production quantities to compensate for poor quality control.

✓ An apparel manufacturer and retailer had products up to 20 years old stashed in its basement. Because the business was sensitive to fashion, the old inventory lost value quickly, while the quantity on hand increased regularly. This was a clue that a strategy was needed to liquidate excess merchandise.

As these cases illustrate, observing the amount, age, condition, and storage of inventory can tell you if problems exist. The next step is to go beneath the surface to try to discover the causes. The underlying operating problems may be caused by ineffective management of:

- Absenteeism
- Bottlenecks
- Down time
- Lead times
- Missing parts
- Obsolescence
- Quality control
- Rework
- Scrap

As the drawing on the previous page demonstrates, these underlying problems must be solved before reducing inventory levels. The remainder of this chapter explores how to uncover and solve some of the underlying problems listed above that are causing you to carry too much inventory.

How Much Inventory?

Effective management of operating problems begins with an analysis of your inventory levels. In addition to inspecting the inventory, what numbers can you look at to tell you how effectively it is being managed?

Turns

A popular and quick measurement of inventory levels can be accomplished by looking at turns — the ratio of the annual cost of sales to on-hand inventory, also referred to as a turnover ratio. This measure compares average on-hand inventory to cost of sales to gauge how quickly stock turns over. Although turns can be calculated for individual items, they are usually stated for the company as a whole. The less inventory your company needs to generate a level of sales, the higher the turns ratio. A high turns ratio is usually considered indicative of more effective management.

To calculate turns, divide your cost of sales — not sales, but the cost of goods sold for the period, including manufacturing cost, storage, and certain overhead costs — by your average total dollar amount of inventory on hand. For example, if you started a year with $90,000 of inventory and ended with $110,000 of inventory, your average inventory was $100,000. If your annual cost of sales was $400,000, your turns ratio was four ($400,000 ÷ $100,000). Compare your turns ratio number with similar companies to see how you are doing.

How often inventory turns over will vary by industry. Supermarkets, for example, turn inventory over more quickly than manufacturers of heavy machinery. The style of operation will also make a difference. A computer manufacturer that makes most of its subassemblies in-house will have more inventory — and thus fewer turns — than a competitor who subcontracts all but the final assembly.

Sometimes, you will hear people discussing months of inventory on hand instead of turns, particularly when discussing individual items. The months of inventory measurement, illustrated by the formula below, is closely related to turns. To determine how many months of inventory you have on hand, divide twelve months by your turn ratio — which is annual cost of sales divided by inventory.

Months of Inventory on Hand Equation

Months of inventory on hand = 12 months ÷ (Annual cost of sales ÷ Inventory)

If inventory turns four times per year, on average, you have three months of inventory on hand.

On-Time Delivery

Other numbers you will want to take a look at in your analysis of inventory are the percentage of customer orders shipped on time and the average time needed to fill backorders. One of the trade-offs to high inventory turns is that lean inventories run the risk of stockouts — inability to fill customer orders. Shooting for 100% on-time delivery may be too costly, but you can establish a target, such as 95% or 98%. Then, if you fall behind, it may indicate that some inventory quantities should be raised.

Balanced Inventory

Another number to examine in your analysis, even more important than the level of inventory, is whether inventory is well-matched or balanced. In aggregate, you may have two months of inventory on hand, but be out of one material, while carrying a two-year supply of another. For example, a clothing retailer may find itself stocking odd sizes and colors. Likewise, most of the old products on the shelves of the medical products company, discussed in the examples at the beginning of this chapter, were low-volume, specialty items. While the overall turns level may have looked healthy, the ratio was driven by the movement of only the top-selling products.

Not only does a poorly matched inventory risk having overstocked items go stale, but you may need additional spending to bring the inventory into balance if you need to fill out a product line in order to market it. Additional spending may also be necessary if component parts only have value when converted to finished goods. Test your inventory regularly on an item-by-item basis to ensure a matched inventory.

Shrinkage

Of course, inventory shrinkage is another factor to look at as a sign of possible problems. As noted in Chapter 9, these losses may only come to light when a physical inventory is taken, perhaps as infrequently as once a year. By the time the losses are discovered, it may be impossible to accurately trace the cause.

Shrinkage is stated as an aggregate measurement and may encompass several underlying problems. Try to isolate individual problems, such as scrap and rework, as they happen until you can identify all the sources of shrinkage and take corrective action.

After analyzing your inventory levels and the problems that need correction, you should examine your inventory control system. The next sections of this chapter discuss various inventory control techniques and how those techniques are related to resolving inventory problems.

Successful System Elements

A wide variety of inventory control systems are in use. Although the shape and form of inventory control systems vary, some basic elements are present in most successful systems.

Software

The most basic element for a modern, successful management system is to invest in a computerized system. Your existing accounting software may suffice, especially if your company does not do manufacturing or only does some light assembly. Most off-the-shelf packages include an inventory module that can track basic ins and outs. Many also handle a simple bill of material (BOM). A bill of material is a listing of all raw materials and subassemblies that go into making a finished product and the quantity required of each. When you add a completed, assembled product to your inventory, the system can use the BOM to relieve the inventory of component parts.

Manufacturing companies, however, may need additional software specifically designed for inventory and production control. Tracking work-in-process; handling complex bills of material, including sub-assemblies; and doing production scheduling are some of the features manufacturers may require. As a starting point, many off-the-shelf accounting vendors can provide you with a list of third-party software compatible with other particular software programs you may want to use. See Chapter 16 for more about choosing financial software.

Physical Controls

Strong physical controls are also important. As is discussed later in Chapter 17, controls are needed less as a deterrent to theft than to ensure that transactions are recorded properly. Simply locking a stockroom can prevent well-meaning employees from grabbing items they need without filling out paperwork or from misplacing parts they are returning to stock. Securing the receiving area keeps employees from moving items onto store shelves or into production before someone can count and log the incoming shipment.

Administrative Controls

In addition to strong physical controls, tight administrative controls are also needed. From verifying the stated quantities of incoming shipments, to cycle counting the stockroom, checking reported production, controlling key punch errors, and comparing shipping records to invoices, a series of checks and balances is needed to prevent the administrative errors that account for the lion's share of reported shrinkage.

Recording scrap, damage, and other losses as they occur is important. As stressed earlier, failing to keep accurate records loses valuable information on the cost and source of these problems. Also, reported on-hand inventory quantities will likely be overstated.

Commitment

The most important component for a good inventory management system is a high degree of commitment from management. Implementation of any inventory control system is not an overnight job. Several tries may be needed to get it right. The new system is likely to meet resistance from employees, as well. Thorough training is important so that the information from the system can actually be put to use. Otherwise, employees will be tempted to either ignore the system or develop alternate, redundant procedures to get information.

Inventory Control Techniques

Before the widespread use of computers, a number of techniques were developed to manage materials, particularly the purchasing cycle. Two techniques that are still popular are EOQ and ABC, which are described below.

Economic Order Quantities (EOQ)

Economic order quantities (EOQ) are calculations of the optimum lot sizes for purchasing items. The simplest EOQ models balance sales demand with handling costs, quantity discounts, carrying costs, and lead times — the amount of time from placing an order to receiving it. More complex calculations can add in the variability of demand and the risks of obsolescence and shrinkage.

Companies also establish formal reorder points based on calculations of the minimum level of inventory desired, taking into consideration demand, customers' sensitivity to stockouts, and the turnaround time to acquire additional stock. If inventory drops below the minimum, a reorder is generated. A maximum, using the same criteria, may also be set, creating what are known as min-max targets.

ABC Classification

Many companies successfully use ABC coding of parts to gain control over inventory. The ABC classification system codes inventory components according to cost and usage. The coding stems from the 80-20 rule, or the theory that a few parts constitute the majority of expense, while a large number of parts are relatively trivial. By focusing the most effort on the relatively few "A" parts, a company can afford to tightly control its most valuable inventory, while removing uneconomical and burdensome controls on less essential items.

A typical breakdown might be as follows:

- "A" parts constitute 1–20% of items but 70–80% of inventory value. The A classification generally includes expensive, hard to obtain, or single-sourced goods. Purchasing is closely controlled to keep holding costs down and ensure adequate supply. A parts are stored in a physically secured location and cycle counted with relative frequency.

- "C" parts are fairly cheap and easy to obtain. C parts may comprise more than 50% of inventory items, but may account for only 10–20% of the cost. C parts are purchased in bulk and cycle counted infrequently.

- "B" parts are items falling between the two extremes of A and C parts. Usually A and C parts are identified first, and whatever parts are left are classified as B items.

After inventory is classified as A, B, or C, each class is managed differently according to importance. The coding decreases costs for management of the inventory, while increasing control where control is critical. ABC coding can be effective in a wide range of settings, from very simple operations to full-blown materials resource planning (MRP) and just-in-time systems, which are discussed next.

MRP and MRP II

Materials resource planning (MRP) was the first production and inventory control methodology to grow out of the use of computers. MRP is a straightforward method that takes projected demand for final products and "explodes" through the bills of material (BOMs). The MRP system calculates through all levels of assemblies to arrive at the demand for component parts. The MRP system then nets this demand against stock on hand and on order to create a buying plan for what is lacking.

The goal is to drive inventory to zero — or desired safety stock levels — by providing precisely the materials needed to meet production demand.

MRP is simply a tool for calculating inventory needed to meet a given production plan. The system answers a need for breaking through multiple level BOMs and for scheduling receipts. MRP does not analyze whether shop capacity is sufficient to meet the plan. And while an MRP system computes what purchases are needed, it does not execute the recommended purchase plan.

A more integrated approach, and one that is a logical progression from the basic MRP system is manufacturing resource planning, or MRP II. MRP II overcomes many of the shortcomings in basic MRP systems by taking into consideration the human and machine capacity of a plant. By including these functional areas of manufacturing, MRP II can ensure that all operations work off the same plan and provide feedback between these areas. MRP II, however, is highly complex; so, while MRP systems are quite common, MRP II is only starting to emerge. The basic elements of MRP II systems are:

- Master production scheduling
- Capacity planning
- Bills of material
- Shop floor control
- Production accounting
- Inventory control

The system starts with the master schedule. The master production schedule is used to determine the quantity and timing of goods needed to meet sales goals. The master schedule is quite comprehensive, taking into account such things as forecasted sales, plant capacity, and the availability of material. The end demands are then exploded through the BOMs to determine the need for component parts. This, in turn, leads to the issuance of purchase orders to vendors and the release of production orders to manufacturing. The progress of these orders is then closely monitored and controlled by the system. Accounting tracks the resources consumed and compares the results to both industry and company standards.

MRP – Problems in Practice

Though MRP systems are capable of dramatic results, research indicates that the majority of systems fail to live up to expectations.[2] Several factors seem critical for successful implementation.

First, MRP works best for manufacturers that produce goods in large batches or repetitive processes where planning of production, ordering and carrying of inventory, and production control are important issues. Job shops may have little use for MRP, since they deal with smaller volumes of production, are less reliant on forecasting, and may use relatively fewer component parts to make a product.[3]

MRP requires accurate recordkeeping. Whatever quantities the system shows for inventory on hand must approximate physical quantities. BOMs must be accurate, or order quantities will be thrown off. Production counts must also be correct.

Lead times need to be measurable and kept up to date. Lead times that are unpredictable or inaccurate undermine the production schedule. Overestimating lead times causes overstocking of items. Underestimating lead times can result in stockouts or extra demands on employees to expedite orders or juggle production schedules.

Most importantly, MRP requires a strong commitment from all managers involved. The system requires a large upfront investment of time and money plus continuous monitoring, data input, and adjustment to run effectively. Implementation of a MRP system is a major undertaking. Given the high failure rate in practice, you will want to consider the benefits you hope to achieve and the commitment level in your company before investing in MRP systems.

In recent years, great attention has been paid to just-in-time (JIT) inventory techniques. JIT has been credited with contributing to much of the success of Japanese manufacturing companies. Greatly reduced production lead times and reduced inventory are just two of the benefits JIT is supposed to deliver. But exactly what is JIT and is it truly a remedy for high inventories and other manufacturing problems?

Just-In-Time

JIT is not simply an inventory control technique; it is more a philosophy. Though JIT seems to mean different things to different people, it seems best described as:

- Doing things right the first time;

- Eliminating costs that do not add value to the final product; and

- Scheduling work on a pull, rather than push, basis.

This last point, pulling instead of pushing, means that production is based on actual orders — not forecasts — with each level of production creating demand for the functions below it.

Some of the underlying concepts of JIT are:

Quality at the source. A commitment to 100% quality eliminates the costs of scrap, rework, and complaints.

No wasted steps. Processes and designs are simplified, leading to shorter set-up times, shorter distances for people and material to travel, fewer production steps and movement, and less paperwork.

Balanced and synchronized workflow. Workforces are organized into cooperative teams of flexible, broadly skilled workers able to do problem-solving.

Preventive maintenance. Ongoing maintenance is emphasized, since equipment breakdowns that cause stoppages will interrupt the synchronized workflow.

Notice that none of these concepts say anything about reducing inventory, but a successful JIT system will reduce inventory in several ways. JIT results in companies ordering goods from suppliers only as needed.

By shortening lead times, fewer of these goods need to be kept on hand. In addition, finished goods inventory is reduced by cutting down production lead times and by producing to actual orders rather than for stock. Finally, streamlining production means less work-in-process.

Combined, all of these measures lead to lower costs. Carrying costs, re-work, handling, inspection time, and paperwork are all lower. Reducing inventory also means less space is needed for storage and you have less exposure to loss.

Remember, reducing inventory levels or shortening lead times is not the starting point of JIT. Rather, reduced inventory levels result from improvements in the manufacturing process and the adoption of the quality-driven philosophy.

Kanban and Combined Systems

JIT and MRP are not necessarily incompatible — although there is controversy on this point. Some companies continue to use MRP to calculate the need for raw materials for the purpose of planning, but under JIT, stop short of actually committing to order materials.

An alternative method for determining reorder points is kanban. Kanban uses visual signals, rather than reports, to authorize making or buying more of an item. In some systems, a colored card is inserted in a parts bin. Usually, the card is filled in with instructions for replenishing the stock. When parts are used to the point that the card is exposed, the card is pulled and the refill order can be processed in a routine fashion by personnel on the shop floor.

Other reorder signals can also be used. Some companies use specially marked containers. When the containers become empty, they are routed to the proper department for refilling.

Kanban was developed in Japan and is used most effectively with JIT. However, even where JIT has not been implemented, the kanban idea can be effective in generating timely reorders of materials used in large quantity.

The Goal

The Goal — Excellence in Manufacturing is one of the most influential books on production and inventory control.[4] A novel written by Eli Goldratt, an Israeli physicist, and Jeff Cox, *The Goal* is more about an operating philosophy than specific analytical tools. The central theme is that the goal of a company is to make money and that some traditional notions about production efficiency are counter to that goal.

Bottlenecks

Two points in particular bear mentioning. One is the idea of attacking bottlenecks. When work in process is held up at one point in production, two things happen.

- Inventory begins to pile up in front of the bottleneck, contributing to higher overall inventory and carrying costs.
- The entire throughput — the amount of material going through a process in a given time — of the plant is affected as operations downstream from the bottleneck don't get the parts they need to keep running.

Basically, the entire operation is only as effective as the weakest link. Goldratt's answer is to do what it takes to move parts through the bottleneck. Don't let the bottleneck area sit idle. Bring in additional resources, if needed, to increase capacity. Even if the added resources seem costly, like reinstating old, slower equipment or adding workers, the benefit of improving total throughput in the plant will greatly outweigh the higher unit cost at the one operation.

Down Time

The other key insight of Goldratt's book is that trying to be efficient by keeping people and machines busy all the time can cost money if you have no orders for the goods they are working on. Building for stock just to keep a plant busy means that cash has to be spent to buy raw materials. That cash ends up being tied up in finished goods sitting in a warehouse. Even though down time means higher unit costs of production and what seems like less efficiency, the overall welfare of your company can be enhanced.

Convert Excess Inventory

In practice, of course, you are likely to have excess inventory on hand at various times. What steps can you take to reduce stock and generate cash?

A common mistake is thinking that all inventory is good inventory. Holding onto slow-moving items because you have one customer who orders them from time to time, or an order for them came out of the blue a few months ago and might again, is a trap. The items can be in excellent condition or been costly to acquire, but if they are not moving, they are tying up cash and probably losing value as they sit on the shelf.

Liquidating Inventory

If you have excess inventory in the form of finished goods, devise a strategy to sell it off in an orderly fashion. Try discounting the goods or paying a higher commission on those items. If they were purchased goods, perhaps the supplier will give you a credit. Discount chain stores may be willing to take production overruns or seconds. Only as a last resort should you have to offer the goods to a liquidator.

For raw materials, you may need to crunch some numbers to see if you generate more cash by selling off the excess or converting the materials to finished goods before selling them. One thing you don't want to do is put excess materials into production just to keep the plant busy. You will spend cash for labor and any additional materials needed and, if the finished products aren't sold, get nothing in return.

Summary

Much attention has been devoted to inventory because, for nonservice businesses, it often represents the greatest area of exposure. To review:

- Inventory ties up large amounts of cash and excess stock is vulnerable to damage, theft, and obsolescence.

- Tracking and accounting for inventory is a complex task, can be costly, and companies frequently are surprised by shrinkage.

- Accurately computing unit costs is critical for pricing and operating decisions.

- In many manufactured products, materials typically make up most of the cost, so the potential payback controlling inventory can be greater than for labor and overhead.

While this chapter has focused on controlling the amount of inventory on hand, for a controller or CEO to decry the high level of inventory and demand a reduction is not enough. Reduced inventory results from good management, not the other way around. Excess inventory often builds up as a buffer against operating problems and a sudden reduction may expose these problems before a company is prepared to deal with them.

A few quick fixes may be available for both manufacturers and nonmanufacturers. On-hand inventory can be scrutinized for overstocked items that if sold, even at a book loss, could generate cash. Inventory can be brought into balance and tighter physical controls implemented. An ABC coding can be devised and, for the A parts, EOQs can be calculated or a min-max system devised. Many just-in-time practices can be implemented without a full-blown conversion.

More sophisticated manufacturing systems, such as MRP and JIT, require long-term investments and, usually, changes in philosophy. These are definitely not quick fixes and a high level of management commitment is needed to succeed. But, in large and small companies alike, the stakes are high when dealing with inventory management and the effort can pay off.

Endnotes

1. Oliver Wright, quoted in *Money Talks*, p. 149.

2. Fisher, Ron and Guy Archer. "MRP: The Problems and Some Solutions." ACCOUNTANCY May 1991: 115.

3. Needle, Sheldon. "Microcomputer-Based Manufacturing Software." JOURNAL OF ACCOUNTANCY June 1990: 115.

4. Goldratt, Eliyahu and Jeff Cox. *The Goal — Excellence in Manufacturing.* North River Press, 1984.

Chapter 11

Cash Management and Liquidity

Cash is King.

Happiness is a positive cash flow.

— Popular sayings

Cash Flow Equals Survival

Nothing matters more than cash. While making a profit is nice, cash flow is vital. Many growing companies find themselves strapped for cash just as their business is taking off. Similarly, a struggling company possibly can stay afloat by finding ways to generate cash.

Cash flow is, perhaps, the single most important element of survival for a smaller business. In a survey of the more than 60,000 businesses that folded in 1990, more than 60% blamed their failure on factors linked to cash flow.[1] And according to a study by the accounting firm of BDO Seidman, 26% of small to medium-sized companies called inability to control cash flow their number one problem.[2]

Admittedly, cash flow problems are often just a symptom of operating shortcomings. However, many cash crunches and resulting crises and failures could be avoided by good planning and effective cash management. Ensuring adequate cash flow provides a needed cushion for companies in unstable situations and also can allow a company to take advantage of opportunities to reduce costs or make strategic investments.

You will need several essential skills to effectively take control of your cash. Effective cash management requires that you:

- Understand the critical differences between cash and profit;
- Have the ability to forecast your cash needs;
- Use strategies to maximize your cash flow; and
- Know how to react to a cash crisis.

Since cash can be the most critical asset necessary for your company's survival, the information in this chapter is important to you.

Cash Flow Versus Profit

Cash flow and profit are not the same thing. Profitable companies can, and do, fail for lack of cash flow. Consider the following examples:

✓ A start-up trucking company enjoyed almost immediate success. By its second year, sales topped $1.5 million with net income of $50,000. Though sales grew only slightly the next two years, profits improved to more than $100,000 per year. But, over those two years, accounts receivable more than doubled to $500,000. The company also moved into a new facility, absorbing $100,000 in pre-paid expenses — carried as assets on the books. Despite being profitable, the company found itself short on cash. With its lines of credit exhausted, when the IRS came looking for $40,000 in back taxes, the company decided to shut down. At the time it went under, the company showed a positive book value of more than $200,000.

✓ A manufacturer of industrial furnaces found itself caught in a frustrating cycle of feast and famine. Most of its jobs were large, up to $1.5 million, and made up a large portion of annual sales, which were growing to about $8 million. Little money was collected on jobs that were in progress, so cash flowed out steadily when large jobs were being worked on. The company was repeatedly thrown into crisis. Many times, the president admitted leaving at night, not sure if the power would still be on the next day.

As soon as a job was done and the invoice paid, the company was flush with cash and all obligations caught up. But because each job seemed to lead to more or larger jobs, there never was a cash cushion. Although sales were growing and the company reported steady profits, the roller coaster cash flow put the company's survival in jeopardy. Fortunately, but only after about ten years, the company finally got over the hump and was able to pay cash out to its investors.

✓ In just its second year, a start-up producer of leather car seats was succeeding in lining up orders from auto repair shops. The operation was capital intensive, but the influx of orders seemed to prove that the risk taken by investing in equipment would pay off. Fixed costs were high due to the payments on the equipment, and margins were modest. But if all the orders could be processed, a solid profit would be made.

Unfortunately, the supplier of leather hides put a cap on credit at $100,000, and no banks or other vendors were willing to extend credit. With payments for the finished seats coming in 30–60 days after the hides were paid for, the owner found that only enough hides could be purchased to get production up to a break-even level. The owner estimated that production would more than double if only enough hides could be secured.

What is it about accounting principles that allows companies like these to show seemingly healthy profits while teetering on the edge of insolvency? The basic answer is that while cash might be the key to survival, it is not the central focus of financial accounting. The bottom line in accounting is net income.

Over the long term, profit and cash flow will be roughly the same, but with significant differences in timing over that period. The differences in timing are a result of the distinction between an expenditure and recognizing an expense, between completing a sale and getting paid.

The gap between net income and cash flow can be very wide. If receivables increase due to rapid sales growth, revenues — and probably profits — will increase ahead of the actual cash receipts. Increases in inventory or fixed assets also consume cash, but have no immediate impact on the income statement. So, while the income statement may look great, cash is scarce. Most commonly found in smaller, growing companies, these circumstances are the reason why even profitable companies are vulnerable to running out of cash.

Something else to be aware of is that inventory and receivables are classified on financial statements as working capital, but clearly are not equivalent to cash.

Conversion, particularly of slow-moving inventory items or troubled accounts, to cash is neither assured nor cost free. Even companies with seemingly healthy working capital balances can be thrown into crisis if cash unexpectedly becomes tight.

The Cash Cow

On the other hand, some companies may incur expenses, but still hang onto cash, even as accounts payable and liabilities are increasing. Expenses, such as depreciation, amortization, and write-offs, do not use cash. Mature companies, which more often have these circumstances, can be lucrative cash cows — companies that generate cash — even when showing only modest profit.

When it comes to survival, cash flow is what ultimately matters. As William McGowan, the former chairman of MCI, said, "No company has ever gone bankrupt because it had a loss on its P&L."[3]

Positive cash flow, however, is no guarantee that a company is healthy. Consider the following example:

✓ A general contracting company that built retail stores collected money from its customers in installments. Generally, the contractor received an initial payment of 25–40% when a contract was signed, two or three progress payments, and then the final 10% when all work was completed and the subcontractors were paid in full.

Margins were very thin, generally 10–15%, but with close to $40 million in contracts, there seemed to be enough margin to more than cover overhead expenses. Certainly, cash flow was very good while the business was growing. The contractor enjoyed the reverse of what most other growing companies see, with receipts upfront, payments deferred, and new jobs bringing immediate cash.

But the cash flow masked serious underlying problems. During a recession, margins deteriorated due to competition, and cost overruns even made some jobs unprofitable. The company started using upfront payments from new jobs to pay off balances due to subcontractors on jobs in process.

This enabled the company to survive as long as there was a steady influx of new jobs. But when business slowed, the cash flow dried up. Subcontractor payments came due with the customers' money long since paid out and few new jobs coming in. Less than a year after celebrating what seemed like a record year, the company was insolvent.

In this case, cash flow was misleading and timely financial statements could have revealed the underlying problems. By matching payments and expenses on each job, the financial statements could have shown how margins were shrinking and even suggested corrective action.

Unfortunately in this case, at the time the crisis hit, the company had gone six months into their fiscal year with no interim financial statements, and its auditors were uncovering critical errors in the preliminary statements for the prior year.

Cash Focus

Both cash flow and profit are important measures, working hand-in-hand to give you a more complete picture of your company's health than either could alone. But because net income is more commonly used, you may need to shift your thinking to give emphasis to cash flow.

Learning to focus on cash and liquidity may actually be easier for a CEO than for an accountant. If you have ever run a business out of a checkbook, this might be a familiar task. You will already know that, at the most basic level, if more cash comes in than goes out, the company is gaining. As long as cash is in the account, the business is solvent.

Only as the business gets more complex, will you need to adopt financial accounting to better classify assets and liabilities and make accrual entries. But the basic practice of keeping on top of the checkbook often remains.

On the other hand, accountants have been trained to focus on net income. They may be less attuned to the importance of liquidity. Therefore, while the accountant should do the work of tracking cash flow and preparing cash forecasts, you may have to take the initiative in getting work on cash forecasts and cash flows started.

Monitoring cash flow also brings an additional and key advantage over just doing accrual accounting. Cash is a very immediate and objective measure. At any point in time, you can know how much cash is on hand. You have no need to wait for a monthly close to get an update.

No timing issues, judgments, or GAAP rules are contended with when measuring cash flow. While a dollar of inventory or goodwill on a financial statement could have varied meaning, you know what a dollar of cash is worth. And, while financial statements can be manipulated, cash flow is a tangible, unbiased measure. If you want an immediate barometer of where you stand, without unraveling accounting jargon and rules, cash flow will provide it.

Cash Flow Forecasting

Cash flow, of course, is not just a method of keeping score, but is a matter of survival for many companies. For others, cash flow may represent the ability to seize expansion opportunities or fund vital product development. Simply reporting on cash flow is not enough. You also need to forecast cash balances and anticipate possible problems.

The cornerstone of cash management is a detailed cash forecast. For most companies, monthly budgets should be done, projecting in advance by at least six to twelve months. Companies in a cash crisis should also do weekly budgets extending eight to twelve weeks. Actual performance should then be tracked against the forecasts to provide warning of potential shortfalls, as well as feedback about the validity of the original assumptions.

The cash forecasts pick up where normal revenue and expense budgets leave off. Forecasts capture the difference in timing between payments and receipts and the financial accounting recognition of income and expense. A typical format for a cash flow forecast is shown in the sample at the end of this chapter.

Unlike business plans and budgets — discussed in chapters 13 and 14 — which are a mix of forecasting and goal setting, cash projections should strictly be forecasts. The purpose is to anticipate cash needs, not set targets or impress investors. Because the cost of running low on cash is severe, it makes sense to inject some pessimism. You can do this by choosing conservative assumptions or by discounting the results. If a forecast becomes outdated, revise it. To wait for the end of the budget period or to match the cash forecast to the regular budget or financial reporting cycles is unnecessary.

In moving from a regular budget to a cash forecast, many items will be the same. Payroll, freight bills, and cash sales are usually booked as revenue and expense very close to the time when cash changes hands. Items such as rent, utility bills, and service contracts are usually paid once a month and only a weekly cash flow would need to reflect the specific timing of the payments.

For other line items, the difference in timing is substantial. Sales and purchases are often on credit, so the cash impact will lag. Inventory purchases, which do not generate an income statement expense until sold, reduce cash flow as soon as they are paid for. Capital expenditures can have a major impact on the cash forecast and cannot be spread out as they are for financial statements. Other expenses that are often smoothed for financial reporting, such as insurance, heat, and taxes, must be adjusted to reflect the actual timing of payments.

When doing cash planning, you might also have to look at items that don't even appear on your balance sheet. Some of your biggest exposures are outstanding purchase orders and contracts. Even if your accounting system doesn't track this number — and it probably won't unless your purchasing system is automated and purchase orders are used for all items — you should ask your controller to have this information available at all times. Contingent liabilities, such as lawsuits, are additional off-balance sheet items that may have to be worked into your projections.

Ideally, the cash budget should have the ability to handle "what if" questions. The "what if" questions allow you to test different scenarios, while emphasizing that any projection has a margin of error. Try changing your assumptions about sales, the timing of inventory purchases, or the speed of collections to see the impact on cash. Develop contingency plans to deal with any potential forecasted problems.

Maximizing Cash Flow

Good cash management does not have to wait for a crisis. Freeing up cash, whether to invest, pay down existing debt, or take advantage of vendor discounts, brings substantial rewards. Your objective is to wring cash out of your business and keep it out. If you do find that you have a potential or actual crisis, you can solve the problem in several ways.

Short-Term Strategies

If your projections indicate a cash shortfall, first ask yourself if you have internal sources of cash that can make up the difference. Start by looking at your balance sheet. Inventory and receivables usually are the biggest cash drains on a company. Both also carry the added risk that the longer they are not converted to cash, the greater the risk they never will be. Issues about controlling and reducing inventory are discussed in Chapter 10. Refer to Chapter 12 for techniques to speed collections of receivables.

Payables also offer an opportunity for generating cash. Stretch out your cash by waiting at least until the due date before releasing funds. Additionally, although you must judge how far you can push, particularly with key vendors, payments can frequently be delayed 15–30 days beyond these due dates. Many vendors are willing to accept a reliable, but slow, payment schedule. Attempt to get terms on all payments, since this type of financing costs you nothing.

You can use other ways to hold onto cash a few days longer or generate a little extra interest income. Having payments wired or mailed to a lock-box gets cash into your account faster. Put as much cash as possible in an interest bearing account and have the bank automatically sweep any excess funds from your checking account into it to generate extra interest income.

Long-Term Strategies

In addition to squeezing the balance sheet, you can use a number of longer-term strategies to reduce cash needs. Some of these include:

- Lease or rent equipment instead of buying;
- Get suppliers to hold parts in their inventory, while charging you only when you order parts;
- Use sales representatives instead of a dedicated sales force to save on fixed costs of salaries and a sales office;
- Do private label manufacturing, where you make the product but someone else's brand name is put on it, to reduce marketing expenses;
- Form an R&D partnership with a larger company instead of paying for all the work yourself;
- Reduce employee hours or encourage opportunities for temporary work elsewhere, rather than simply cutting headcount outright; and
- Subcontract manufacturing work to a third party to eliminate payroll and overhead costs, plus reduce or defer the carrying costs of inventory.

These strategies can be particularly helpful to smaller companies seeking to reduce upfront outlays, control risk, and preserve cash. However, each also brings a potential cost, such as sharing profits or loss of control over operations. You can work with your controller to develop additional strategies for conserving cash and to weigh alternative approaches.

Financing and Investors

As hard as the work might be to generate cash internally, going to outside sources is generally more difficult and more expensive. Start ups will find few sources of seed capital and even successful entrepreneurs report spending close to half their time the first year in business trying to raise financing. In addition, selling equity to outsiders raises the issue of valuation and how much control you must surrender.

Once your company is successfully launched, your cash needs may only increase. As discussed earlier, one of the ironies of rapid growth is the creation of greater cash needs. At this point, assuming a company is profitable or close to it, possible investors should show greater interest. As earlier examples demonstrated, however, investor interest is not guaranteed. To reduce dependence on outside sources, you may want to hold down growth to what can be financed with internally generated funds.

Debt is an option for companies with assets — which can be used for collateral — or a history of positive earnings and cash flow. Debt does not dilute ownership, but it does increase the risk of the company. Interest payments on the debt raise your break-even point and your company must also generate sufficient cash to meet any principal payments.

Expect your bank to attach covenants to your loan agreement specifying targets for earnings and various liquidity ratios.

Capital structure for any financing you seek will depend on:

- What ownership percentage you want to maintain;
- How much leverage you are comfortable with;
- Your tax strategies; and
- The availability of money.

The basis for calculating how much financing you need is your cash forecast. Follow your forecast out to find the future point where your cumulative cash flow is the most negative. This point determines the minimum amount of cash needed.

Be conservative in calculating your cash needs to make sure that you borrow enough. Just as you would tuck away money for a rainy day in your personal savings, you will want a cash cushion for your business. Run a worst case scenario to see what your maximum cash need might be. Allow for some unexpected expenditures and for shifts in the timing of transactions. Raising financing now will be easier and cheaper than if you find yourself in the midst of a crisis.

A complete evaluation of financing strategies is beyond the scope of this book. However, two books available from The Oasis Press, *Raising Capital: How to Write a Financing Proposal* and *The Money Connection: Where and How to Apply for Business Loans and Venture Capital*, can help you develop financing strategies and find financing for your business. Check the Related Resources pages at the back of this book for ordering information.

Crisis Management

Cash planning and management are not simply strategies for dealing with a cash crisis. They are tools for avoiding a crisis in the first place. In spite of the fact that a crisis can seem to come on with unexpected suddenness — the loss of a key customer, a lender or key supplier cutting off credit, or an unanticipated expenditure — most cash shortages are avoidable. As venture capitalist Stanley Rich has said, "There's no excuse for running out of money."[4]

In a crisis, the role of cash is magnified and you shift to a cash mentality. How much cash is coming in? What customers can be called to speed payments? How much money is available to meet payroll and pay vendors? Who can wait and who must be paid?

One of the hardest adjustments in a cash crisis, particularly for a controller, is understanding how irrelevant typical financial statements and accounting valuations can become. The focus becomes very short-term as assets and operations are evaluated based on their ability to generate immediate cash, rather than long-term profit. Bankers, who are nervous about their collateral, may stop looking at book values and start to assess assets at liquidation values.

The key to resolving a cash crisis is to generate cash by speeding collections and slowing payments, even if it means taking a book loss. Strategies you can implement are:

- Reduce inventory, especially obsolete or excess items, even if they are liquidated below cost;
- Settle disputed accounts receivable;
- Sell excess fixed assets;
- Finance purchases wherever possible, even at high interest rates; and
- Prioritize all payables and pay only the most essential items and vendors.

Clearly, no business can operate long term under these conditions. But your job is to first survive the crisis and then turn the practices of tight cash management into an ongoing habit to prevent a relapse.

Lenders and Investors in a Crisis

Lenders and outside investors can play a key role in rescuing a company from an impending crisis. Sometimes, however, they are the ones that precipitate the crisis. Venture capitalists often try to limit their exposure, and keep entrepreneurs hungry for cash by keeping each round of investment as small as possible. Although entrepreneurs who anticipate upcoming cash needs and meet their operating targets can usually get additional funds, they may have little margin for error. Failure to realistically forecast cash needs can leave those entrepreneurs scrambling.

Dealing with banks is not much easier. A banker is said to be someone who will lend you an umbrella when it is sunny out and wants it back when it starts to rain. Bankers are extremely risk averse and cannot be expected to step up with more money during a crisis. In fact, they are more likely to react to a crisis by restricting credit. Here again, good cash management is needed. A forecast will help you communicate your plans and needs with the bank.

If you achieve your targets and can demonstrate control over the situation, your bank is more likely to keep supporting you. Reducing your cash needs is the best plan, since you will reduce borrowing and minimize exposure to any actions by the bank.

Cash Keys

Ultimately, the keys to cash management are to understand the sources and uses of cash and to anticipate potential problems. The feedback you get from cash flow is timely and objective. Persistently poor cash flow is usually a symptom of operating problems. For growing companies, though, poor cash flow may be quite normal. Regardless of the cause, running out of cash is almost always avoidable and the consequences range from costly to catastrophic.

Careful planning and aggressive management are the keys to maximizing cash flow, starting with inventory and accounts receivable. A large part of a controller's job should be to keep these exposures under control. The next chapter looks at managing credit and collections.

Endnotes

1. Branch, Shelly. "Go With the Flow — Or Else." BLACK ENTERPRISE November 1991: 77.

2. Ibid.

3. William McGowan, quoted in *The Manager's Book of Quotations*, p. 6.

4. Andrews, Edmund L. and Stanley R. Rich, quoted in "Running Out of Money." VENTURE January 1986: 33.

Cash Flow Forecast – Sample

	Jan.	Feb.	Mar.	Apr.	May	Jun.
Beginning Cash Balance	30,500	9,590	28,760	20,930	71,270	86,610
Cash In:						
Cash sales	20,400	21,290	19,230	21,290	20,600	21,290
Collections on receivables	270,200	279,500	252,600	279,900	271,200	280,400
Sales of fixed assets			15,000			
New borrowing				50,000		
New equity						
Total Cash In	290,600	300,790	286,830	351,190	291,800	301,690
Net Cash Available	321,100	310,380	315,590	372,120	363,070	388,300
Cash Disbursements						
Operating Expenditures:						
Inventory purchases	150,400	135,900	150,600	145,900	150,800	155,800
Payroll	77,500	70,000	77,500	75,000	77,500	78,500
Benefits	25,300	22,500	24,300	23,000	23,300	23,600
Rent	10,000	10,000	10,000	10,000	10,000	10,000
Utilities	4,710	5,120	4,060	2,350	1,060	1,060
Repairs & maintenance	500	500	500	500	500	500
Travel	3,000	2,000	8,500	3,000	2,000	3,000
Leases	1,300	1,300	1,300	1,300	1,300	1,300
Insurance	27,000	0	0	27,000	0	0
Phone/postage	2,000	2,000	2,000	2,000	2,000	2,000
Other	9,800	7,300	7,800	10,800	8,000	8,600
Subtotal	311,510	256,620	286,560	300,850	276,460	284,360
Interest			8,100			8,100
Principal on Loans						50,000
Fixed Asset Purchases		25,000				
Net Disbursements	311,510	281,620	294,660	300,850	276,460	342,460
Net Cash Flow	−20,910	19,170	−7,830	50,340	15,340	−40,770
Ending Cash	9,590	28,760	20,930	71,270	86,610	45,840

Bottom Line Basics: Understand & Control Business Finances

Notes

Chapter 12

Credit and Collections

Creditors have better memories than debtors.

— Ben Franklin[1]

Good cash management depends on a strong credit and collections program. Together with inventory, receivables often are the greatest drain on cash, tying up funds that could be used to fuel other aspects of a business. Growth, as well as protection from cash crunches, also requires a predictable cash flow, something that can only come from an effective collections strategy.

Collections often get inadequate attention because bill collecting is one of the least favorite activities of managers and controllers. The work is mundane, disputes with customers can be emotionally charged, and, in the words of one CEO, "Receivables don't create sales."[2] However, no sale is complete until payment is received. And few businesses can prosper when squeezed between demands for payment by creditors and slow receipts from customers.

Collecting receivables is not simply a matter of chasing after customers with phone calls and letters, but results from having a total credit strategy. To implement an effective credit strategy, you must:

- Decide on payment terms;
- Perform credit checks;

- Choose which personnel to involve;
- Monitor receivables;
- Follow up problem accounts; and
- Identify when to look outside your company for assistance.

The following sections of this chapter cover each of the above-listed topics, so that you can put your own strategy for handling credit and collections into effect.

Extending Credit

The first step in your credit strategy is determining whether to extend credit. Consider the following example:

✓ One company claimed to have no receivables problems. Few accounts were past due and someone always followed up with phone calls as soon as accounts went even a few days beyond terms. "The accounts we have written off," the office manager said, "are all customers we can't do anything about. They are in bankruptcy or have shut down." On closer examination, it turned out these write-offs had totaled several hundred thousand dollars the year before on sales of about $10 million. The issue was not how the company collected past due bills, but who they extended credit to.

The key to making good credit decisions is gathering pertinent information upfront. While nationally published credit reports, the best known of which is Dun & Bradstreet (D&B), are popular sources, they have limited value. Although subscribers can obtain information about a firm's management, products, number of employees, credit history, financial relationships, debts, and records of payments from these published credit reports, the financial data is provided by the company being reported on.

The financial information is often quite old and nearly all of it unaudited. Bureaus, such as D&B, verify little of the information on credit histories, and you have no way of determining who supplied that information. Bad news about a company may never show up on their credit report because most of the information comes either from the company itself or from vendors who may be reluctant to damage the reputation of a customer.[3]

Rather than rely solely on these national services, your company should develop its own sources of information. Ask for bank and credit references when setting up a new account, and call them promptly so that problem customers can be spotted before credit is issued.

If financial statements are desired, get them directly from the customer. Up-to-date credit information, similar to what is available from D&B, may also be available from local credit bureaus or through exchanges of information with suppliers.

One of the best sources of information can be your company's own sales-force. A single visit to a customer's plant or conversations with their employees may provide more insight than reports and phone calls. Use salespeople for this task with caution, since there is a risk that their selling relationship with the client may be affected if the credit process becomes adversarial.

Involving the Salesforce

In addition, limit salespeople's role in the final credit decision. Depending on the commission structure, salespeople may have a built-in incentive to ship merchandise to marginal accounts. Consider the example below:

✓ A company experienced nearly half its bad debt losses in a sales territory that contributed just 10% of sales. The salesperson, through bad judgment or self-interest, convinced the home office to continue shipping to several delinquent accounts in that territory. The salesperson racked up commissions and the company ended up writing off several hundred thousand dollars.

If possible, tie a portion of commissions to successful collections. Salespeople can also be helpful following up on delinquent accounts, since they may have an easier time than corporate staff getting their calls taken by the customer. For the most part, expect some resistance to these measures. Many salespeople view bad debt losses as an administrative cost. In addition, waiting for collections can delay their commission, and they may fear losing future sales if their rapport with customers is damaged by collections efforts.

Not every sale is a good one. Unfortunately, selling to troubled accounts is often easier than selling to sound ones because your company may be the only one willing to extend credit. Walking away from a sale is hard, particularly in tough times, but sometimes you have to.

Once you have reached the decision to extend credit, set a credit limit and stick to it. Review the limit periodically or as events demand. If a customer has reached the credit limit and an increase in the limit is not justified, do not ship additional product without payment of at least part of the oldest outstanding invoices. Even though putting a customer on hold may threaten a sale, this action is also your greatest source of leverage.

Credit Limits and Terms

Payment terms should fit your overall credit strategy and be varied by customer. For new or high risk customers, you may want to make terms tight, such as net ten days or even cash on delivery (COD). As you gain experience with a customer, you can gradually loosen the terms.

Early payment discounts are effective in encouraging rapid payment, but can be very costly. For example, a 2% discount for payments within 10 days, when normal terms are 30 days, is a 36% annualized interest rate —

on the flip side, when paying bills, try taking advantage of such discounts if cash flow allows. In addition, many companies will take offered discounts, but continue to pay in 30 or 45 days as usual. Because of this, offering cash discounts usually makes sense only when early payment by customers is critical.

One exception may be in dealing with government agencies. Consider what one manufacturer discovered.

✓ The manufacturer was selling to the federal government and its typical invoices were close to $100,000. Though the agencies were notoriously slow payers, they were required to take advantage of any offered discount, even if fairly small. By offering a 0.5% discount for paying in 15 days, the manufacturer greatly improved cash flow at a low cost.

At the other end of the spectrum, what if a customer pays late? Should you assess interest or late fees? How much should you charge? How late is the payment before you assess a charge? These charges are very much a judgment call.

Additional charges can add some leverage when negotiating with a troubled account and do represent an attempt to recoup a very real cost. However, many companies simply ignore these charges, and other customers may be annoyed by the charges. The best strategy of all is to put effort into collecting on time to prevent the need for tacking on late fees.

No matter what your payment terms, they can best be met only if you mail invoices promptly and the terms are understood by your customers. Communicate terms upfront when the order is placed or an account is set up. Make sure your invoice is intelligible and the due date is clear. Observe how unclear terms can affect payment in the example below.

✓ One company stated its terms as "3%/10 Net 30." The intention was that customers invoiced by the 25th of May could deduct 3% if paying by the 10th of June; otherwise, the net amount was owed on the 25th of June, 30 days after the date of the invoice.

While nearly all customers understood the deadline for taking a discount, there was great confusion, even among employees of the company, on when balances were due for customers not taking a discount. Many thought the balances weren't due until 30 days after the discount period, or July 10. As a result, many customers routinely paid 60–75 days from the invoice date.

Even when you make sound decisions about extending credit and have clearly communicated your credit terms, you will probably have some customer accounts that become delinquent. The next step in your credit strategy is to learn how to manage those delinquent accounts.

Nothing is more pleasant and courteous than a customer who pays bills promptly and in full. Unfortunately, payments slide all too commonly. Whether due to cash flow problems or simply an effort to improve float, some customers simply pay late. They can also tell many different stories why, such as:

- We do not have a copy of your invoice.

- We pay everyone in [45, 60, or 75] days.

- We do not pay partial shipments.

- There was an error on the original. We are waiting for a [correction or credit].

- We do not start the payment clock until the invoice is in our system.

- We cannot pay you until we get paid.

- I think it is scheduled for next week.

Effective Responses

How do you effectively respond to these delinquent accounts? The first rule is to take an active, not passive approach. Don't wait to take action. The odds of collecting an account diminish greatly as time passes. In addition, companies with revolving lines of credit will find that banks generally will not lend against invoices older than 90 days. Call as soon as an account becomes past due. For large invoices, you may want to call before payment is due just to be sure all paperwork is in order and that payment will be processed on time.

Call, don't write, as a first approach. Since letters are expensive, easily ignored, and avoid confronting the issue, make your first approach to the problem effective. Many companies send dunning letters to customers and yet continue to have conversations totally unrelated to the collection effort, effectively dodging the issue.[4]

A cordial, but firm, approach usually works best. Do not threaten or browbeat customers. Politely explain why it is important for terms to be adhered to, and listen carefully to why your customer is not paying. If a problem exists with the product or the invoice, the customer may provide valuable feedback on your own operation.

Conversations should be carefully documented. Documentation helps to avoid future misunderstandings and will record any promises made. If a customer acknowledges a debt and does not dispute the amount owed or raise a problem with goods or services provided, confirm the conversation in a letter. This confirmation will strengthen your position in the event of future litigation.

If a customer will not, or cannot, pay the entire debt, try to get a commitment to pay at least a portion of the bill and be willing to spread payments out over time. This flexibility may make payment manageable for a customer as well as reduce your overall exposure. You can also clearly establish agreement that the amounts are indeed owed by getting a commitment to pay.

Troubled Accounts

In spite of extending every effort to work with your late payment accounts, you will undoubtedly end up with a few very troubled accounts. When you sense that a customer with a past due balance is at risk of defaulting, the most important thing is not to wait. Maintain a sense of urgency and don't be afraid to be the "squeaky wheel." Consider the case below.

✓ A company that had filed for Chapter 11 bankruptcy still got letters a year later from creditors asking for payment to "avoid the embarrassment of legal action." These letters were both futile and costly. They also demonstrated how lax, and out of touch, some creditors are with their accounts. By contrast, another creditor had successfully attached the company's bank accounts six months before the filing and gotten paid in full for an $8,000 debt.

Letters and calls are most effective when the content and style of the message is varied. If calls do not get a response, a variety of letters — legal, registered, or telegrams — are possible. Numerous types of action give alternate media a chance to work and also keep the debtor's attention.

Collection agencies and lawyers are costly options. Troubled accounts should not be turned over to them as a first response. Do consider these options — discussed in more detail later in this chapter — but only after failing to collect with calls and letters.

Try some creative techniques. You may be able to minimize your risk by getting a lien against assets of the customer, especially the product you shipped. Accept post-dated checks or negotiate more favorable terms on pending orders. One possibility is to work down an outstanding receivable balance by insisting that future sales be COD, plus an additional 5% to be applied to old invoices.

At some point, you may need to cut your losses. While no one likes to take a loss, persistently chasing an undesirable credit risk may not be worth your time and expense. However, you may be able to negotiate a settlement of the account that would allow you to salvage something.

Bankruptcy

Particularly in tough times, a working knowledge about bankruptcy laws can pay off. If you have many troubled accounts, you can expect that some of those may choose bankruptcy to solve their debt problems. In recent years, close to one million Americans and American businesses annually have filed for bankruptcy.[5] Usually coming on the tail of a string of broken promises, bankruptcies can leave a creditor feeling betrayed and angry. However, an understanding of the law and the particulars of each case can help you deal with a customer's bankruptcy.

In all cases, companies filing for bankruptcy have an automatic stay on any debt incurred before the filing. Creditors are not allowed to pursue collection of the old debt or offset subsequent payments against it. Any pending lawsuits are also stopped and the bankrupt company has the option of accepting or rejecting contractual agreements, including leases. As a creditor, if you wish to protest any aspect of the bankruptcy, or have the automatic stay lifted, you must go through the bankruptcy court. Contesting a bankruptcy is a costly process and usually not worth the effort.

A bankruptcy does not necessarily mean you will not be paid — although that may happen. But you will have to wait in line with the other creditors. The pecking order for payment is:

- Secured debts — those tied to specific assets, or collateral;

- Priority debts — unsecured debt, usually amounts owed to taxing authorities like the IRS; and

- Unsecured debt — not tied to any assets or collateral.

Most trade debt is unsecured. Clearly, if you can secure your receivable before the bankruptcy filing, which is unlikely unless you have substantial negotiating leverage, your odds of payment are greatly improved.

Three main classes of bankruptcy can be filed. Chapter 13 is for individuals and involves setting up a payment plan over three to five years to satisfy the debt. Chapter 7 is for both individuals and businesses. In Chapter 7, the trustee simply sells the assets of the debtor — certain property is exempt — and distributes the proceeds. Chapter 11 is a business bankruptcy that allows the debtor to continue to operate. The company must submit monthly reports to the court and file a plan for paying the creditors.

Emotionally, you may want to stop doing business with companies that file for Chapter 11, but they can still be excellent customers. Often, you can extract favorable credit terms, and a customer who defaults on a debt in Chapter 11 risks being shut down involuntarily. Plus, what better way to get even with a company that stiffed you by filing for bankruptcy than to continue to sell to them and make a healthy profit?

A customer on the verge of bankruptcy may approach creditors and propose a settlement of debt at a discount in lieu of filing for bankruptcy — an out-of-11 settlement. Taking a loss may be hard to swallow, but could be preferable to waiting in line for an uncertain payment during a bankruptcy. In bankruptcy, payments to creditors up to three months before the filing may be considered preference payments and the creditor may be forced by the court to refund them. So, your sense of urgency with a troubled account must be followed immediately with action.

Alternatives to Internal Collections

The risk and effort of collections can be transferred to outsiders in several ways. One possibility is to turn nearly the entire effort over to a factoring company — sometimes called factors. For a fee that runs roughly 1–2% of qualified receivables, plus an interest charge several points over prime for funds advanced, factors essentially buy your receivables from you. They operate much like an in-house credit department, performing all credit checks, setting credit limits, and pursuing collections. Factors generally assume the risk of nonpayment and pay you upfront so your cash flow is accelerated. The down side is that factoring, as a means of generating cash, is more expensive than a bank loan and, by handing credit activity over to the factors, your company may lose control over some business decisions.

Another possibility is to buy credit insurance. Structured like most other forms of insurance, for a premium the insurer assumes the risk of loss from default on receivables. The cost is roughly 0.2–0.4% of sales, although the exact premium will depend on a company's risk profile. Generally, deductibles and liability limits are included in the policy. Sometimes coinsurance provisions are included, as well. Credit insurance works best for companies at risk of catastrophic loss. This category includes companies that sell to a few, very large accounts or are at risk in case of a general industry slump.

While both factoring companies and insurance companies are interested in healthy receivables, collection agencies specialize in tracking down bad debt accounts. Most agencies are paid on a contingent basis, which limits your out-of-pocket cost if efforts are unsuccessful. But, their fees generally range from 20–35% of what is collected. Most will also insist that you turn the account over to them exclusively. The high fees and loss of control over how the collection is handled makes agencies desirable only after internal options have been exhausted.

Lawyers can be used at several stages. If phone calls have been ineffective, a letter on legal letterhead may provoke a response. Attorneys can help in securing a security interest in a debtor's property. In the case of default, the attorney may seek a writ of attachment, placing a lien on a debtor's assets, or a writ of possession, taking possession of assets in which your company has a security interest. Many lawyers also provide the same services as collection agencies. If needed, legal action should be taken quickly because other creditors may try the same remedies. Legal action is also, of course, a very expensive option and may not make sense with smaller accounts.

Collections Made Easier

If you decide to keep collections in-house, you can make the process easier and more effective by establishing some foundations in your accounting procedures. Keeping good records is the key. Your controller must ensure that records are accurate, timely, and complete to avoid sabotaging the collections efforts. By keeping poor records, many companies become their own worst enemy when it comes to collections.

To get paid in time, invoices should go out on time. If you ship products, get bills out by the next day. If you bill professional services, consider billing weekly rather than monthly. Use the date product ships or services are performed on your invoices, rather than the date the invoice is cut. This starts the payment clock sooner. For very large invoices, consider using overnight mail to send invoices or receive payment.

Eliminate any excuses a customer may have for not processing invoices immediately. Make sure quantities, prices, and extensions are correct and that terms have been agreed on and are clearly stated. Follow up by phone before payment is due to make sure the customer has found the invoice in order and has it "in the system."

A good computerized accounting system is a valuable asset. The system can provide current account agings, alert clerks to credit limit problems, and assist in tracking changes in payment patterns — often the first indicator of problems with an account. The computer system can also ensure a good audit trail, needed for tracing the history of orders, invoices, and payments.

Accurate posting of transactions to the receivables system is also essential. Most accounts have a stream of invoices, partial payments, credits, and adjustments made to them that complicate recordkeeping. Taking the time to keep account changes straight and up-to-date is worthwhile, especially to ease the resolution of discrepancies. For example:

✓ A company with a complicated billing structure, including third-party payments and several layers of discounts, often had difficulty matching payments and invoices. As a result, the company became frustrated tracking receivables and started simply applying all payments to the oldest open invoices. Resolving payment disputes with customers quickly became nearly impossible because their records disagreed on which invoices had been paid and which were open. It took six months to restore order, during which time customers expressed frustration at having to repeatedly explain the history of their accounts. Many disputed balances were written off for lack of supporting detail.

Finally, to repeat, document all conversations with debtors. Documentation provides a record of promises made and makes it easy to track the history of an account.

Involve the Right People

Collections often end up in the hands of a lowly clerk, overburdened with other daily chores and untrained in credit procedures and collection techniques. This situation can happen when collecting is not given high priority or is considered such an unpleasant task that it keeps getting handed down until it can go no further. That approach is a recipe for failure.

Sales without collections are meaningless and collections should be given as high a priority as sales. A starting point is to hire or train a qualified credit professional and give that person the resources and support needed to make credit decisions. Like sales, collections is a total company effort. The effort starts with the salesperson who first decides to approach an account and continues with the customer service employees who take an order, explain terms, and get references. The credit manager must check the references, approve terms, and monitor payment history. The accounting department is responsible for issuing invoices on a timely basis and providing accurate records. The effort then continues, if an account becomes past due, with follow-up calls and letters from appropriate personnel, including you if necessary.

Slow, Steady, and Persistent

While collections may never be the highlight of your day, neither does it need to become emotionally charged. You should not need to issue threats or hire muscle-bound henchmen to collect funds. A persistent, professional approach will usually convince customers you are serious about collections and bring results. And if customers are not willing to pay, be willing to enforce your claim and walk away from future sales. After all, who needs a customer who doesn't pay?

Now that you know the essentials of managing your assets, and you understand the basic accounting functions involved, you are ready to really take charge. Part IV – Taking Control will show you how to look forward by using planning and forecasting, and how to stay on target with techniques in budgeting and project evaluation. You will also find out how a computer can really help you accomplish your goals. Finally, you will see how to pull all of your financial information together to make comprehensive decisions and maintain a firm grasp on your business' finances.

Endnotes

1. Quoted in *The Apollo Book of American Quotations,* p. 66.
2. Fraser, Jill Andresky. "Getting Paid." INC. June 1990: 58.
3. Ibid. pp. 68–69.
4. Seder, John. *Credit and Collections.* David McKay Company, Inc., 1977, p. 82.
5. Anderson, Dan Goss and M. J. Wardell, American Bankruptcy Institute, quoted in *Surviving Bankruptcy.* Prentice Hall, 1992. p. vii.

Part IV

Taking Control

Chapter 13

Planning and Forecasting

Men don't plan to fail, they fail to plan.

— Anonymous

It is hard to forecast, especially the future. If you have to forecast, forecast often.

— Paul Samuelson[1]

Just about everyone knows that if you want to raise or borrow money, a formal plan that includes financial projections is a necessity. Venture capitalists, bankers, and the U.S. Small Business Administration (SBA) will all require projections when reviewing a loan or investment. But how useful are projections the rest of the time or for internal use?

Smaller business owners and CEOs alike often become too immersed in daily operating issues to look at long-range issues. Or they may perceive budgets and projections as mere financial exercises that don't reflect reality or quickly go stale.

Stories abound of very successful companies that never followed their business plan. "Nobody ever volunteers to give you a copy of their business plan, even when they're successful, because nine out of ten times that plan didn't come true," says Joseph R. Mancuso, who has authored several books on preparing business plans.[2]

Ben Cohen and Jerry Greenfield of Ben & Jerry's Homemade, Inc. knew they needed a forecast for the SBA to consider their loan proposal. They projected first year sales of $90,000, a figure Cohen thought was impossible. Said Cohen, "I remember sitting around trying to figure out how many cones per hour we'd have to sell in order to get that $90,000 ... we had absolutely no way of gauging what our sales were going to be. But we had to put in numbers to play the guessing game."[3]

In Ben & Jerry's first year, they did $200,000 in sales and in just a few years they went from operating out of a garage to being a public company with sales of more than $10 million. "It occurred to me," said Cohen, "that that's how all these major businesses get millions of dollars, doing this crazy little exercise that probably has as much bearing on reality as the one we did."[4] And at the headquarters of Newman's Own, Inc., a sign hung with the following quote from founder Paul Newman. "If we ever have a plan, we're screwed."[5]

Why Plan?

If so many companies succeed without following a business plan, why should you do financial projections? Note first, the companies discussed above were start ups with short operating histories and products having little market exposure. They were forced to project sales based on not much more than unbridled optimism or were graced with explosive sales growth that quickly rendered sales targets obsolete. Established companies have a base level of performance from which they usually make reasonable assumptions of future results. A 1990 survey of 1,650 business owners revealed that 69% had a strategic plan. Of those with a plan, 89% said the plan had been effective.[6]

A 1993 survey by AT&T of 500 businesses with less than $20 million in sales provides even further, concrete evidence of the importance of planning. In that survey, 59% of the companies with growing sales used formal business plans, while just 38% of those with declining sales did.[7]

Even if your sales projections are difficult or prove off the mark, you can and should revisit the planning process as often as needed. The purpose of planning is not to produce a document written in stone. If your company's plan no longer reflects reality, update it — don't toss it aside.

The formal plan and projections are often less important than the process itself. If nothing else, strategic planning allows you to "come up for air" from the daily problems of running the company, take stock of where your company is, and establish a clear course to follow.

Regular planning also helps your company deal with change, both inside and outside the company. By constantly reevaluating your company's strengths, markets, and competition, you are better able to recognize problems and opportunities. You can react to new developments, rather than simply plugging along.

For some top managers, planning can be a response to vague feelings that profits should be better. Take the case of the small business owner who complained:

✓ "I feel that my store should be doing better. I guess I should be glad we're making a profit at all." But when asked what the store's sales and profit should be, possible ways to meet those goals, or how other retailers in the community were doing, the owner confessed to not knowing the answers. Unease about the company's performance resulted from not knowing where the company was headed or how to get there.[8]

For other entrepreneurs, getting down into specific financial benchmarks and targets allows them to understand the ramifications of operating decisions. For example:

✓ The owner of a small furniture manufacturing and retailing company had experienced five years of losses. Unwilling to finance the business any further, the owner wanted to know if the business was worth keeping alive. By putting together a pro forma projection and break-even analysis both the owner of the business and the business' controller determined what level of sales were needed from a new retail location, together with cuts in operating expenses, to become profitable. Encouraged that the goals were attainable, the owner succeeded in both increasing sales and cutting expenses, returning to modest profitability within six months. Furthermore, knowing the company's break-even point has enabled the owner to quickly gauge performance by tracking monthly sales, and to gain a gut feel for the proper level of operating expenses.

Projections and planning can be a rather tortuous exercise, especially the first time through. Translating headcount to dollars; digging up the running rate of everyday expenses, such as telephone and electricity; adding up the full cost of an hour of direct labor; and determining a break-even level can be painstaking efforts. For example:

✓ One small company president dreaded every minute that went into putting first projections together, complaining that it was a grinding process that caused a constant search for numbers. But, the finished product was invaluable for understanding the business and evaluating strategies, not to mention essential for working with the bank and obtaining the SBA funding.

What if you feel your company's strategic goals and direction are clearly established and you do not need a formal plan to raise financing? What is accomplished by preparing projections and budgets? What keeps it from just being a number crunching exercise?

Not Just Number Crunching

■ First, the financial plan translates your company's goals into specific targets. It clearly defines what a successful outcome entails. The plan is not merely a prediction; it implies a commitment to making the targeted results happen.

- Second, the plan provides you with a vital feedback and control tool. Variances from projections provide early warning of problems. And when variances do occur, the plan can provide a framework for determining what the financial impact will be and the effect of various corrective actions.

- Third, the plan can anticipate problems. If rapid growth creates a cash shortage due to investment in receivables and inventory, the forecast should show this. If next year's projections depend on certain milestones this year, the assumptions should spell this out.

In the example of the furniture manufacturer, an annual three-week shutdown during the summer and payment of Christmas bonuses, combined with a seasonal slowdown, strained cash during the year. The projections anticipated the cash needs and how much needed to be set aside ahead of time.

Ongoing Communication

As already mentioned, plans play a vital role in raising financing and communicating with outside investors. If your company is dealing with outside investors or lenders, you need to be able to convey how investments will be paid back and the timetable and milestones involved.

Not only is this true at the time the funds are sought, but ongoing communication of progress against projections, explanations of variances, and any revised projections are critical. In loan workout situations, lack of communication between the bank and company is often a key reason for the bank calling, or threatening to call, a loan. Updated projections, followed by monthly updates of performance versus plan, are key tools for keeping bankers and other key creditors updated.

Your plan not only communicates with outside investors, but also reveals your goals and expectations to people within the company. It educates employees about planned actions, guides them in what is to be done, and provides a basis for ongoing communication.

Crunching the numbers will also help ensure coordination and consistency between the various stated goals of your company. Commonly, companies will adopt a number of objectives — perhaps for sales growth, ROI, R&D spending, or debt to equity ratio — only to find, that while each goal is admirable, together they are impossible to reach.

Consider the following example of a company with an outstanding planning process that recognizes the need for coordinating financial goals.

✓ Analog Devices, Inc. has grown steadily from a start up in the mid-1960s to a company with more than a half billion dollars in sales in 1991, building much of its long-range planning around what it calls its "fundable growth rate." Analog had a goal of self-funded growth, plus a target profitability level. These, plus other inputs, helped define an achievable target for long-term sales growth.

information on margins, headcount, ownership, data on past performance, and market share; and preparing the projections — anticipated revenues and expenses — included in the plan. The controller, who is usually knowledgeable in all areas of a business, is also in a strong position to evaluate the nonfinancial aspects of the plan.

Even the projections must be the responsibility of top management — not the controller or other financial specialist. This does not mean you have to sit at the computer and bang out spreadsheets. But the projections should be driven by the assumptions and goals you established in the other sections. And you should work with the controller on any additional assumptions that are needed. This way, the numbers and the written plan are consistent, plus you will understand how the projections were derived and can answer questions posed by investors and key personnel.

Mechanics of Long-Range Projections

A sample set of projections are included at the end of this chapter for you to look at. Typically, long-range projections, including those in business plans, are prepared going out five to seven years. Projections should be broken out by months for at least one year, by quarters for another year, and annually after that.

The projections should include an income statement and a balance sheet. Cash needs should be clearly identified, possibly by adding a separate summary. If you usually include financial ratios or expenses as a percent of sales as part of your financial statements, include them as part of the projections, too. Expenses can be summarized by department. You can hold line-item detail, except for large expense categories, for the budget.

Projections are an ideal computer application and can be prepared on spreadsheets or business planning software. Many different factors can be incorporated in the projections and, if programmed properly, can handle multiple scenarios or "what if" analysis. However, this should not be taken as an opportunity to dazzle your readers with brilliant programming or baffle them with pages of printouts. Communication is an important goal of the projections and, therefore, you need a clear, professional presentation. Good presentation is particularly necessary for business plans, where your audience consists of potential investors and bankers.

Assumptions

As in the sample projections at the end of the chapter, all assumptions should be laid out very clearly. Rather than simply showing that annual sales will be $5 million, show how that figure was reached. Did you take last year's sales and assume a certain percent growth? Is it based on a customer-by-customer sales forecast? Maybe it includes factors for seasonality, price changes, or changes in market size and share. Spelling these assumptions out has several advantages.

- First, computer printouts can be very impressive looking, but important logic and assumptions are too often buried in formulas and hidden from the reader. To make an informed judgment about the validity and consistency of the projections, the reader must know what went into the figures, not just the final result.

- Second, spelling out the assumptions clearly can make it easier to track variances. Sales may be a function of variables such as product mix, the number of days in a month, and prices. If these assumptions aren't known, there is no basis for evaluating future differences.

- Finally, on a technical programming note, laying the assumptions out makes it much easier to play with multiple scenarios. For example, referring to the sample projections at the end of this chapter, if you quickly change the average selling price per unit by 10%, you can see the impact immediately.

As you go out several years, confidence in the projected figures will clearly decline; however, do not let this deter you from including them in the projections. Investors understand the uncertainty involved and will not hold you to those numbers. Just pick a reasonable basis for those future year assumptions. Modest year-to-year growth rates are one possibility. Another method is to develop a model of where you would like to be in five to seven years and move slowly toward that target. Looking at the published financials of companies similar to yours will give you possible targets for the distribution of expenses among departments.

One exception to using modest assumptions is for business plans designed to attract venture funds. For these, showing the potential for exceptionally high returns is often useful — so use your most optimistic forecast.

Be sure to employ consistent assumptions about the economy and the industry in all your calculations. If inflation is built into your sales assumption, it must be part of your costs as well, including interest rates.

Because of the uncertainty inherent in long-range projections, try preparing several scenarios — such as best case, worst case, or best guess scenarios, for example. You can either present each separately or combine them by using a weighted average of the different scenarios.

Check the Math

Although, seemingly an obvious suggestion, if you have written your own spreadsheet, be sure to double check the calculations. Because spreadsheets easily handle so many complex formulas and look impressive, you may have an impulse to assume they are accurate. If you don't check the numbers, you can be sure readers of the plan will. At the very least, it is an embarrassment to issue projections that don't add up properly or have balance sheets that don't balance.

Timing and Budgets

When, and how often, should plans be prepared and updated? While raising financing, the plan should be kept current, even if frequent revisions are needed. Be careful, though, to advise potential investors of any changes and to throw away outdated copies. And watch out for too much tinkering. Trying to go into too much detail or achieve perfection can be paralyzing.

Since the long-range plan forms the basis for preparing operating budgets, annual planning cycles need to be completed early enough to allow timely completion of the budgets. For a smaller company, one to two months prior to the start of the next budget period should be sufficient.

As mentioned earlier, one complaint about formal plans is that they quickly become obsolete. When this happens, the plan either gets ignored, as in the start ups discussed at the beginning of the chapter, or there is a risk it will restrict managers' ability to react to change, simply because it is not in the plan.

Rather than let your plan go stale, review it and, if needed, revise it at regular intervals. This is particularly true in small, fast-changing companies. How often you need to revise your plan will depend on your company and its environment.

One method for updating the financial projections is to define a benchmark plan and a rolling plan. The benchmark is the plan prepared at the start of the year or your first version of the business plan. As time passes, actual figures will become available and your assumptions may change. Incorporating this new information into the projections creates the rolling plan, which you can update as often as needed.

Monitoring Results

While the main use of your plan may be to set the direction of your company, don't forget to monitor actual performance against targets. Failure to reach key objectives may jeopardize other goals, as well as indicate possible operating problems. Successfully meeting your targets can be the basis for rewarding managers.

Variances from your plan should be investigated quickly and corrective action taken. Some questions to ask might include:

- How large was the variance and is it significant?
- Was the variance caused by actions within the company or by factors beyond its control?
- What corrective action is needed?
- What feedback should be given to managers?
- Should assumptions about the market or operating environment be changed?
- What are the implications for the company's strategy and operating plan?

When it comes to the financial plan, don't be discouraged if your first few efforts stray off the mark. Forecasting is partly art, partly science.

Forecasting sales, in particular, can be extremely difficult, not to mention frustrating when shortages cut into profit or pessimistic estimates cause opportunities to be missed. In general, operating expenses are much easier to both project and control.

Planning is a repetitive process. Each time around, you will get a little bit better at it. A few planning cycles may be required before you can accurately predict the flow of receipts and expenses. But the very act of investigating variances and challenging or refining assumptions about your business can be more valuable than having an accurate forecast.

Planning or Control?

With both long-range plans and operating budgets, comes an important, but sometimes subtle, trade-off between the planning and control aspects. You have the opportunity to use these plans to set the general direction of your company and establish guidelines for operating managers. Or you can use the plans to specify actions to be taken, set spending limits, and evaluate performance. Often, some combination is used.

The degree of emphasis you give to planning and control will vary depending on management style, company size, and how stable the environment is. For example, a small company, with a limited number of management layers and a need to react swiftly to changes in its environment, will place a higher emphasis on the planning aspect. The goal is assistance in allocating resources and anticipating operating problems, not restricting or measuring management decisions.

A larger company usually operates in a more stable environment and with many levels of management. They have a need to coordinate the actions of their managers to ensure corporate goals are achieved. They often require more formal spending guidelines and performance evaluations. Here, the control aspect is paramount.

In a large organization, top management's only control over spending may be a budget. In a small company, the president may be personally involved in all spending decisions, minimizing the control issue.

Another trade-off comes when the operating environment changes. For example, if the economy improves and sales take off unexpectedly, should plans and budgets be revised or not? Revising will provide the most accurate guide for ongoing operations. But having moving targets makes it difficult to measure managers.

Seeing the Big Picture

Planning can seem like a distraction and doing the homework needed to produce a thorough plan may be arduous. But failure to plan can leave your company drifting and unprepared for reacting to crises. In the words of business writer Ronaleen Roha, "The fact is poor management is the biggest cause of business failure. And the basis of poor management almost always comes down to lack of planning."[9]

Planning is not just an exercise done to please bankers or raise financing. The very process elicits new ideas and visions, anticipates problems, challenges and refines your perceptions of operations, and sets the course of your business.

And even if explosive growth is your goal, don't assume any plan will become obsolete. Consider the case of Stratus Computer.

✓ A maker of fault tolerant computers, Stratus' original business plan called for sales of $75 million in their fifth year — and they hit that total almost exactly. CEO William Foster said the next year, "That plan was something we took very seriously. I'm convinced that if the original plan had a lower goal, we would have achieved less."[10]

If your sales explode and render your original plan obsolete, as with Ben & Jerry's, terrific. But use the opportunity to update your plan and set new targets. As a proverb says, "If you don't know where you're going, any path will get you there."

Your long-range plan addresses the big picture. The next chapter focuses on budgeting, which translates your goals to detailed actions and targets, and makes it possible to get where you are going.

Endnotes

1. From a lecture at Sloan School of Management, 19 Oct. 1991.

2. Larson, Erik. "The Best Laid Plans." INC. February 1987: 60.

3. Ibid. p. 61.

4. Ibid.

5. Ibid. p. 62.

6. BDO Seidman. "Pulse of the Middle Market 1990." A survey reprinted in SMALL BUSINESS REPORTS July 1991: 55.

7. Bygrave, William D. "Small Business Has Key to Success." BOSTON BUSINESS JOURNAL 6–12 Aug. 1993: 15.

8. Ibid. p. 53.

9. Roha, Ronaleen R. "10 Ways to Scuttle Your New Business." CHANGING TIMES July 1990: 63.

10. Larson, p. 62.

Financial Projections – Sample Assumptions

	Jan.	Feb.	Mar.	Apr.	May
# of Working Days	22	20	21	22	22
Av. Unit Sales/Day	183	250	240	270	275
List Price – Contract Sales	$87	$87	$87	$87	$87
List Price – Regular Sales	$115	$115	$115	$115	$115
List Price – Discounters	$60	$60	$60	$60	$60
Net Av. Selling Price	$96	$96	$96	$96	$96
Total Sales Volume	387,000	480,000	484,000	570,000	581,000
Customer Breakdown					
Contract – PA	17%	17%	17%	17%	17%
Regular – PA	26%	26%	26%	26%	26%
Contract – NY	20%	20%	20%	20%	20%
Regular – NY	32%	32%	32%	32%	32%
Discount	3%	3%	3%	3%	3%
Other	2%	2%	2%	2%	2%
Cost of Materials					
Contract Sales	52%	52%	51%	51%	51%
Regular Sales	46%	46%	46%	45%	45%
Discounters	70%	70%	70%	70%	70%
Sales Impact on Inventory					
Contract Sales	2%	2%	2%	2%	2%
Regular Sales	0	0	0	0	0
Discounters	−22%	−22%	−22%	−22%	−22%
Indirect Labor Pay/Month	20,500	20,500	20,500	20,500	20,500
Direct Labor Wages/Day	2,000	2,000	2,000	2,042	2,052
Benefits Rate	30%	30%	30%	30%	30%
Freight/Unit – PA	$6.90	$6.35	$6.43	$6.21	$6.17
Freight/Unit – NY	$3.45	$3.18	$3.21	$3.10	$3.09
Co-op Advertising – Reg. Sales	4.0%	4.0%	4.0%	4.0%	4.0%
Commissions – Contract Sales	4.0%	4.0%	4.0%	4.0%	4.0%
Commissions – All Other Sales	5.0%	5.0%	5.0%	5.0%	5.0%
Depreciation	8,030	8,370	8,700	8,700	8,700
Av Days A/P Outstanding	32	32	32	35	35
Av. Days A/R Outstanding	52	50	50	49	49
Fixed Asset Purchases	0	20,000	20,000	0	0
Interest Rate	9.0%	9.0%	9.0%	9.0%	9.0%
Debt Principal Payments		25,000			

Financial Projections – Sample Assumptions (continued)

	June	July	Aug.	Sept.	Oct.	Nov.	Dec.	Total Year
	20	22	22	20	23	20	20	
	280	240	270	290	290	305	210	
	$87	$87	$87	$87	$87	$87	$87	
	$115	$115	$115	$115	$115	$115	$115	
	$60	$60	$60	$60	$60	$60	$60	
	$96	$96	$96	$96	$96	$96	$96	
	538,000	507,000	570,000	557,000	640,000	586,000	403,000	6,303,000
	17%	17%	17%	17%	17%	17%	17%	
	26%	26%	26%	26%	26%	26%	26%	
	20%	20%	20%	20%	20%	20%	20%	
	32%	32%	32%	32%	32%	32%	32%	
	3%	3%	3%	3%	3%	3%	3%	
	2%	2%	2%	2%	2%	2%	2%	
	51%	50%	50%	50%	50%	50%	50%	
	45%	45%	45%	44%	44%	44%	44%	
	70%	70%	70%	70%	70%	70%	70%	
	2%	2%	2%	2%	2%	2%	2%	
	0	0	0	0	0	0	0	
	−22%	−22%	−22%	−22%	−22%	−22%	−22%	
	20,500	20,500	20,500	20,500	20,500	20,500	20,500	
	2,062	2,000	2,042	2,083	2,083	2,114	2,000	
	30%	30%	30%	30%	30%	30%	30%	
	$6.14	$6.43	$6.21	$6.07	$6.07	$5.97	$6.67	
	$3.07	$3.21	$3.10	$3.03	$3.03	$2.98	$3.33	
	4.0%	4.0%	4.0%	4.0%	4.0%	4.0%	4.0%	
	4.0%	4.0%	4.0%	4.0%	4.0%	4.0%	4.0%	
	5.0%	5.0%	5.0%	5.0%	5.0%	5.0%	5.0%	
	8,700	9,370	9,370	9,370	10,030	10,030	10,030	109,400
	38	38	38	38	38	38	38	
	48	48	48	48	48	48	48	
	0	40,000	0	0	40,000	0	0	120,000
	9.0%	9.0%	9.0%	9.0%	9.0%	9.0%	9.0%	
	25,000			25,000			25,000	100,000

Financial Projections – Sample P&L

	Jan.	Feb.	Mar.	Apr.	May
Sales					
Contract & Regular – PA	166,400	206,400	208,100	245,100	249,800
Contract & Regular – NY	201,200	249,600	251,700	296,400	302,100
Discount	19,400	24,000	24,200	28,500	29,100
Total Sales	387,000	480,000	484,000	570,000	581,000
Manufacturing Costs					
Purchases	192,660	238,944	238,853	278,331	283,713
Inventory Change	940	1,152	1,162	1,368	1,406
Direct Labor Wages	44,000	40,000	42,000	44,915	45,144
Indirect Labor Pay	15,375	20,500	20,500	20,500	20,500
Benefits	19,350	18,150	18,750	19,625	19,693
Rent	10,000	10,000	10,000	10,000	10,000
Utilities	4,710	5,120	4,060	2,350	1,060
Depreciation	3,210	3,350	3,480	3,480	3,480
Other Overhead	800	800	800	800	800
Total Cost of Sales	296,170	338,016	339,605	381,369	385,796
Gross Margin	90,830	141,984	144,395	188,631	19,5204
	23.5%	29.6%	29.8%	33.1%	33.6%
Expenses					
PA Trucking	11,900	13,700	13,900	15,900	16,100
NY Trucking	10,300	11,800	12,000	13,600	13,800
Depreciation	4,820	5,020	5,220	5,220	5,220
Co-op Adv. – PA	4,025	8,256	8,324	9,804	9,992
Co-op Adv. – NY	4,954	9,984	10,068	11,856	12,084
Commissions – PA	7,663	9,504	9,583	11,286	11,504
Commissions – NY	9,288	11,520	11,616	13,680	13,944
Warehousing – PA	2,500	2,500	2,500	5,000	5,000
G&A Salaries	15,000	15,000	15,000	15,000	15,000
Benefits	4,500	4,500	4,500	4,500	4,500
Leases	1,300	1,300	1,300	1,300	1,300
Insurance	9,000	9,000	9,000	9,000	9,000
Travel & Entertainment	2,000	2,000	2,000	2,000	2,000
Phone/Postage	2,000	2,000	2,000	2,000	2,000
Other	3,700	1,200	1,200	3,700	1,200
Total Salaries, G&A	92,949	107,284	108,211	123,846	122,644
Operating Income (loss)	−2,119	34,700	36,184	64,785	72,560
	−0.5%	7.2%	7.5%	11.4%	12.5%
Interest Expense	5,300	5,300	5,300	5,100	5,100
Net Income	−7,419	29,400	30,884	59,685	67,460
%	−1.9%	6.1%	6.4%	10.5%	11.6%

Financial Projections – Sample P&L (continued)

June	July	Aug.	Sept.	Oct.	Nov.	Dec.	Total Year
231,300	218,000	245,100	239,500	275,200	252,000	173,300	2,710,200
279,800	263,600	296,400	289,600	332,800	304,700	209,600	3,277,500
26,900	25,400	28,500	27,900	32,000	29,300	20,200	315,400
538,000	507,000	570,000	557,000	640,000	586,000	403,100	6,303,100
262,703	245,400	275,880	266,704	306,432	280,578	193,014	3,063,212
1,292	1,228	1,368	1,348	1,536	1,406	978	15,184
41,248	44,000	44,915	41,664	47,914	42,288	40,000	518,088
20,500	20,500	20,500	20,500	20,500	20,500	20,500	246,000
18,524	19,350	19,625	18,649	20,524	18,836	18,150	229,226
10,000	10,000	10,000	10,000	10,000	10,000	10,000	120,000
1,060	1,180	1,180	1,350	2,808	3,850	4,260	32,988
3,480	3,750	3,750	3,750	4,010	4,010	4,010	43,760
800	800	800	800	800	800	800	9,600
359,607	346,208	378,018	364,765	414,524	382,268	291,712	4,278,058
178,393	160,792	191,982	192,235	225,476	203,732	111,388	2,025,042
33.2%	31.7%	33.7%	34.5%	35.2%	34.8%	27.6%	32.1%
14,800	14,600	15,900	15,100	17,400	15,700	12,000	177,000
12,700	12,600	13,600	13,000	15,000	13,500	10,400	152,300
5,220	5,620	5,620	5,620	6,020	6,020	6,020	65,640
9,252	8,720	9,804	9,580	11,008	10,080	6,932	105,777
11,192	10,544	11,856	11,584	13,312	12,188	8,384	128,006
10,652	10,039	11,286	11,029	12,672	11,603	7,981	124,802
12,912	12,168	13,680	13,368	15,360	14,064	9,674	151,274
5,000	5,000	5,000	5,000	5,000	5,000	5,000	52,500
15,000	15,000	15,000	15,000	15,000	15,750	15,750	181,500
4,500	4,500	4,500	4,500	4,500	4,725	4,725	54,450
1,300	1,300	1,300	1,300	1,300	1,300	1,300	15,600
9,000	9,000	9,000	9,000	9,000	9,000	9,000	108,000
2,000	2,000	2,000	2,000	2,000	2,000	2,000	24,000
2,000	2,000	2,000	2,000	2,000	2,000	2,000	24,000
1,200	3,700	1,200	1,200	3,700	1,200	1,200	24,400
116,728	116,791	121,746	119,281	133,272	124,130	102,366	1,389,248
61,665	44,001	70,236	72,954	92,204	79,602	9,022	635,793
11.5%	8.7%	12.3%	13.1%	14.4%	13.6%	2.2%	10.1%
5,100	4,900	4,900	4,900	4,700	4,700	4,700	60,000
56,565	39,101	65,336	68,054	87,504	74,902	4,322	575,793
10.5%	7.7%	11.5%	12.2%	13.7%	12.8%	1.1%	9.1%

Financial Projections – Sample Balance Sheet

	Beginning Balances	Jan.	Feb.	Mar.	Apr.	May
Assets						
Cash & Investments	30,463	53,382	60,543	10,192	60,858	79,533
Accts Receivable	699,872	674,470	738,000	804,000	876,530	942,000
Inventory	535,773	534,833	533,681	532,519	531,151	529,745
Less: Reserves	−45,000	−45,000	−45,000	−45,000	−45,000	−45,000
Prepaids/Other	72,211	71,700	71,700	71,700	71,700	71,700
Fixed Assets (Net)	318,971	310,941	322,571	333,871	325,171	316,471
Land	22,160	22,160	22,160	22,160	22,160	22,160
Total Assets	1,634,450	1,622,486	1,703,655	1,729,442	1,842,570	1,916,609
Liabilities & Equity						
Trade Payables	201,405	205,504	254,874	274,776	324,720	330,999
Accrued Wages	24,696	24,500	22,000	22,000	18,500	18,200
Accrued Liabilities	101,848	93,400	98,300	98,300	105,300	105,900
Long-Term Debt	700,000	700,000	700,000	675,000	675,000	675,000
Equity	200,000	200,000	200,000	200,000	200,000	200,000
Retained Earnings	406,501	399,082	428,482	459,366	519,051	586,511
Total Liabilities & Equity	1,634,450	1,622,486	1,703,655	1,729,442	1,842,570	1,916,609

Financial Projections – Sample Balance Sheet (continued)

June	July	Aug.	Sept.	Oct.	Nov.	Dec.	Total Year
178,348	221,830	294,112	310,861	347,554	403,643	492,759	18.2%
886,600	829,800	874,200	899,000	974,200	970,000	754,700	27.8%
528,453	527,225	525,857	524,509	522,973	521,567	520,589	19.2%
−45,000	−45,000	−45,000	−45,000	−45,000	−45,000	−45,000	−1.7%
71,700	71,700	71,700	71,700	71,700	71,700	71,700	2.6%
307,771	338,401	329,031	319,661	349,631	339,601	329,571	12.2%
22,160	22,160	22,160	22,160	22,160	22,160	22,160	0.8%
1,950,032	1,966,116	2,072,060	2,102,891	2,243,218	2,283,671	2,146,479	79.2%
332,757	310,840	349,448	337,825	388,147	355,399	244,484	9.0%
18,100	19,200	17,300	17,900	15,400	17,000	22,500	0.8%
106,100	103,900	107,800	106,600	111,600	108,300	97,200	3.6%
650,000	650,000	650,000	625,000	625,000	625,000	600,000	22.1%
200,000	200,000	200,000	200,000	200,000	200,000	200,000	7.4%
643,075	682,176	747,512	815,566	903,071	977,972	982,294	36.2%
1,950,032	1,966,116	2,072,060	2,102,891	2,243,218	2,283,671	2,146,479	79.2%

Notes

Chapter 14

Budgeting

*The budget should be a door open to more satisfying and profitable
work — not an instrument of torture. Then it will be known that
what you can do without a budget you can do better with one.*

— James L. Peirce[1]

While the long-range plan identifies the goals of a company over several
years, the budget process identifies the actions and milestones needed
over a shorter time span — usually one year — to carry out the long-term
strategy. Where the long-term plan lays out fairly general guidelines out-
lining the big picture, the budget provides a specific and detailed allocation of resources.

Budgets, particularly in smaller companies, have a tarnished reputation.
Some common complaints and perceptions include:

- Budgets unnecessarily restrict managers' actions. Who wants an in-
  spired idea zapped because "it is not in the budget?"

- Budgets quickly become obsolete and either hold managers to unrealistic targets or get ignored.

- Managers play "budget games." To make their numbers, they may shift
  expenses between accounting periods, play with accounting practices,
  or unwisely freeze or cut vital spending.

- Budgets are simply a number-crunching exercise.

- Budgets are unrealistic because top management dictates the targets
  rather than encourages managers' inputs.

These problems are real, but usually result from poor implementation. Done properly, budgets are vital for coordinating the company's activities, anticipating possible problems, gaining the commitment of managers, and providing control and motivation. As was argued for long-term planning, the consequences of not having a budget are often worse than the drudgery of pulling it together.

Planning and Control

You can use budgets for both planning and control. Preparation of the budget gets you and your managers involved in identifying and choosing between operating strategies. The budget also lays down specific targets and milestones. This planning aspect sets the direction of your company and provides a basis for predicting financial performance.

Budgets are also powerful tools for coordinating, motivating, and evaluating the performance of managers. Many companies base some portion of compensation on performance versus budget. Just the act of setting targets and providing regular feedback motivates many managers. The budget also can define spending limits and communicate expectations so that top management can harness the actions of line managers.

Many budget decisions involve some degree of trade-off between planning and control. Should sales goals be set aggressively to motivate performance or at lower levels that more realistically predict expected performance? Should budgets be revised during the year to improve their accuracy or should managers be held to their original targets?

How you prepare and use a budget will depend on your company's structure and your management style. In general, though, smaller companies are more likely to use budgets as planning instruments. Larger companies, with more complex operations and layers of management, tend to use budgets for control.

Regardless of how the budget is used, it is more than simply a forecast. A forecast is a prediction of future results. Budgeting asks for a commitment from management and provides a blueprint to make the results happen.

Size and Complexity

Developing a budget does not need to be a complex procedure. Smaller companies with few, if any, layers of management and one very focused line of business might be able to draw up a budget in one meeting between the president and the controller.

But even a simple budget is valuable if for no other reason than to ensure that cash out doesn't exceed cash in. Take the example of a family household. The typical family determines how much income it expects and identifies goals, such as saving for college and retirement, taking a vacation, and improving the house. These goals are then translated into dollars and then necessary expenses, such as food, clothing, and paying off the mortgage, are added in. The numbers are then compiled, and massaged as necessary, to see if the household budget balances or leaves a little extra money for a rainy day or emergencies.

For small companies, whose operation is expected to continue largely as is, the budget might be little more than an extrapolation of previous years' spending. In most companies, past spending is the best clue to future expenditures. Once the sales target is set, determining how expenses should change is a fairly straightforward exercise.

Before putting the budget to rest, take a critical look at whether the projected profit is really in line with long-term goals. If possible, compare key assumptions, such as gross margin or G&A spending, with that of other companies or even past performance. If savings are needed, challenge current spending and try to identify sufficient savings to bring the budget in line with the new targets.

Budget Cycle

Larger companies will have a more formal budget cycle that involves key managers. Starting with the completion of a long-range plan, the cycle would include preparation of an operating budget, some form of feedback and control, plus possible updates. Some of the questions to answer include:

- Who prepares the budget?
- Should the process be top-down, driven by upper management, or bottom-up, driven by department needs?
- What time period should the budget cover?
- How will it be linked to the long-range plan?
- When should the budget be prepared?
- Should it be fixed or updated regularly?
- What is the balance between planning and control?
- Will compensation or performance reviews be tied to the budget?
- How will intangibles be measured?

Top-Down or Bottom-Up?

A budget can be prepared "top-down" or "bottom-up." Top-down refers to a budget that is dictated by upper management, based on their vision of the company and knowledge of its goals and resources. Department managers may budget specific line items, but their overall budget is set from above.

Bottom-up budget processes are initiated by department managers, taking advantage of their detailed knowledge of the operation or marketplace. Starting with only broad guidelines from top management, the line managers identify and request projects and staffing they feel are needed. The department budgets are then added together to form the company budget.

The advantages of top-down budgets are that they enhance coordination of department budgets and can be implemented quickly, particularly in crisis situations. If department managers lack the training or support staff to effectively participate in planning, a top-down budget may also be needed. On the other hand, because line managers are closer to the market and day-to-day operations, bottom-up budgets may be better at recognizing opportunities for innovation. In addition, the higher degree of participation helps win the commitment of managers to the budget goals.

In practice, a combination of these approaches is usually used. The long-range plan is prepared at the top and incorporates the vision and objectives of the owner or top management. The basic assumptions of the plan — such as sales, inflation rate, and capital investment — are given to the department managers who are asked to prepare their budgets consistent with these assumptions. These budgets are totaled and compared to the targeted spending of the long-range plan. Any inconsistencies are then resolved by revising either, or both, the budget and long-term plan.

A Nonaccounting Function

No matter which process is used, you and your managers should do the budgeting. It is not an activity owned and operated by the accounting department. The purpose of budgeting is to:

- Evaluate operating options;
- Set targets; and
- Provide a basis for monitoring performance.

These activities are management, not accounting functions. Your accounting personnel can and should assist you and your managers in preparing projections and compiling relevant figures. During the year, the accounting department should also track actual and budgeted performance, providing essential feedback. These functions are important, but they make up a supporting, not a leading, role.

The accounting department also lacks the clout and leadership needed to implement the budget. Accounting will probably be required to carry out the mechanics of compiling the budget. But gaining the commitment of line managers, allocating resources, and controlling operations is your job.

Timing

For most companies, the budget cycle will start with completion of the long-range plan. A normal target for a smaller company to start the budget cycle is one to two months before the beginning of the period covered by the budget.

A typical budget covers a one-year period — more by convention and a conformity with the fiscal year than by necessity — and is usually broken down further by month or quarter. A company with lengthy projects will probably want to budget each project separately over its expected lifespan. Other companies may have a quarterly budget cycle in which only the upcoming quarter is budgeted by month, and the remainder of the year is budgeted by quarter. Every three months, a new budget is prepared that goes out one year, even though the budget year does not correspond to the fiscal year.

Your first step in starting your budget cycle is to communicate the assumptions and targets contained in your long-term plan to each manager. Each manager must work from the same set of assumptions about factors such as sales, the economy, and target raises. If one manager budgets on the assumption sales will be flat or inflation negligible, and another predicts a sharp sales increase or 10% inflation, the combined budget will be seriously flawed.

As a starting point, the controller should provide historical financial information to the managers. As mentioned earlier, the best clue of what a particular expense will be is usually the past run rate. History is only a guide, though. One trap to avoid is having managers simply project the results of the old year onto the next.

Your controller can also help to model certain expenses — an especially useful tool for salary expenses. A department head can supply headcount figures with projected raises, and an accountant can extend that into dollars, including a proper allowance for benefit expenses. As salaries are often the largest departmental expense, a careful headcount projection contributes greatly to an accurate budget.

Another calculation the controller can help with is figuring the impact of seasonal variations or a rapid growth in sales throughout the year. Few companies have flat expenses from month to month, so managers cannot simply take annual targets and divide by twelve to get monthly budgets. But the mechanics of figuring out how to spread the expenses is often a task better suited to an accountant than a line manager.

Arriving at the final budget is a repetitive process. The initial input from the line managers is totaled and compared to the targets set forth in the long-range plan. Top management reviews both the spending levels projected, as well as the merits of any new projects proposed. Any disagreements with the proposed spending is then communicated to the line managers. Through give and take, the budget is revised and projects agreed on until all parties agree and the budget is in line with the long-range plan. The budget is continuously restated until all issues are resolved. Unless top-down control is essential, you should not simply impose your will on subordinates. Instead, selling any proposed changes will help you ensure commitment to the budget.

If the budget does not fit within the targets of your long-range plan, consider changing the projections. Often, doing a budget points out inconsistencies in the more general, long-term projections.

Most companies will find that two or three budget cycles will be needed for the process to be effective. Remember, the entire budget process is repetitive, so don't be discouraged by early difficulties.

People and Budgets

So far, the discussion has focused on the planning role of budgets. The budget process is where ideas are generated, compared, and tested for financial soundness. Spending targets are set at the department and company level and form a guide for the upcoming period.

In planning, the budget is shaped by a company's managers. But once the budget is in place, the focus shifts to the control function. You ask your managers to achieve the targets that have been laid out, and you monitor their progress. Often, their compensation or career advancement depends on how well they do compared to the budget.

Attainable Goals

The budget can shape the behavior of managers, which of course, is one of the reasons for doing a budget in the first place. If the targets are set, and management is committed to them, the people responsible will look for ways to meet those targets. What gets measured, gets done.

Note that you may have a gap between a target that is set to motivate a manager, particularly if it is a stretch, and the best prediction of what will actually happen. For example, a salesperson might be given a quota 25% above the prior year's figure and be compensated based on how well this quota is met. But for planning purposes, you may want to use a more conservative growth figure.

One prerequisite for motivating managers is ensuring that the person assigned a budget item believes the target is attainable. Targets set too tight may discourage managers or, as discussed below, encourage accounting games. In addition, the more the budget is dictated from the top, the greater the risk of managers not buying into it.

Responsibility

Responsibility for budgeted expenses should be assigned to specific people whenever possible. With many overhead expenses, such as health and workers' compensation insurance, facility maintenance, or heat, you may be tempted to treat them as uncontrollable or simply allocate them to various departments. Though these expenses can be controlled, they probably won't be if no one is held responsible.

Of course, you need to choose an appropriate person. Where possible, this should be an operating manager. Consider the following story:

✓ A company thought the cleaning expense for its factory was exorbitant. The manufacturing employees claimed the expense could not be reduced, so responsibility was assigned to the controller. Sure enough, cleaning costs were quickly reduced — and the facility became a mess.[2]

Incentives

While setting goals and monitoring progress are powerful motivation tools, tying a portion of compensation to achieving budget goals can provide a further incentive to managers. You can design a bonus system to reward meeting or exceeding department, division, or company goals. Since the bonus is primarily a control tool, alignment with your goals for the company is important. Regular feedback to managers on their progress is also key for motivating them.

One risk of compensating managers based on performance versus budget is the possible introduction of budget games. To make their performance look better, some managers may:

- Build padding into the budget;

- Attempt to shift expenses to other departments;

- Slash expenses, such as advertising, maintenance, or R&D, for short-term gain at the expense of long-term performance; and

- Make deals with vendors or customers that accelerate sales or defer expenses.

To defuse these games, either you must set compensation to reward actions that work toward long-term, corporate goals or you must have enough understanding of possible games to be able to detect and counteract them.

Other Budget Structures

Budgets can be used to plan and control more than just expenses. Many managers control not only costs, but revenues, intangibles, or a combination, and their departments should be measured accordingly. In addition to the traditional cost center, which is measured strictly on the basis of expenses, some of the following structures are possible:

Standard cost centers. Standard cost centers are structures usually used for a production department where volume and, therefore, total cost cannot be controlled, but unit costs can be. Supervisors are evaluated based on performance versus standard cost for direct costs and for staying within budget on overhead items.

Revenue centers. Revenue centers are structures typically used for a sales department. Managers are expected to spend no more than budget and maximize sales.

Discretionary expense centers. Discretionary expense centers are applicable to administrative departments where there may be no relation between the amount of money spent and the quality of work performed. Managers are asked to spend the budget and obtain the best quality output.

Profit centers. Profit center structures are useful when departments or divisions control both revenues and expenses. Managers concentrate on achieving the best combination of activities for generating income.

Defining Profit

The definition of profit, if you are using a profit center structure, can range significantly, depending on the focus you encourage. Profit can be affected by the methods you choose to account for indirect costs. Some possibilities are if you:

■ Include only revenues and direct costs to show what each department contributes toward overhead;

■ Add in overhead costs a manager controls, at least in the long-term, such as capital equipment and use of space and accounting resources; or

■ Allocate a portion of company costs a manager has no control over, such as interest.

By including allocations, you risk passing on costs that are beyond a manager's control. If the allocations are based on inappropriate measures, they may distort both reporting and decision making. The benefit is that your managers can gain an appreciation for the total costs of the company.

Customize Your Budget

Because budgets rely on accounting information, they are often subject to the limitations of accounting that have been discussed earlier. Perhaps the most important information to remember is that budgets only measure financial items. Budgets can track where the money was spent or motivate managers to control spending or headcount. But they say little about the quality of the spending.

With intangibles, such as quality or customer service, increasingly becoming a major part of strategic objectives, the budget process must include some measurement or feedback on nonfinancial measures.

Aligning the activities managers control with budget responsibility may require breaking up traditional account groupings. If a production unit contributes directly to expenditures for R&D or accounting, these costs should be included in the production department's budget, even though GAAP statements would place the expenses in different categories. In addition, where R&D or accounting costs can be directly attributed to several departments, you can break them up. Rather than assigning the entire R&D budget to one manager, give various pieces to the departments that actually control them.

Decisions on allocating expenses should be based on the planning and control objectives of top management, not accounting conventions. For example, GAAP requires that manufacturing costs be spread to inventory, but there is no need for budgets to allocate manufacturing overhead. If management chooses to assign a portion of corporate overhead to profit centers, that would also differ with GAAP presentation.

Because department managers can engage in some of the creative accounting described in Chapter 5, as well as other budget games, you may need to set up some safeguards. These might include setting some targets and monitoring statistics, such as bookings to shipments ratios, inventory levels, or customers served per employee.

Flexible Budgets

Usually, the largest variable in budgeting is predicting the sales level. Not only do sales vary more, and less predictably, than expenses, but many expenses are related directly to sales mix and volume. Sales variances can cause large swings in departmental expenses that are beyond the control of the line managers.

In addition, as part of your planning process, your company will want to identify the impact of higher or lower sales. You can then prepare strategies to respond to different levels of sales.

A common budget technique that adjusts for variations in sales is the flexible budget. One method of flexible budgeting is to construct several budgets for different sales levels. More commonly, the flexible budget figures are accomplished by expressing expenses as a function of sales or activity levels. With a straightforward calculation, you can arrive at the expense level for any level of activity.

The next illustration demonstrates the use of a flexible budget, assuming the following simple budget for a shipping department:

Flexible Budget

Budget Item	Original Budget	Actual	Flexible Budget
Units shipped	10,000	9,000	9,000
Boxes ($1/unit)	$10,000	$ 9,900	$ 9,000
Freight ($5/unit)	$50,000	$47,000	$45,000
Salaried labor	$30,000	$29,000	$30,000
Total	$90,000	$86,900	$84,000

At first glance, the department seems to have spent less than budget — $86,900 versus $90,000. However, you can see that both box and freight expenses vary directly with sales — and that sales were 1,000 units less than planned. Using the flexible budget, you can see that at the lower volume, total spending should have been only $84,000. Thus, total spending actually exceeded the budget.

By having the flexible budget and comparing it with the actual figures, you are made aware of any important variances that occur within your business.

Budgets as Working Documents

Managers get beaten on both sides by budgets. CEOs hit the managers over the head about performance, while accountants paddle them from behind about expenses.

Although large companies may use budgets to restrict the actions of managers, smaller companies should seek to use budgets to enhance managers' performance. Budgets aren't written in blood and should not deter managers from pursuing unexpected opportunities. Budget busting may need to be encouraged if new opportunities or challenges arise.

To ensure that budgets are effective motivation and feedback tools, timely reporting and adequate follow up of results are needed. Soon after the end of each accounting period, the controller should provide each manager with a package showing actual results compared to the original plan with the variance calculated. The controller should then work with the managers to follow up on any reported variances.

As a first step in investigating a variance, have your controller identify all transactions posted to the account during the period. Your controller can then make a first attempt to explain the difference. The controller will usually be able to isolate causes of variances related to:

- Timing of transactions
- One-time expenses
- Significant price changes by vendors
- Increases in the overall level of activity

In these cases, no corrective action is needed. The controller may just want to summarize the findings in brief comments to the appropriate people.

Unexplained variances should be investigated by you or your operating manager. While the controller may be able to identify which transactions to investigate, the line manager is in the best position to determine the underlying cause. The problem may well be poor assumptions in the original budget. But if an operating problem exists, the budget and interim results will have provided an early warning.

Your controller should also be prepared to explain the results to outsiders. Investors and bankers, in particular, will want to understand how a company is performing against its business plan. In turnarounds and startups, for example, early losses are often expected, so progress against the business plan is usually more important than the actual bottom line. By breaking down the financial results and explaining the source of any variances, your controller can greatly enhance relations with outsiders.

Rolling Budgets

For many companies, budgeting is only an annual exercise. Of course, as the end of the year approaches, the budget no longer looks out many months ahead. In addition, the original budget may be hopelessly outdated because of changes in operations or assumptions.

Rather than toss the budget aside, you can update it using a rolling budget — similar to the way you use a rolling plan, as discussed in the previous chapter in the section on timing and budgets. In an annual rolling budget, as one quarter ends, another quarter is added to the end of the budget. This way, a company is always looking forward nine to twelve months. While a rolling budget can be prepared without revising the existing budget, the entire budget is usually redone.

Any budget revision, of course, requires additional management time. The additional time can be viewed as an unnecessary disruption or, preferably, as a way to force managers to take time to plan up to four times a year.

But revisions also raise another important planning versus control trade-off. A revised budget will probably be more accurate, which is important for forecasting. It also provides some flexibility for managers who might have been constrained by the original budget. However, constant revisions may make it difficult to judge managers against earlier targets.

If benchmarks constantly shift, using the budget as a tool for control becomes difficult. Even though you risk some confusion, one solution may be to monitor performance against both the original and the current budget.

Capital Budgets

Annual budgets typically cover operating expenses for a company. These operating expenses include spending decisions for ongoing departments and existing equipment. However, planning also requires investment decisions: what equipment to buy, whether to open a new plant, or which division to close.

The process of making these decisions is called capital budgeting. Much as individuals compare the costs of buying a new car to the expense of maintaining their old vehicle, plus the risk of major repairs, department managers must decide on the best long-term investment strategy.

Capital budgeting involves calculating the risk and estimated return of investments and choosing between competing strategies. The tools used in capital budgeting, including discounted cash flow, payback, and internal rate of return, are discussed in the next chapter.

Budget Dynamics

The long-range plan and the budget go together to express the goals of the company in a clear and objective manner. The plan expresses the long-term vision while the budget identifies the specific steps and resources needed. Budgets and planning are more than just number-crunching exercises. They provide a framework for clearly expressing where your company is, where it wants to get to, and the basis for measuring its progress against those goals.

Depending on the structure and style of your company, the budget may either be used for planning, for control, or a combination of both. Either way, both you and your top managers must be committed to the goals set forth in the budget. Lack of top management commitment on your part or the failure of line managers to buy into the budget will almost surely make the budget process ineffective.

Budgeting can be time consuming and your managers may complain that they have no time to plan, but the time is well invested. The next chapter discusses another area of planning on which spending time is also well invested — project evaluation. Many times you will need to choose between two or more projects. How do you tell which one is best? Chapter 15 deals with making investment decisions.

Endnotes

1. Peirce, James L. "The Budget Comes of Age." HARVARD BUSINESS REVIEW May–June 1954: 66.

2. Viscione, Jerry A. "Small Company Budgets: Targets are the Key." HARVARD BUSINESS REVIEW May–June 1984: 48.

Chapter 15

Evaluating Projects

One accurate measurement is worth a thousand expert opinions.

— Rear Admiral Grace Hopper, U.S. Navy [1]

In capital budgeting, and throughout every year, your company will make a number of important investment decisions. These might include whether to open a new store, start a new product line, buy a piece of equipment, or go from buying to making a component. An investment decision may require a comparison of several alternatives, including the option of doing nothing at all. How do you sort out the alternatives?

The good news is that the techniques for evaluating projects are very straightforward and can be applied to a broad range of investment decisions. What is usually difficult is gathering good projected figures and dealing with the uncertainty inherent in them.

Whatever the project, "running the numbers" is important. Do not rely on gut feelings. Valuing projects provides a clear-cut basis for choosing among alternatives. The analysis may turn up unexpected problems and help avoid costly mistakes.

In making this point, one manager described his company's computer museum. "Any rudimentary analysis," he said, "would have shown that most of the computer equipment we bought was uneconomical." Instead, the equipment sat idle, a constant reminder of wasteful spending.

Like budgets, project evaluation also provides concrete financial targets and clearly communicates expectations. Unlike budgets, however, evaluation and tracking of projects extends over their entire lifetime, which may cover several accounting periods.

As with budgeting, the controller can assist you with the mechanics of valuing projects. However, developing reasonable cost and revenue assumptions requires the active involvement of the managers closest to the project. Each investment decision you make merits an individual appraisal. Although project evaluation may seem like a time-consuming task, this chapter can help you with techniques for evaluating projects and investments, and includes tips and pitfalls. At the end of the chapter is a worksheet that you can use to evaluate projects.

Determine Net Present Value

The first step in valuing a project is to estimate all the associated costs and revenues — or cost savings. These should be calculated for the entire life of the project, though there may be a practical limit to how far out these can be projected.

Only actual cash outlays, savings, and revenues should be included. If a new machine is housed in an existing building, no cash outlay is needed for the space. Even if your accountants allocate a portion of facilities expense to the project, that expense should not be included in your valuation of the project. Similarly, if you depreciate your investment over several years, show the cash outlay in the period it occurs, not when you record the expense for book purposes.

Clearly, you are interested in projects that return more cash than you pay out. However, for a project to simply bring in more revenue than it costs — or reduce expenses — may not be enough. You may not find it worthwhile to spend a dollar to save two dollars if the return only comes in the far distant future. Some recognition has to be given to the fact that a dollar today is worth more than a dollar in the future.

The technique for recognizing this time value of money is called present value (PV). If you can invest money in a sure thing, like treasury bills at 10%, you will be indifferent about having a dollar today or $1.10 a year from now — $1.00 plus 10% interest. Restated, the $1.10 you will receive one year from now only has a present value (PV) of $1.00. The equation below expresses this algebraically.

Present Value Equation

$$PV = \$1.10 \div (1 + 10\%)$$

Translated into words, the mathematical equation states that the present value is equal to the future value, divided by one plus the interest rate.

If you will not receive the cash until two years from now, the formula below is applied.

Present Value Equation – Two Years

$$PV = \$1.10 \div (1 + 10\%)^2$$

In the equation above, the present value equals $0.91, so having $1.00 today would be preferable.

Formulas for additional years are computed in the same way by changing the exponent to reflect the number of years. Since competing investments are assumed to earn a continuous and compounding return, the more into the future the earnings are, the less they are worth today. For example, if interest rates are 10%, $2.00 received seven years from now would only have a present value of about $1.00.

Most projects involve a stream of cash flow. If you invest in a piece of equipment or open a new store, you will have an initial outlay of cash, followed by several years of increased cash flow. Here is an example of how to use the net present value method for determining the worth of a project.

Net Present Value Method

Time Period	Cash Flow ($)	Discount Factor at 10%	Present Value ($)
Day 1	− 1,000	1	− 1,000
Year 1	+ 300	$(1 + 10\%)^1$	+ 273
Year 2	+ 300	$(1 + 10\%)^2$	+ 248
Year 3	+ 250	$(1 + 10\%)^3$	+ 188
Year 4	+ 250	$(1 + 10\%)^4$	+ 171
Year 5	+ 200	$(1 + 10\%)^5$	+ 124
Sale of Equipment	+ 100	$(1 + 10\%)^5$	+ 62
Total Cash Flow:	+ $400	Net Present Value:	+ $66

Although this project returns $400 more than it costs, due to the time value of money, the net present value (NPV) is only slightly positive. But the fact that it is positive means the project is better than the alternative of investing at 10%. Therefore, this is a good investment.

The golden rule is that a negative net present value indicates that other investments are more attractive and a project should not be undertaken. A positive NPV means a project is attractive.

Sometimes, two or more projects are mutually exclusive. You may not have enough money to invest in all the projects or several projects may be directed toward solving the same problem, so adopting one project eliminates the need for others. In these cases, you want to choose the combination of projects that provides the highest total NPV. To determine the net present value for one of your projects, use the Net Present Value Project Evaluation worksheet at the end of this chapter. Follow the instructions to determine what numbers you will need.

Alternative Methods

Two popular methods, which are commonly used to evaluate projects, are also worth mentioning here, even though each is technically flawed. These are the payback method and the internal rate of return (IRR) method.

The payback method measures how long it takes for a company to recoup its investment. In the example above, this occurs approximately halfway through the fourth year — or a payback of three and one-half years. A company may insist that projects meet a maximum payback period, such as two to three years.

This method fails to take into account the time value of money. To adjust for this, some companies use a discounted payback, where the cash flows are discounted using the present value method. Under this measure, the project would have a payback of five years.

The payback method has several weaknesses. It fails to take into account cash flows beyond the point where payback is achieved. If the project returned an additional $1,000 in years six through ten, the payback method would not pick it up. The payback method also fails to reflect the magnitude of the returns, only reflecting the timing, not the size of the cash flow.

The IRR is closer to the NPV in theory. In the example, the discount rate was assumed to be 10%. Because the NPV is positive, you know that the rate of return on the project is better than 10%, but not how much better. That is what the IRR calculates. Put another way, the IRR is the interest — or discount — rate that makes the NPV exactly equal to zero. In the example above, the IRR works out to about 12.6%.

Firms may set a target IRR, sometimes called a hurdle rate. Projects with a rate of return that exceeds the target rate are accepted. This is the same as saying the project has a positive NPV.

The weakness in using IRR instead of NPV is that, like payback, IRR does not reflect the magnitude of a project. This can be a problem when you have to choose between two mutually exclusive projects, like the following:

IRR Versus NPV Comparison

Evaluation Technique	Project A	Project B
Internal Rate of Return (IRR)	25%	20%
Net Present Value (NPV)	$100	$5,000

Even though Project A has a higher IRR, the company is worse off than if it chooses Project B because the net return is $4,900 less.

Valuing a Business

NPV can be used to value a business as well as a project. Instead of projecting cash flows for an isolated investment, use the cash flows for the entire business. The total discounted value of the cash flows equals the current value of the business.

Many factors must be considered in valuing a company. While NPV is theoretically sound, other valuation techniques are often used in practice.

Your Choice of Technique

Your choice of a valuation technique may depend on your background. A recent survey showed that accountants and financial consultants prefer present value for valuing a business. Techniques that use a multiple of expected earnings or cash flow ranked second. Business owners and brokers, on the other hand, overwhelmingly relied on appraisals of tangible assets, such as customer lists, fixed assets, and inventory.

These findings may indicate that business owners are most comfortable with more tangible, less abstract, measures of value. In addition, the survey concluded that, "Business owners may envision a worth for their business that turns out to be quite different" from what is established by a consultant.[2] To avoid a surprise, or inadvertently establishing too low a value, you should apply the present value technique in valuing your company.

Technical Issues to Remember

As was briefly mentioned earlier, only incremental cash flows directly associated with the project should be included in the NPV calculation. This implies three things:

- Sunk costs should be ignored. If you are considering making a new investment in a struggling store or product line, you must ignore any previous investments. You are only interested in whether you make money on this additional investment. Frequently, human nature makes you want to recoup earlier money or cautions you about throwing good money after bad, but only the incremental investment and return is relevant.

- What matters is when cash is spent or received, not when the money shows up on the income statement. If you buy equipment with installment payments, the cash flow is different than when you pay upfront. Also, noncash entries, such as depreciation or accruals, are not included.

- Only spending and revenue directly associated with the project are included. If you invest in an advertising campaign, only the incremental sales generated, not total sales, are included. By the same token, include any incidental effects of the project. If the advertising spurs sales of other products, allow for this in your investment decision.

You need to have consistent assumptions about inflation in determining cash flows and the discount rate. When you project revenues and expenses, you can either assume that prices are stable or apply a factor for inflation. For example, if your expenses include payroll, you can either use salaries in effect today throughout the life of the project or assume you will make cost of living adjustments.

Either approach is acceptable as long as your choice of discount rates reflects the same assumption. If the quoted or nominal interest rate on a mortgage or bond is 10%, roughly 6–7% of that can be attributed to inflation. The remaining 3–4% is the real return, what you will earn after adjusting for the effects of inflation. When you build inflation into your projections of cash flows, you should discount the cash flows at nominal interest rates. If current price levels are used, then use a real discount rate. For example:

✓ The types of errors that can occur when real and nominal figures are mixed occurred in Ireland in 1974. The government created a furor when it purchased a stake in Bula Mines for 40 million pounds when some consultants valued it as low as 8 million pounds and others as high as 104 million. A large part of the difference in valuations was attributed to confusion between real and nominal rates.[3]

Finally, be sure to factor taxes into the cash flows. Taxes are a very real cost, plus the tax treatment of investment options may vary greatly. Some investments qualify for tax credits, others for capital gains treatment or accelerated write-offs.

Calculate Risk Factors

Another issue is how to incorporate risk into the calculation. A bond is a safer bet than starting a new product line. If your investment choices offer the same cash flows, you would clearly choose the less risky option. How do you incorporate this into the NPV?

The answer is to adjust the discount rate according to the risk of the venture. Basically, the discount rate of a project should be what you could expect to earn investing in a competing project with the same risk.

The discount rate for the bond might be compared to returns available on other government issued or insured investments; the new product line's discount rate could be set equal to the stock market returns of companies in the same industry. The higher the risk, the higher the discount rate — and therefore, the lower the NPV.

What if there is great uncertainty over just what the future cash flows will be? If you are launching a new venture, you face the possibilities the project will be a bust, a moderate success, or a home run. Rather than compromise on one possible outcome, prepare discounted cash flows for several scenarios and then assign probabilities to each case. The weighted average then becomes your expected outcome, as illustrated on the next page.

Determining Weighted Average

Case	NPV ($)	Probability (%)	Weighted Average ($)
Bust	− 1,000	15	− 150
Break Even	0	20	0
Most Likely	+ 200	60	+ 120
Home Run	+ 2,000	5	+ 100
Total Weighted Average			+ 70

Even if no cash actually changes hands, the cost of a resource may be relevant. Consider in your calculations some of the types of opportunity costs that may apply to a project. For example:

Consider Opportunity Costs

✓ One manufacturer was evaluating the option of opening outlet stores. The business had a lot of excess merchandise that had been returned, was out of season, or slightly imperfect. Selling through outlet stores could generate enough cash to cover the operating costs of the store. Since the merchandise was already paid for, the stores would generate cash and the company went ahead with the project. What had not been considered, was that the merchandise could have been sold to wholesale discount stores or liquidators with little out of pocket expense. So, even though no cash was needed to move the merchandise from storage to the outlet stores, the opportunity to sell to discounters was lost.

This type of lost revenue is called an opportunity cost. This cost is very real and you must always consider it whenever you choose one option that excludes another. Put another way, instead of asking whether cash flow is better after opening the stores, the right question for the manufacturer in the above example would have been, "Do the stores generate more cash than selling the excess merchandise to discounters?"

For smaller companies that can only focus on a few projects at a time, the opportunity cost of a time or resource consuming project can be enormous.

✓ The founder of a specialty book publisher told the story of the consulting work the business accepted from a Fortune 500 company. Though the money seemed good, the work required different skills than the core business and new people had to be hired. Cash was also tied up as the new employees were paid promptly, but the Fortune 500 company stretched its payments out. When the dust settled about a year later, the project had broken even, but the publisher had missed a year's opportunity by focusing on consulting rather than books.

Cash is clearly a scarce resource in many companies and can also carry a high opportunity cost.

✓ A software developer with a modest 10% market share in a primary market spent $100,000 to develop an unrelated product, a touch screen system for executive information retrieval. Not only was the money lost, but so was the return that could have been earned building market share for the core product.

Another type of opportunity cost not normally picked up by accounting systems is lost time in getting products to market. For high-tech companies where product life cycles are relatively small, lost time can be critical, and missing a window of opportunity can be very costly. The NPV calculation can reflect this cost, provided market opportunities lost due to slow product development can be measured.[4]

Using Break-Even Analysis

A simple, but effective, tool for evaluating risk in your projects is the break-even analysis. This analysis usually assumes a very simple relationship between sales and expenses and shows the profit a company or project will earn across a range of sales volumes.

In the classic break-even analysis, expenses are classified as either fixed or variable. As sales increase, it is assumed that fixed expenses don't change, but both revenue and variable expenses increase in proportion to volume. At low volumes, fixed costs exceed the total contribution margin — which is revenue less variable costs — earned on sales, and the business is unprofitable. At some level of volume, however, the contribution margin will exactly offset fixed expense. This volume is called the break-even point. At volumes above this, the business is profitable. The break-even analysis is commonly shown in graph form, like the one shown below, with dollars plotted along the y-axis and volume on the x-axis.

Break-Even Classic Analysis

Fixed costs = $1,000
Price per unit = $10   Variable cost per unit = $6   Margin per unit = $4

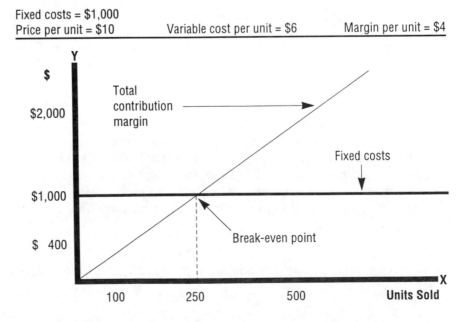

The graph on the previous page shows the break-even point for a project in which each unit brings in $10 (revenue) and has expenses as follows:

Interpreting the Graph

Project Costs	Fixed	Variable
Administrative salaries	$600 per month	
Commissions		$0.60 per unit
Direct labor		$2.00 per unit
Equipment leases	$150 per month	
Raw materials		$3.00 per unit
Rent	$250 per month	
Shipping		$0.40 per unit

First, the expenses are classified as either fixed or variable. The fixed expenses, expressed as a dollar amount per month, are those that do not change as volume changes — such as administrative salaries, rent, and equipment leases. The fixed costs in this project add up to $1,000 and are represented by the horizontal line drawn at $1,000 on the y-axis. The fixed cost line remains the same for any level of volume that is shown on the x-axis, since fixed costs will not change.

The variable expenses, expressed as costs in dollars per unit, change in proportion to volume. Expenses, such as direct labor, raw materials, commissions, and shipping are typical variable expenses. Total variable costs in this project add up to $6 per unit. Since each unit sells for $10, the contribution margin per unit — revenue less variable cost — is $4.

The break-even point is reached when the total contribution margin is equal to the fixed costs ($1,000). To draw the diagonal, cumulative contribution margin line, select any level of sales volume, for example, 100 units. Multiply the sales volume (100 units) by the contribution margin per unit ($4), to get the total contribution margin ($400).

This point is plotted on the graph by locating 100 units on the x-axis and $400 on the y-axis. Draw a diagonal line, starting at the origin — when volume equals zero and the contribution margin equals zero — and continuing through the plotted point and beyond. This line shows the total contribution margin for all levels of volume. Where this line crosses the fixed costs line, is the break-even point, since fixed costs and the contribution margin are equal at that intersection.

To compute the break-even point directly, divide your total fixed costs by the contribution margin per unit. In the example above this equation is:

Break-Even Equation – Cost per Unit

$1,000 fixed costs ÷ $4 contribution margin per unit = 250 units

If the contribution margin is expressed as a percentage of sales, break-even volume in dollars can be calculated by dividing your total fixed costs by the contribution margin percentage. For the previous project, this equation is:

Break-Even Equation – Percentage of Sales

$1,000 fixed costs ÷ 40% contribution margin per unit = $2,500 of revenue

At the end of this chapter are two different worksheets you can use to calculate your break-even point on either a project, a product, or a business.

Nonclassic Break-Even Analysis

In practice, revenues and expenses rarely follow this simplistic relationship. So-called fixed costs, such as indirect labor, will likely change with volume, while per unit costs may decline at higher volumes. You can devise a break-even analysis that uses other than straight-line functions, such as the nonclassic analysis shown below, in which fixed costs increase in steps.

Nonclassic Break-Even Analysis

Fixed costs = $1,000
Price per unit = $10   Variable cost per unit = $6   Margin per unit = $4

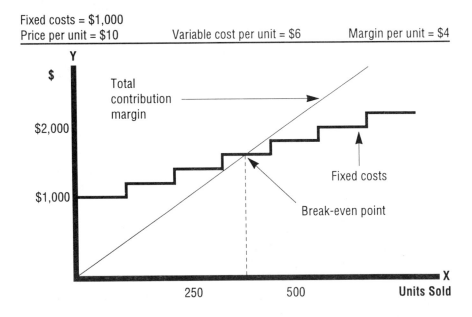

The graph above depicts a simple nonclassic analysis for the same project shown in the first graph. Assume that for the project above, administrative salaries were not truly fixed, but that, in addition to the $600 already being spent, one person had to be added at a cost of $166 per month for each 100 units produced.

Instead of fixed costs staying flat, they would start at $1,000 when volume was zero, increase to $1,166 when volume reached 100, and continue to increase in a step-wise manner. On the nonclassic break-even graph, "fixed costs" are no longer a horizontal line, but a line that shifts in discreet steps. The break-even point is still where this line is met by the total contribution margin line, but at a different volume than before. In the nonclassic analysis, the new break-even point is at 375 units.

== **Homework**

Investment analysis techniques are quite simple and straightforward. The difficulty in evaluating projects generally is not in finding the proper analysis tool, but in developing reasonable estimates of revenues and expenses and trying to quantify factors such as opportunity costs. This problem can be more acute in smaller companies, which do not have the same access to in-house expertise or historical data as larger firms.

To deal with this risk, use more than one tool or evaluate several scenarios of the same project. Even though NPV is theoretically sound, you can gain some further comfort if a payback analysis shows a swift return of the initial investment or a pessimistic case indicates the down side is limited. As a starting point, use the worksheets at the end of this chapter to calculate net present value on your projects and determine your break-even point.

As with long-term projections and budgets, there likely will be a large degree of uncertainty in the calculations. Forecasting is always more art than science. But just the act of running the numbers will improve the decision making process by both introducing some structure and by asking managers to take a hard look at the assumptions behind their investment proposals. A little homework upfront can prevent you from accumulating your own computer museum.

On the other hand, the next chapter takes a look at how computers can be useful in your business and save you many hours of homework.

== **Endnotes**

1. Quoted in *The Manager's Book of Quotations*, p. 390.

2. "Is Value in the Eyes of the Beholder." SMALL BUSINESS REPORTS July 1992: 7.

3. Brealey, Richard and Stewart Myers. *Principles of Corporate Finance.* McGraw-Hill, 1981. p. 88.

4. Smith, Preston G. and Donald G. Reinersten. "Developing Products in Half the Time." SMALL BUSINESS REPORTS Jan. 1992: 65.

Net Present Value Project Evaluation Worksheet – Instructions

Expected Life of Project

Enter the number of years between the first expenditure on the project and the final cash flows expected. If the expected life is greater than ten years, enter ten.

Discount Rate

Choose a discount rate. This should be the rate of return you expect to earn on investments of similar risk. The rate should reflect both the time value of money — a dollar today is worth more than a dollar in the future — and the risk of the project. The higher the risk, the higher the rate of return must be. The discount rate will probably vary from project to project depending on the risk involved. Because the risk of an individual project will usually differ from the risk of your company as a whole, the discount rate you should choose is probably not the interest rate you pay on debt. Once you have chosen a rate, check off whether it is a nominal rate that includes a premium for expected inflation or a real rate — the return over and above inflation. You can choose either, but you should be careful make a consistent assumption when computing your expected cash flows.

Incremental Cash Flows

What will the net cash inflows and outflows be over the life of the project? Start by computing your upfront costs and enter those on the first line as a minus. Then, for each year in the life of the project, enter the incremental cash flows, plus or minus, expected. In your calculation, be sure to:

- Ignore sunk costs — which are costs for past investments. Include only new spending.

- Include only the cash that will be received and paid out directly on this project. Ignore any allocated costs.

- Be consistent about using real or nominal cash flows.

- Include the impact of taxes.

At the end of the project, there may be a residual value. Perhaps you are starting an operation that can be sold to an outside investor, or equipment you purchased can be sold for a salvage value. Or perhaps the project will continue to operate beyond ten years and you want to place a value on the continuing cash flows. Whatever you estimate that value to be, if any, enter it on the last line in the Incremental Cash Flows column for the residual value.

Discount Factor

Enter the discount rate you chose above on each line in the Discount Factor column — for example, 1 + 10%. For residual value, enter the number of years in the expected life of the project from above in the exponent field. Compute each period's discount factor.

Present Value

Divide the cash flows by each discount factor and enter the result in the Present Value column.

Total

Add the numbers in the Present Value column to get the net present value. If this number is greater than zero, the project is worthwhile. Less than zero, the project should not be undertaken. Other statistics you might wish to compute:

- Internal Rate of Return: The discount rate at which the net present value exactly equals zero.

- Payback: To calculate, add the figures in the Incremental Cash Flows column until the cumulative total reaches zero — the number of years where this occurs is your payback period.

- Discounted Payback: To calculate, add the figures in the Present Value column until the cumulative total reaches zero — the number of years where this occurs is your payback period.

Net Present Value Project Evaluation Worksheet

Project: _____

Expected Life of Project: _____ years.

Discount Rate: ____%

Check One: ☐ Nominal   ☐ Real

Brief Description of Project: _____

_____

_____

_____

_____

Time Period	Incremental Cash Flows		Discount Factor		Present Value
Initial start up	$_____	÷	1	=	$_____
Year one	$_____	÷	$1 + \_\_\_\%$	=	$_____
Year two	$_____	÷	$(1 + \_\_\_\%)^2$	=	$_____
Year three	$_____	÷	$(1 + \_\_\_\%)^3$	=	$_____
Year four	$_____	÷	$(1 + \_\_\_\%)^4$	=	$_____
Year five	$_____	÷	$(1 + \_\_\_\%)^5$	=	$_____
Year six	$_____	÷	$(1 + \_\_\_\%)^6$	=	$_____
Year seven	$_____	÷	$(1 + \_\_\_\%)^7$	=	$_____
Year eight	$_____	÷	$(1 + \_\_\_\%)^8$	=	$_____
Year nine	$_____	÷	$(1 + \_\_\_\%)^9$	=	$_____
Year ten	$_____	÷	$(1 + \_\_\_\%)^{10}$	=	$_____
Residual value	$_____	÷	$(1 + \_\_\_\%)^-$	=	$_____

Total Cash Flow: $_____   **Net Present Value:** $_____

Payback: _____ years.

Discounted Payback: _____ years.

Break-Even Analysis Worksheet – Cost per Unit Basis

Depending on the types of numbers you have for your business or project, use either this worksheet or the one on the next page to calculate your break-even point. If the numbers and projects you work with are based on per unit costs, use this worksheet. If your figures are expressed as a percentage of sales, use the worksheet on the next page.

☐ Classify all expenses for your business or project as either fixed or variable. Fixed expenses are items you expect to basically stay constant as sales volume changes. Typically, these include expenses such as rent, administrative salaries, and insurance. Classify as variable any expenses that change in proportion to volume, such as raw materials, direct labor, and commissions. Recognize that these divisions are highly simplified, since in practice, expenses are rarely totally fixed or variable.

☐ Enter your expenses in the correct columns below. Fixed expenses are entered as the total expense for the month or any other period of time you are using. Variable expenses are listed as cost per unit.

Fixed Expense	Amount	Variable Expense	Cost per Unit
	$		$
	$		$
	$		$
	$		$
	$		$
	$		$
	$		$
	$		$
	$		$
	$		$
	$		$
	$		$
Total Fixed Expenses:	$	**Total Variable Expenses:**	$

☐ Total both columns.

☐ Enter your sales price per unit here: $_____.

☐ Then, subtract your total variable expenses per unit (calculated in the column above) from the total price per unit to determine the contribution margin. Enter the contribution margin here: $_____.

☐ Divide your total fixed expenses by the contribution margin to determine the number of units needed to break even.

Unit sales needed to break even: _____ units.

Break-Even Analysis Worksheet – Percentage of Sales Basis

You can use either the worksheet on this page or the worksheet on the previous page to figure out your break-even point for your business or a particular project. This worksheet is for businesses or projects that generally encompass a variety of activities, where costs are expressed as a percentage of sales.

☐ Classify all the expenses for your business or project as either fixed or variable. Fixed expenses, such as rent, administrative salaries, and insurance, are expenses that do not vary as sales volume changes. Variable expenses, such as raw materials, direct labor, and commissions, do vary in proportion to volume.

☐ List your expenses in the appropriate columns below. For fixed expenses, enter the anticipated total expense for the period of time you are using. For variable expenses, enter a percentage of sales volume.

Fixed Expense	Amount	Variable Expense	Percent (%) of Sales
_____	$_____	_____	____%
_____	$_____	_____	____%
_____	$_____	_____	____%
_____	$_____	_____	____%
_____	$_____	_____	____%
_____	$_____	_____	____%
_____	$_____	_____	____%
_____	$_____	_____	____%
_____	$_____	_____	____%
_____	$_____	_____	____%
_____	$_____	_____	____%
_____	$_____	_____	____%

Total Fixed Expenses: $_____   **Total Variable Expenses:** ____%

☐ Add up the columns.

☐ To calculate your break-even volume, use the following equation:

Break-even volume = (total fixed expenses) ÷ (1 – total variable expenses).

Break-even volume: $_____.

☐ Enter your price per unit: $_____.

☐ To figure your break-even volume in units, divide your break-even volume (calculated in the step above) by your average price per unit to determine the unit sales needed to break even.

Unit sales needed to break even: _____ units.

Notes

Chapter 16

The Computer

*If accountants don't understand that all double-entry bookkeeping today
is computer driven, they don't understand the accounting environment.*

— Anthony M. Santomero [1]

Computers and accounting are inextricably linked. Accounting is repetitive and transaction based, making it an ideal computer application.
Starting in the 1960s, most companies' first computers were bought to
handle accounting functions. In the 1980s, it was Lotus 1-2-3 — a financial spreadsheet software program used for planning, cost estimating, and
other number-crunching tasks — that created the boom for IBM personal
computers. Computers provide a wide range of benefits in accounting,
such as:

Speed. The computer can look up, calculate, and print information far
faster than manual processing.

Detail. The computer can collect, store, retrieve, and manipulate detail
efficiently.

Control. Computer systems can build in checks and balances, control
access to information, and provide audit trails.

Integration. Computers make it possible to only enter data once, ensuring
that information from one entry automatically appears in related modules. For example, part numbers and descriptions entered for inventory
control can be accessed for billing and purchasing.

Flexibility. Data can be viewed in different manners, shared by different users, and traded among programs.

Accuracy. Calculations are performed correctly and consistently.

Ultimately, these intangibles translate into an essential cost and time advantage. The computer — with its promise of faster information, tighter controls, and a better database — supports you and your controller in all areas of financial management. This chapter will help you make the right choices in selecting a computer system for your business. You will also learn how to avoid mistakes that are costly in the long run.

Resistance to Computers

Despite their proliferation, computers have not yet taken smaller businesses by storm. Many small businesses continue to use manual systems, while others have minimal setups that, for example, might have just general ledger or automated billing. Other computerized businesses are running outdated equipment.

Why aren't computers more of a factor in smaller businesses? Inexperience and discomfort with computers, especially among older businesspeople, is surely a factor, but it is hardly the only barrier to change. Other sources of resistance are discussed below.

Manual Systems Work

One reason many smaller business owners resist computers is because their existing manual systems work, whether writing checks, preparing invoices, or keeping track of inventory. These manual systems may be cumbersome and time consuming — such as writing out 50 checks or keeping inventory stock cards current — but they do the job. With no urgent reason to change methods, and the risk that a conversion may be unsuccessful, business owners often decide to stay with manual systems.

Technology Changes

In addition, changes and choices in technology are very rapid. Since the early 1980s, the life cycle of hardware has been quite brief. A new generation of machines seems to appear every 18 months and within five years, equipment is usually obsolete. Operating systems, like CP/M, and programming languages, like Basic, have largely vanished. Operating systems, such as Windows NT, OS/2, and UNIX, are set to supplant the DOS operating system. In addition, much of this new software demands large amounts of storage and memory and will not even run on older machines.

This frequent shifting of hardware and software capabilities and prices introduces added risk, which is an incentive for many to delay decisions. The rapid obsolescence means a quick payback is needed to justify any investment. Furthermore, businesses need assurances that software vendors will provide continued support and product upgrades.

Initial costs for setting up a computerized system keep many smaller businesses from taking the plunge to computerize their accounting departments. Computers require a substantial upfront investment in equipment, software, and training. If the money isn't there, the expenditure is deferred. However, if there are potential savings, deferring the transition can eventually become a losing strategy after a while, as illustrated by the following example:

✓ At one apparel company, staying on top of what items were in stock required order entry personnel to either take frequent physicals or run out to the stock room while a customer was on the phone to check. Since cash was tight, the project of upgrading the inventory system was repeatedly tabled. Meanwhile, the costs of lost orders and extra labor piled up, quickly surpassing the projected cost of a new system.

Initial Costs

Other small business owners wonder if computers will truly provide great savings and perform as well as promised. Most of the benefits of using computers are intangible or hard to quantify. Some claim that, to date, computers have created as much extra paper, busy work, and maintenance as they eliminated, so that no net savings have been realized by businesses. Without a clear picture of how a system can be used and how it could contribute to the bottom line, many business owners have serious doubts about computer benefits that are hard to overcome.

Vague Benefits

Many of the benefits of computerization may not be immediately evident. For example, the initial task of typing a letter, paying a bill, or preparing a simple spreadsheet is often no faster or slower using a computer. But if you need to do revisions, have repetitive tasks, or need rapid access to information, the savings pile up quickly. For a clerk generating a stack of invoices, a customer service rep trying to trace a transaction, or an accountant making the same entries each month, the computer allows for great efficiency.

Money is easily wasted on computers. But for certain applications, especially accounting with a high volume of repetitive transactions, automation pays large dividends. And with careful planning, particularly in choosing stable and proven hardware and software, you can successfully convert.

Many companies have attempted computerization only to be frustrated by inflexible or inadequate software and a lack of proper training. These companies, who are "once bitten, twice shy," sit with an unproductive mix of partially installed software and manual systems, unsure of how to move forward.

Making the Investment

For many of these companies, feelings of discomfort are aggravated by the high price tags their systems carried or fees paid to consultants for installation and training. Investing additional money or writing off the investment and starting anew is a bitter pill for a small company.

The good news is that many solutions are now available at a fraction of their cost of even five years ago. A fresh look at the options available today may relieve some of the anxiety of making a new investment in financial systems.

Up until recent years, a minicomputer was needed to run a typical small company's software. Price tags for hardware and software routinely ran $50,000–100,000 and higher, not including fees for installation, training, customized forms, and maintenance. With no clear-cut choice of hardware or software, there was a high risk of choosing an unpopular platform that could quickly be obsoleted or lock a company into a particular vendor. If special features were needed, customization or development of in-house programs was even more costly. In addition, data exchange between mini-based accounting systems and popular personal computer-based spreadsheet packages was difficult, if it was even available.

While the minicomputer still provides more power and may be needed by some smaller companies, personal computers (PCs) are increasingly the machine of choice in smaller to mid-sized businesses. PCs have increased dramatically in speed, storage, and connectivity.

For little more than the cost of a dumb terminal — consisting of a keyboard and screen only — hooked to a central computer, each desk can be equipped with a fully functional PC networked to the accounting system. This option eliminates the need to:

- Maintain a mix of PCs and a minicomputer; or
- Force spreadsheet and word processing users to log onto a minicomputer, slowed down by the demands of the accounting system.

If you explore all of the options available, you will likely find that computerizing your system will assist the overall smooth functioning of your business' accounting functions, without an extreme cost burden.

PC Accounting Software

An excellent selection of PC accounting software is available to you. Although the divisions are somewhat blurred, there are basically three levels of programs.

Low-End Level

At the low end are packages that handle checkbook functions, such as writing checks, recording deposits, and reconciling bank statements. Most can print simple financial reports and some can do billing and track payables. These programs typically sell for $50–100 and are most appropriate for personal finances or very small, cash-based businesses.

Programs are usually designed for ease of use with entry screens that actually look like checks, invoices, and checkbook registers. Entries usually require just filling in the blanks as you do with a paper system.

Though these programs do double-entry accounting, you are spared from having to know debit and credit bookkeeping.

For businesses needing more than basic checking and invoicing features, a number of well-supported, integrated accounting packages sell for under $300. These packages usually include:

Mid-Range Level

- General ledger
- Accounts payable
- Accounts receivable
- Billing
- Inventory
- Purchasing

Many software packages work on networks, can support point-of-sale functions, have integrated payroll modules, and can transfer data to spreadsheet programs. Most, however, lack order entry — although independent third party add-ons may be available — and have only very simple inventory tracking capabilities. They also have limited flexibility and usually cannot be customized.

These integrated packages are usually quite easy to install, but do require a basic knowledge of accounting. Expect to set up a chart of accounts — sample ones are usually provided — make debit and credit entries, and define accounting periods.

Companies needing more flexibility or features, such as manufacturers needing inventory and production control, will want to step up to a high-end package. High-end packages bear tremendous similarity to the minicomputer software of a few years ago, with good reason — many packages are directly adapted from minicomputer applications. The cost for these programs typically runs $500–1,000 per module, sold separately, with most companies needing anywhere from five to twelve modules. Still far cheaper than their minicomputer brethren, you have the choice of several well-established packages.

High-End Level

For companies needing customization, some high-end programs can be modified — preferably by a consultant trained by the software company to ensure the integrity of the programs. Almost all high-end programs have substantial third-party libraries that have modules or customization tailored to certain industries.

Sorting Your Options

While the number of quality, PC-based packages available is good news, it can introduce confusion into the selection process. In sorting through the options, you will discover that all the major packages can handle the basic accounting and reporting functions very well. Concentrate on features that may be unique to your company or industry and see how each package handles these. Rather than focusing on general ledger, receivables, and payables, which are usually very straightforward, zero in on inventory, order entry, job costing, and similar modules, if appropriate for your type of business.

Total Costs

A commonly asked question is, "What is the least expensive package?" This is the wrong question because your upfront outlay for hardware and software is only a fraction of your total cost. Training, installation, maintenance, and specialized forms, such as preprinted invoices, will account for most of your cost. The wrong system will also cost you in aggravation, fixes, and work-arounds — procedures that get the job done but don't correct the root cause. Be sure to figure all these costs into your budget.

When software is cheap, you may be tempted to say, "If I don't like it, I can just toss it out and try something else." But when you factor in the time and hidden expenses of converting, the cost of even a cheap package can get high. In addition, don't lock yourself into a system that is less than you need because it costs less initially. If you need to start small, look for a package that provides an easy upgrade path.

Custom Programs

Try to avoid custom programming. Custom programs not only add additional expense, but they are more prone to bugs, often lack proper documentation, and are usually hard to maintain. Consider the following examples:

✓ At one company, which modified an existing package, the programmer moved away. The only way to modify the system was to have the programmer call in via modem at night — if available and at $40 an hour, plus phone costs.

✓ Another company was stunned to learn it had spent $60,000 per year just for maintenance on their custom system. Even minor adjustments, like changing a report heading, required a costly programming change and, since they had never been given documentation, switching to a new programmer would have entailed a struggle deciphering the existing code.

If an off-the-shelf product can give you 80–90% of what you need, you are usually better off to go with it rather than customizing. Most newer packages even allow a large degree of customization by letting the user choose and change numerous options. These options might include report and entry screen layouts or whether to track sales history by item, customer, or salesperson, or all three. If necessary, some of these packages do allow modification of the underlying software. Be aware, however, that software companies are constantly enhancing their programs, and the custom features may not be compatible with the upgrades. Retaining the changes may require passing up the improvements in the upgrade or customizing the software a second time.

A related problem is trying to do everything on a database, spreadsheet, or checkbook program. For example:

The Wrong Program

✓ One entrepreneur, like many others, started out entering a price list and printing invoices on a database program — a software program that maintains records such as names, addresses, inventories, and price lists. Because this approach worked, the owner became comfortable using the program, and additional features were programmed in as the business' needs grew. The system was awkward and had the occasional glitch, but the entrepreneur was getting by with it. Eventually, though, when the owner needed to produce financial statements to attract financing, the programming effort became too much work.

Others have repeated this approach, writing complex accounting routines in spreadsheets like Lotus 1-2-3 or finding tricks to use a basic checkbook program for payables, receivables, and more. This type of effort, however, just reinvents the wheel. Even worse, these hybrid programs usually lack important controls, have only very basic features, and may be nearly impossible for all but the programmer to use or modify.

Even if you have been successfully doing accounting functions, such as invoicing, in a database or word processing program, you should convert those functions to your accounting package when you upgrade. Off-the-shelf, integrated programs deliver the advantage of sharing data between modules. If you do your billing on one system, but track your receivables or do your general ledger on another, at some point, you will need to transfer or reenter information. This is a cumbersome and error-prone process. You will be much further ahead to enter data once and have it automatically update all related modules.

A common trade-off is between the number, and sophistication, of features built into accounting software and the ease of installation and use. No one program seems to combine the best of both. Larger packages provide impressive functionality, but can overwhelm you with the number of reports, data fields, or options. Simpler programs are easier to set up and maneuver through, but often lack flexibility or are quickly outgrown. Older, more mature, programs often have built up an impressive list of features and third-party applications, but may be written in older, less sophisticated languages, like COBOL, or have arcane data entry screens. Newer programs may take advantage of snazzier interfaces, like Windows, but have yet to develop a full library of modules or their installed base — number of users — is too small for you to have confidence the program will be fully supported in the future.

Features Versus Ease of Use

The trade-off between features and ease of use can pit users without significant accounting or computer experience against more sophisticated users or outside consultants. If you ask for recommendations from a dealer or outside accountant, they likely will lean toward more complex, more mature products. These are the ones that usually provide the most features and build in the tightest controls. In addition, these professionals have usually used the products before and understand how to make them work.

By contrast, less experienced users are willing to trade off some features to ensure the system can be up-and-running easily and can be run without constant hand-holding. The inexperienced user usually feels the less knowledge of accounting needed to use the system, the better.

The final choice is an individual one. Try to achieve a good balance between features and ease of use. Test drive the systems you are considering and do not buy on features alone. But make sure the system you choose has the functionality you need, especially room to grow.

Do you have to become an accountant to use or set up a system? Not entirely, but a basic understanding of accounting is important. Low-end integrated programs increasingly have become much easier for nonaccountants by eliminating accounting lingo, simplifying the initial setup, and providing more intuitive data entry screens. But you should still get involved in designing a chart of accounts, establishing procedures for accurate and timely data entry, and spending time reviewing reports.

You should have a similar involvement even if you need a more complex, module-based, system. But by the time you need a more complex system, you will probably have financial managers who can handle many of the technical aspects of the system.

Spreadsheets

Financial managers have other software tools at their disposal. Electronic spreadsheets, made popular by Lotus 1-2-3, have replaced the columnar pad for preparing projections and financial schedules. Modern controllers and CFOs should be adept at using spreadsheets to tackle their planning and analysis roles.

The power of spreadsheets is multifold. The main advantage has always been the ability to create, and then replicate, fairly sophisticated formulas. Spreadsheets can also perform simple database functions, as well as create presentation graphics from the numbers. Spreadsheets can often accept data from other programs, including the accounting system, to allow manipulation or an alternate presentation.

Spreadsheets are continuing to evolve. The newest packages handle multiple scenarios with ease and allow data to be viewed in multiple dimensions — "sliced and diced" — at the click of a button. Coming soon is software that could eclipse spreadsheets by anticipating financial questions and simultaneously processing historical, projected, and external benchmark data.

The danger of spreadsheets is that their complexity and slickness can mask underlying problems or legitimize weak logic. Spreadsheets give any user the ability to build impressive looking models, but don't ensure that the assumptions used are valid or provide any checks and balances. Digital Equipment Corporation's founder Ken Olsen, a strong proponent of understanding accounting statements, warns that many spreadsheet users, "Take garbage and reprocess it, contributing nothing but confusion .... If you say 'Lord bless my spreadsheet,' I guarantee you He won't."[2]

The key is to use spreadsheets as a tool, not a crutch. Users should be able to see the source of any inputs and follow the flow of the worksheet. Make sure assumptions are laid out clearly, so they can be carefully examined to make sure the logic behind the calculations is evident, and test the conclusions to see if they are consistent with external data and past experience.

Databases

A technology rapidly finding new uses is database software. At their simplest, databases store information, such as names and addresses, in a user-defined format: records can be easily entered, updated, viewed, and printed. A familiar use is for making mailing labels or personalizing form letters written on a word processor.

Over time, databases have grown more powerful and easy to use. Relational databases can take several independent files, such as a mailing list, customer file, and invoice log, and use the three files as if they were one file — provided at least one piece of information, such as the customer name, is common to all three files. Most have powerful commands for sorting, updating, or printing a selected range of records. This technology has also given the newest accounting packages the ability to display a transaction or piece of data and allow the user to quickly display any supporting detail or jump to related records.

Even more impressive are the programming tools that make it possible to design data input screens, reports, and even processing logic in very little time. While this sort of programming has a less universal appeal than spreadsheets, the newest generation of databases has put the ability to design simple applications in reach of the financial professional.

Specialty software is also available for a wide range of financial and administrative functions. These include programs to track fixed assets, write personnel manuals, and draft legal forms. Once again, much of this software is inexpensive and provides one more reason to make the investment in computers.

Data Input Technology

New technology is also changing the way data gets entered into accounting and control systems. Bar coding, familiar to most of us from supermarket checkout lines, is used to track inventory in many manufacturing companies. Much like early adopters of computers, users who have repetitive data entry and a high need for accuracy will find a rapid payback in bar coding. Studies show that the error rate for bar codes is one per three million characters entered against one per every 300 characters entered by a keyboard operator; inventories for automated systems average 98% accurate versus 73% for nonautomated systems.[3]

Other companies routinely transmit information over telephone lines using modems. A common application is that of a subsidiary transmitting transaction information, such as shipments completed, to a centralized computer at the parent company for billing, then receiving the next day's orders via a return transmission. Accessing PCs or a network directly from remote sites via a modem hookup is also possible.

Pen-based computers will soon bring more portable and user-friendly data entry and processing within reach of many users. Scanners are capable of quickly entering whole pages of text into computers, although these are used primarily for word and graphics processing rather than accounting. Scanning technology, though, does promise to change the way records are stored and retrieved. Voice recognition technology has made great strides and may find its way into accounting departments before long.

Excess Data

As computers are used to collect increasing amounts of data, you need to know what is relevant, where to draw the line between data and information. By having such easy access to data, you risk flooding managers with irrelevant reports. On the other side, users may request numerous special reports and there is the risk that, once run, these become institutionalized.

You and your controller should occasionally weed out reports that aren't being used. One effective technique is to simply stop printing certain reports to see if anyone notices. Don't do this arbitrarily or allow it to be used as an excuse to skip the cash forecast one month. But done right, this technique can uncover what actually gets read, as one controller found out.

✓ One controller using this technique was grabbed in the hall by a manager who complained about not getting a monthly sales analysis. When told it had not been run in six months, the manager left, mumbling something about maybe not needing it right away.

Errors

In the early days of computers, mistakes and mix-ups were commonly blamed on computer errors, which is, of course, a misnomer. While there are rare hardware glitches, computers do what they are told and problems can almost invariably be traced to human error. One joke says that computer errors really involve two errors, the first of which is blaming it on the computer.

In reality, software is the culprit of most errors. Unfortunately, even best-selling software can contain bugs, especially new releases. Avoid the first release of new software versions and wait instead until updates are released. Internally developed applications are even more risky. Be sure to test all software thoroughly, even minor updates. Save backup copies of older, working versions until new programs have been fully evaluated.

Most errors in the actual processing of transactions result from weak internal controls. As discussed in the next chapter, computers can enhance and automate certain control procedures, but they cannot atone for weak manual controls. Inaccurate data entry, failure to establish checks and balances, and an inappropriate reporting structure will carry over from a manual system to an automated one. As programmers say, "Garbage In, Garbage Out" (GIGO). The computer is a fantastic tool for accounting and financial management, but the backbone of any system is strong internal controls.

Endnotes

1. Anthony M. Santomero, quoted in *The Manager's Book of Quotations,* p. 8.

2. Rosenberg, Ronald. "A Little Moralistic Curmudgeonry from the Master Himself." Ken Olsen, quoted in THE BOSTON GLOBE 1 August 1993: 80.

3. Denalli, Jacquelyn. "Bellying up to the High-tech Bar." SMALL BUSINESS REPORTS May 1991: 64.

Notes

Chapter 17

Internal Controls

Let giving and receiving all be in writing.

— *Apocrypha*, Wisdom of Ben Sira 42:7

Effective checks and balances are the bedrock of any accounting and control system. Employees make mistakes, theft is a concern, and the perpetual question of managers seems to be, "The numbers look good — but are they right?" Strong internal controls — systematic procedures for verifying information, detecting errors, and ensuring proper authorization for all transactions — provide the needed level of confidence in the accuracy of financial systems.

Internal controls should also be efficient. At many companies, accuracy and control are achieved only by constantly recounting inventory, double-checking data entry, or having the owner or CEO personally approve almost every expenditure. These are signs that something is almost certainly wrong and resources are being wasted. Tight control does not mean constant oversight and redundant processing. Instead, control can be achieved with fairly simple, routine procedures, plus the discipline to enforce them.

The thrust of internal controls should be to ensure accuracy in everyday processing. Though theft and fraud are clearly of concern, the cost of errors in routine data collection and entry is insidious and usually far greater. Duplicate payments, billing errors, and lost paperwork are more common than dishonesty and routinely cost companies significant amounts of time, money, and goodwill.

Strong controls are also needed to ensure timely information. A system that fails to provide current balances, such as for stock on hand or cash in the bank, results, at best, in costly "workarounds" — employees developing personal files or procedures to override information in the system. At worst, these systems simply get ignored.

These problems apply to both manual and automated systems. While computers have altered the look of accounting systems and greatly expanded what can be accomplished, basic internal control procedures are little changed. In fact, strong manual controls are a prerequisite for an effective computerized system. The computer will only magnify weaknesses in manual controls, not compensate for them.

The core of any accounting system — manual or computerized — is strong controls. This chapter explains the role of controls and describes some basic procedures to implement and enforce controls. You can use the Internal Control Questionnaire for Cash Disbursements at the end of this chapter to check some of your basic procedures for cash disbursements.

Your Personal Checkbook

You, like most people, probably apply basic controls to the handling of your personal checkbook. You start by keeping tight physical control over your checks, storing them in a safe place or carrying them securely in your pocket or purse. Even if a check were to fall into the wrong hands, certain procedures help prevent losses. The checks cannot be used at most stores without also presenting proper ID, and the bank will compare the signature to a card on file.

Checks are numbered so that, if each check written is recorded in the checkbook, you can quickly see from the register whether every number in a sequence is accounted for. Recording each check and deposit also enables you to keep a running balance of money left in the bank, so spending can be budgeted and overdrafts avoided. At the end of every month, reconciling the checkbook to the bank statement can detect any errors. When the statement is reconciled, you can be secure in knowing exactly how money was spent and the balance remaining in the account.

Of course, many people keep their checkbooks a bit less rigorously than this. Whether they fail to reconcile their statements, forget to record every check, or don't keep running totals of cash in the account, they pay a price. Some of these consequences are:

- Uncertainty about cash on hand, perhaps causing overdraft or other bank charges to be incurred;

- Lost information such as, "Where did all the money go?";

- Poor tax records;

- Inability to spot bank errors;

- Extra effort needed to "catch up" or to reconcile statements months later;

- Difficulty finding cancelled checks if a proof of payment is needed;

- Lost interest if extra funds are kept in noninterest bearing checking accounts, rather than invested; and

- A disorganized or unprofessional appearance.

At the same time, some people make effective use of personal computer programs to pay bills and do budgeting. The use of a computer requires an upfront investment in buying software and forms and learning the programs, but these costs are offset by advantages that include:

- Calculations that are automatic and correct;

- Time savings for repetitive transactions;

- Information that can be broken down to the desired level of detail and is easily summarized;

- Credit cards, investments, and other assets that can be tracked in the same program; and

- Excellent tax records and historical information.

The issues that face businesses are much the same and involve not only cash, but payables, receivables, inventory, and other subsystems. A combination of strong physical controls, clearly defined authorization levels, transaction logs, timely recordkeeping, and reconciliations work together to ensure control over assets and accurate information. Properly done, the transactions and procedures are routine and nonobtrusive. Conversely, lack of discipline and controls is costly in terms of lost information, duplication of effort, errors, and unprofessional appearance.

Businesses must deal with an additional problem — having more than one person entering information and controlling the movement of assets. Individuals and sole proprietors have no problem keeping their best interests at heart and ensuring accurate communication. But once a business includes even two people, the protection provided by internal controls becomes an even greater necessity.

Basic Concepts

A few basic underlying concepts and techniques are all you need to set up an internal control system.

Separation of Duties

The first concept is to maintain distinct separations of duties. Loss of an asset, whether from theft, unauthorized expenditure, or error requires both physical access to the asset — including authority to approve expenditures — and a failure to detect or stop the loss. Writing a check does not appropriate funds; it must also be signed and is scrutinized during the reconciliation process. Inventory shortages in a warehouse or stockroom require removal by authorized personnel, but can be detected by comparing on-hand quantities to perpetual accounting records.

If you give a person access to an asset, and at the same time, control of the relevant recordkeeping, you are inviting trouble. However, simply splitting the duties, so that at least two different people control access to the asset and review of the transaction, can provide adequate control.

Some examples include:

- The person preparing checks should not have authority to sign them or reconcile the bank statement.

- Different people should authorize purchases, place orders, and issue payment for goods and services.

- Data entry should be performed and reviewed separately, including batch control totals.

Another simple example can be seen the next time you go to an entertainment event where tickets are sold — a movie, a cash bar, or a club. One person takes the money and hands out the tickets, and another person takes the tickets. The tickets collected provide an independent check on the number sold and, therefore, the cash that was collected. If just one person sold and collected tickets — or there were no tickets — that person would have sole control over both the money and any recordkeeping. Proper payment to the owner would depend entirely on the cashier's diligence and honesty.

Physical Controls

The second concept you do not want to overlook is the role of physically restricting access to assets. To help safeguard your assets:

- Keep checks and possibly other important forms and documents locked.

- Put inventory into stockrooms.

- Label all your equipment.

These types of controls are especially important for inventory, since parts and finished products may be easy to remove and detection of small losses is unlikely. In many companies, inventory is not subject to precise recordkeeping, or shrinkage is almost expected, so loss of a few items is shrugged off. In contrast, fixed assets may be so large, or easy to identify, that they are hard to remove without someone noticing. Cash can be reconciled to the penny, so loss from theft of cash or a check can be detected quickly.

The records of your company must also be physically controlled to maintain both confidentiality and prevent unauthorized changes. Lost records can also be damaging if needed to research a payment, tax, or legal dispute.

For computer records, not only should you restrict physical access to computers and terminals, but passwords should be used as well. Password restrictions can be fairly sophisticated because many software programs allow access to be defined by report, transaction, and even fields of data. Passwords should be changed regularly, kept confidential, and not be shared by users.

Reconciliations

The third concept for establishing internal controls is maintaining timely reconciliations of general ledger account balances. When your ledger balances can be compared to an objective, independently determined balance, a reconciliation can and should be performed. Tying cash to a bank statement — as for a personal checkbook — is the most common type of reconciliation. The bank statement provides an opportunity to verify that all checks and deposits have been recorded and for the right amount. These are errors that routine processing may not detect.

Other important reconciliations you should perform include:

- Make ledger balances for payables and receivables agree with detailed agings.
- Maintain a fixed asset register that foots — adds up — to the book balance. You can use the same register to compute depreciation. Periodically, fixed assets should be inventoried.
- Match vendor payable balances to any statements received. Resolve discrepancies promptly.

Ledger account balances are interconnected, so reconciling one account may clear up problems in another. For example, if receivables records differ from a customer's because a payment was not recorded, the bank reconciliation will catch this error. The bank statement will show a deposit not reflected on the internal records, and the reconciliation will not balance until this discrepancy is resolved.

In practice, because so many transactions involve cash, the bank reconciliation is, perhaps, the best control for ensuring that all revenues and expenses have been booked properly. The bank statement can be an excellent tool for a controller or business owner who is not routinely involved in handling the checkbook to gain insight into how cash flows and how well the accounting is being controlled. Many top managers reserve this task for themselves.

Smaller business owners should also insist that bank statements be sent directly to their home to gain added physical control over these records.

Self-Interest

An understanding of the concept of self-interest will help you make some correct choices. When a business or merchant makes an error in a customer's favor, like failing to bill for a purchase, the customer is likely to keep quiet and pocket the windfall. Of course, if the customer is billed twice, a credit will be demanded or the second bill ignored. Simply put, people can be expected to act in their own best interest. And this expectation is a powerful influence on the effectiveness of controls and should be considered in shaping any system.

If you have to choose between a procedure that prevents double-billing or one that ensures all shipments get billed, it is the latter that most tightly closes the control loop. Though neither type of error is desirable, the protection against double-billing is somewhat redundant since the customer is almost sure to notice. However, no such built-in safeguard exists for failing to bill.

The same logic applies to internal transactions. If a stockroom clerk is responsible for shortages, he or she will have an incentive to properly count incoming shipments or insist on having proper paperwork before releasing goods out of stock. Similarly, a salesperson, who is not reimbursed for expense reports having missing receipts, has a strong incentive to collect the documentation.

Control Numbers and Logs

Finally, the concept of using control numbers and logs can be an important control issue. While an incorrect transaction may be quickly spotted, you may not notice a missing one. You also need a way of identifying transactions so they can quickly be researched or followed up on later. Using control numbers and logs — an extension of the concept of using check numbers and a checkbook — will enable you to solve problems quickly.

Suppose you need a control against failing to bill a customer. In addition, once the bill has been issued, you need a record for tracing payments owed and made. A way to do this is to assign numbers to sales orders and shipments and record them either in a log book or on a computer.

When an invoice is issued, assign a number to it and cross-reference that with the order number. Orders not matched to invoices indicate items yet to be shipped — or items shipped and not billed. Similarly, for any invoices without a payment against them, create a list of open receivables.

This concept extends to a wide range of accounting documents. For example, many restaurants assign servers prenumbered pads and account for all checks at the end of the night; for a physical inventory, tag numbers issued are carefully logged and must all be accounted for at the end of the count.

Assigning and accounting for the transaction numbers ensures that many items do not slip through the cracks and also provides a useful means of cross-referencing them.

Now that you have an understanding of the basic controls you should implement, you will need to fine tune your internal controls to fit your business and to keep control.

If you personally approve every expenditure, a high degree of control might exist, but little gets done. You will devote too much energy to minute details, while managers waste time interrupting their work for approvals and standing in line outside your office. At an early stage in any company's growth, authority to initiate or approve transactions must be passed down.

To do this, and maintain adequate control, give your line managers spending authority, but with specifically defined limits. At that designated dollar limit, transactions should require joint signatures or review at a higher level. For the checkbook, this might take the form of requiring two signatures above a certain figure.

Formal approvals are not just required for the spending of money. Many noncash transactions involve a commitment of resources. You may need formal approvals to provide a paper trail to establish accountability or to use as a systematic vehicle of communication in an organization. Situations where you should require formal authorizations include:

- Sales orders — Make sure to include credit checks and price verifications. Without controls, salespeople will often push through orders at unfavorable terms.

- Purchase orders — Many companies allow managers to order directly, leading to poor price negotiation and little control over the amount and timing of expenditures.

- Return authorizations — Specify terms under which products are accepted back. Customer complaints need special handling.

These authorizations should be obtained early in the processing cycle. For example, the time to do a credit check is before an order is processed, not after an invoice is cut. Dollar limits for approving transactions should apply even on noncash transactions — such as return authorizations.

Maintain Control

Several problems may occur within your system that require preventive maintenance to keep the system running smoothly. The credibility of your system must be kept high. Once information is perceived as unreliable, people begin to work around systems.

Late information can have the same negative effect. Improper training can produce either discomfort with the system or a failure to understand the interdependency of each department and lead to a breakdown. Operators may adopt a technique that gets their job done, even though it forces adjustments downstream. Observe the following illustrations of these types of problems:

✓ At one manufacturer, the purchasing manager routinely added 10% to certain raw material orders because inaccurate bills of material distorted projected usage. The same manager would also physically count on-hand quantities before ordering because of inaccuracies in the perpetual inventory. At other companies, salespeople request extra copies of invoices, or clerks keep personal files or reference cards because they do not trust information they get from a computer system.

✓ At another manufacturer, the production manager did scheduling manually because daily updates to the computer system were routinely processed first thing in the morning — which meant they were completed after the day's work had begun in the plant.

✓ In a company where a new production system was installed, many orders came in that included new part numbers. When this happened, the order entry clerk found it quicker to type the sales orders by hand, using the old forms rather than adding the new parts to the system and then entering the order. This not only forced clerks from production through shipping and invoicing to adopt special manual steps to deal with these orders, but eventually caused the production control aspects of the system to be abandoned altogether.

Enforcing controls may seem to slow work down and create temptation to take shortcuts. However, time lost on the front end is invariably recouped later. Creating exceptions leads to confusion and errors.

Doing things right usually saves time, even if procedures that ensure control seem cumbersome. Ironically, what seems like more work can often take less time to do. For example, when an invoice must be adjusted, should you void the original and issue a new invoice or should you just print an invoice for the difference?

While voiding and reissuing seems to add an extra step, these are very routine transactions. Issuing an adjustment may require stopping for an added calculation and perhaps attaching a note to the customer. Doing two routine steps is often faster than one special one. In addition, when the transaction is reviewed — perhaps when payment arrives — you can see the steps involved more clearly with the two-step procedure.

Audit Trails

This last point leads to a vital internal control feature — the audit trail. Any accounting system must provide a way to easily trace transactions from the ledger or any summary back to supporting detail. Examples include:

■ The balance in accounts payable should tie to an accounts payable aging, listing all open items by a reference number, such as invoice number. Summary information about the invoice should be retrievable on-line and the paper copy should be in an easily accessible file.

- Salary expense for the month may be the total of several weekly entries. Within each week, pay for each individual should be available together with the check number. Hours paid should be verifiable to a time card and the pay rate to a personnel file.

A breakdown in the audit trail makes assigning accountability for transactions and doing reconciliations extremely difficult. A breakdown can also prove costly when disputes over payments with vendors or customers arise. A company may show a vendor invoice as paid, but not be able to identify the check number used — and therefore cannot provide a proof of payment. Similarly, a customer may claim to have paid an invoice and provide a cancelled check — yet you show the invoice still open. If you cannot demonstrate where that check has been applied, perhaps to a different invoice, your customer's claim will stand.

Make Controls Routine

A key factor to successful internal controls is to make the control measures you implement routine. For example:

✓ A car dealership chain was having problems controlling cash down payments given to its sales managers. Rather than submitting them right away to the home office, the sales managers would wait until all paperwork for the sale was complete and submit the cash with it. At times, this meant the managers were carrying a large amount of cash. Occasionally, the company experienced a loss if the sales manager was fired. More frequently, the cash would get used as petty cash to pay miscellaneous expenses, making reconciliation of the paperwork for the sale and office expenses next to impossible.

A very simple check was devised, calling for accounting to randomly compare the sales managers' cash receipt books to cash turned in. This raised the ire of the sales managers who were singled out; they objected to being treated like thieves.

The solution? The company instituted two random checks per month of every sales manager's cash receipt book. This allowed a needed control to be implemented — without the overtones that came with singling people out.

The job of your controller is to ensure that these proper checks and balances exist. Not because the controller suspects people of being dishonest or incompetent, but because it is simply part of the job. Quite the opposite of being a burden, good checks and balances ensure accuracy and eliminate the need for constant policing and monitoring.

Controls must treat people with respect. An example is the monitoring of expense reports. If a manager with full responsibility for running a major department is missing a $20 receipt on an expense report, don't badger him or her over it. The information is not critical to your company and you have no reason to worry that the company is being ripped off — if there is, and that manager controls a large budget, you have a greater exposure than the $20.

If necessary, in order to gain employees' acceptance, consider blaming the need for controls on your outside auditor. CPAs are perceived as straight and narrow, so people are likely to accept their recommendations.

Computers and Controls

The computer has changed the way accounting is done and, therefore, impacted the structure of internal controls. Computers are not quite mysterious black boxes, but they do force a company to more tightly control the processing of financial information. In fact, an entire field of auditing is devoted just to the issues of the computer.

In addition to having the potential to repeat or magnify problems that exist with the manual systems they replace, computers introduce the ability to rapidly access entire files for viewing or altering data, even from a remote site. While, as with manual systems, you still have the threat of theft or fraud, the most dangerous risk is of accidental error. You have the risk of losing data to disk crashes or operator error.

Basic Controls

Some basic controls should bring you peace of mind. As mentioned earlier, passwords should be used to tightly restrict access to data. Physical controls should be established, including locking up data disks, using key locks on PCs, and placing minicomputers in secured rooms. Loss of data from disk crashes and accidental erasure may occur, but daily backups can minimize any losses.

Daily backups also provide the best protection from routine processing errors. Mistakes, such as prematurely closing an accounting period or using the wrong transaction date on a string of entries, can often be corrected by restoring the previous day's data from a backup and starting over. Proper storage and handling of computers and using devices such as surge suppressors can prevent equipment failures.

Commercial accounting software can be relied on to process data accurately and reliably. Software that is developed or modified in-house is prone to bugs and should be tested thoroughly before changing over your entire system. Keep a backup of earlier software versions and data so changes can be reversed.

Despite these risks, the computer should actually enhance overall control. Software can be designed to include a wide range of checks and balances that otherwise would require tedious human review. Programs routinely check to see that entries are in balance, and issue and track invoice and other control numbers. They can test payables invoice numbers to avoid duplicate entries, alert order entry clerks when customers have exceeded credit limits, and flag inventory reorder points to avoid stockouts.

Computers assure that all transactions are processed consistently and calculations done accurately. Because they can store detail easily, they also provide better audit trails, plus rapid and flexible access to information. The physical handling of files is reduced, helping to prevent records from becoming lost or misfiled.

The biggest control risk in a computerized system, as discussed earlier in Chapter 16, is not the computer itself, but manual procedures and disciplines. The computer system will not solve problems due to poor manual controls. Those controls must be fixed before attempting to install a computerized system, or confusion and duplication of effort may grow out of hand.

To return to the example of the checkbook, the computer can open up a range of opportunities for more efficient recordkeeping, but only with the proper discipline. A person who fails to physically control checks, properly categorize expenses, or reconcile the bank statement will have problems using a manual or computerized checkbook.

Audits

A review of internal controls is a standard part of a CPA's audit. In addition, the extent of transaction testing done in an audit is related to how reliable the CPA feels your internal controls are. At the end of the audit, the CPA should issue a management letter that discusses weaknesses in internal controls with recommended corrections. You and your top managers — not just the controller, because the controller's work is being reviewed in the letter — should carefully review these comments and either implement changes or justify current practices.

Examinations of internal controls are not to be confused with searching out fraud. As discussed in Chapter 2, typical audits are not designed, or intended, for detecting fraud. In fact, cleverly disguised fraud, particularly if top management is involved, is nearly impossible to detect in a routine audit.

If fraud is suspected, and has not been detected with basic controls as described in this chapter, you may want to call in a forensic accountant. These specialists, who generally work individually or in small accounting firms, dig deep into transactions. Where a routine audit may only send out confirmation letters to customers, a forensic accountant might examine all invoices and contracts, research the ownership of the outside firms, and search for signs of collusion.

Conclusion

Not all desirable internal control features will be cost-effective. Small companies with few clerical employees will find separation of duties harder to implement. Requiring multiple signatures on checks or purchase orders may delay and impede operations. In these cases, you must weigh the relative costs and benefits of controls in deciding what to implement.

Once in place, internal control procedures become routine, providing unobtrusive, but effective, protection against loss and errors. While you may experience initial resistance to adding procedures or paperwork, the upfront investment usually reduces work down the line — not to mention giving you added security that will let you sleep at night.

To help you evaluate your internal controls, ask your auditor or accountant for any literature or checklists he or she may have on the subject. In addition, you can use the Internal Control Questionnaire for Cash Disbursements on the following pages to check your internal control procedures for cash.

Putting into place everything that you have learned is not something you can do overnight. However, the next chapter can help you get started with a ten-step basic plan of attack.

Internal Control Questionnaire for Cash Disbursements

Internal controls can provide protection from loss and errors. Use this questionnaire to determine if you have established effective internal controls in the area of cash disbursements. Check with your accountant or auditor for checklists, questionnaires, or more information on internal controls in other areas of your business.

Accessibility or Safeguarding

Physical controls and restricted access are important control tools. Review this section to see if your procedures can use improvement.

Yes	No	
☐	☐	Are all payments made by check or other negotiable instrument?
☐	☐	Are checks made payable to specific payees?
☐	☐	Are your checks prenumbered and used in sequence?
☐	☐	Are voided, special, or mutilated checks saved and filed?
☐	☐	Does someone check the sequence of checks periodically?
☐	☐	Do you store unused checks in a restricted area in the possession of a specified person?
☐	☐	Are checks made of protective paper?
☐	☐	Is a check protector used?
☐	☐	If you use facsimile plates or similar devices for check signatures, have you identified who is to have custody and use of the plates?
☐	☐	Do you keep facsimile plates in a restricted, secure place apart from blank check stock, and the plates are only used in the presence of the person designated as responsible?

Separation of Duties

Maintaining a distinct separation of duties is one of the most important practices you can establish for controlling unauthorized expenditures, theft, and errors.

Yes	No	
☐	☐	Are checks prepared by persons other than those with voucher approval authority?
☐	☐	Is the person who prepares checks independent of purchasing and receiving functions?
☐	☐	Are checks signed by persons other than those preparing or having approval authority?
☐	☐	Are authorized signatures limited to employees having no access to accounting records, cash receipts, or petty cash funds?
☐	☐	Is there a dollar limit at which all checks must be countersigned?
☐	☐	Are bank reconciliations prepared monthly by an employee who does not sign checks, record cash transactions or have access to cash?
☐	☐	Does this person receive the bank statement unopened?

Internal Control Questionnaire for Cash Disbursements (continued)

Processing and Recording

Review the questions below to check whether your processing and recording procedures provide enough checks and balances to detect incorrect transactions.

Yes   No

☐   ☐   Are all regular disbursements that you make by checks prepared and based on adequate and approved documentation?

☐   ☐   Does the person who signs checks verify whether the amounts are approved and have adequate documentation?

☐   ☐   Do you pay only against original invoices and not against statements or photocopies?

☐   ☐   Do you mark invoices after payment and check for duplicate numbers to avoid paying twice?

☐   ☐   Are only complete checks — not blank — ever signed?

☐   ☐   After signing, are all checks recorded in a cash disbursement record that gives enough detail to allow accurate summarizing and posting?

☐   ☐   Are actual disbursements periodically compared to forecasted disbursements and large or unusual variances investigated and accounted for?

Answer Key

Ideally, you have answered all of the questions with a "Yes" answer, but a "No" answer to any of the questions does not necessarily indicate a problem. Not all internal controls are cost effective or even possible for many companies. You will have to weigh the costs versus the benefits of the controls you decide to use, as applied to your unique business situation. This questionnaire has only dealt with internal controls for cash disbursements — don't forget to look at other internal controls, as well.

Conclusion

A Ten-Step Plan for Control

Never ask of money spent
Where the spender thinks it went
Nobody was ever meant
To remember or invent
What he did with every cent.

— Robert Frost, *The Hardship of Accounting*

You have completed your survey of controllership. The concepts covered in this book are some of the nuts and bolts of business. Financial management is rarely exciting or the thing that sparks new ventures. As business consultant and author Tom Peters has written, "Inspiring visions rarely (I'm tempted to say never) include numbers."[1]

But a command of the numbers, plus a strong system of controls, are critical for steering your company towards success. If you can measure the activities in your company, you can manage them. If you can quantify goals, you can evaluate your progress and determine if corrective action is needed. As former ITT Chairman Harold Geneen sums it up, "The professional's grasp of the numbers is a measure of the control he has over the events the figures represent."[2]

To accomplish this, you do not have to become an accountant. Your controller is the chief numbers person. But what *Bottom Line Basics* has tried to provide is enough of a working knowledge of financial management to enable you to direct your controller's work.

You do need to find the right numbers. As discussed, too often the only numbers a manager has to work with are those provided by the financial accounting system. This information is often too late, too aggregated, and too hard to interpret to be of the greatest use.

Return to the analogy of an owner being the pilot of a company. The controller has to provide more than financial accounting or it is like navigating with just a little black box — the flight recorders carried by commercial planes. As you travel along, accounting faithfully records everything that happens. However, since the information is historical and hard to access, it cannot be used to help navigate. Worse, no one might take the time to analyze the information unless something goes terribly wrong.

An effective control system is not a black box. Rather, it should function like the instrument panel on a plane. The feedback must be timely, accurate, and accessible. You should have tools for spotting problems and helping steer past them. You must be able to interpret the readings but also be free to exercise judgment in making the ultimate decisions that run the company.

What is often more important than a knowledge of accounting is developing an instinctive understanding, or ownership, of the numbers driving your business. What is your break-even point, what should your target profit margins be, or when do you add an employee? In addition, run the numbers to project cash or evaluate projects. The numbers can't replace judgment, but they do provide support.

The Payback

How much should you invest in a controller and, possibly, a staff or systems? How do you measure the payback? Sometimes, putting a dollar figure on a controller's work is easy. The savings can be directly measured, if:

- Your controller identifies places where costs can be cut.
- You are able to reduce the use of your outside CPA firm.
- Your systems that are put in place allow you to reduce headcount.

Other savings can be determined over time, including improvements in collections or reductions in inventory waste.

Many benefits, however, are intangible or hidden. It is hard to place a definitive value on having better, more timely information or avoiding errors in processing billings and payments. The cost of a cash crisis can be enormous, but if a controller's efforts prevent a crisis from occurring, the work may go unnoticed.

Maintaining good relationships with your banker and investors can be largely dependent on your controller's work. Timely and informative financial reports, the ability to communicate your plans through projections and budgets, plus being able to demonstrate control over the business will earn the confidence of investors. Their confidence will help ensure their support during a downturn. Again, to put a value on this may be hard.

Finally, consider the benefit to yourself of having a strong command over the numbers driving your business. Here is what one owner had to say after turning around his out-of-control, nearly bankrupt film company with the help of a financial management consultant:

> "There are still things I can't do. I can't post information into the books, and I can't analyze four or five years of past P&Ls and such. What I can do, though, is on a daily basis see that only X dollars are being used in Y areas and know that I have only so many dollars to apply in so many different departments.

> "Damn, I am running the company. I have a new controller who handles my finances. I have a sales manager who handles my sales. I have a production head, and I have a creative head. They all come to me with questions, and I know most of the answers. I am a CEO and I'm not ashamed of the title anymore. I deserve it. For the first time I get just as excited by doing business as I did before by producing films....

> "I like the respect that I get now. I didn't enjoy being the head of a financially failing company. Furthermore, once I took away the fear caused by my own ignorance, I was able to relax and be more comfortable, even before all the problems got solved. Now I can sleep nights."[3]

No single formula can determine what to spend on the controllership function. But the starting point is realizing that the job is much more than just accounting and, therefore, requires more than just a number cruncher. As one veteran financial manager wrote:

> "The main blunder made by the owners I've worked for was sticking with a bookkeeping type for too long before hiring a capable financial manager. I think that's because they think of the number one finance person as the head bean counter. That is a huge mistake."[4]

Much is at stake in the financial management of your company. The potential return is large, but also easy to underestimate. Add up both the possible tangible and intangible benefits of strong controllership. Look at successful competitors in your area and see what sort of reporting and systems they have. Then choose the areas that have the best payback and move forward.

Getting Started Now

On the next few pages, is a basic plan of attack that can get you started on taking control. These are ten things you can do right now to improve cash flow, reduce costs, and give you a better understanding of the numbers driving your business.

Step One

Develop at least a one-year projection for your company. Include a profit and loss statement and statement of cash flow. This does not need to be a full-blown business plan or budgeting exercise. Use a format like the sample projection at the end of Chapter 13 to develop a top-down forecast. If cash is tight in the short term, also do a cash flow forecast on a weekly basis going out two to three months. Working with your controller or accountant, these projections should take about two days.

The benefits of doing forecasts are:

- Preparing forecasts is an educational process. Having to review expense trends and what drives revenue, costs, and cash flow can provide insights you would not get just reading financial statements. You are forced to get into the numbers and learn what is behind them. You also get the big picture, a summary of a year's operation and how the dollars flow from month to month.

- Forecasts clearly spell out milestones and expectations for your company. They are something you can monitor your progress against. Also use the projections to communicate with investors and employees.

- Forecasts will tell you in advance if you need to worry about a cash crunch or if your current path will generate sufficient profits. By anticipating problems or highlighting profit or margin weakness, forecasts give you time to take timely corrective action.

- Building models allows you to play what-if games. For example, what happens if sales fall below expectations or if you can speed collections?

Step Two   **Come up with the key numbers you need.** These numbers are used to tell you how your business is doing. These can be financial or nonfinancial, such as:

- Daily sales and cash receipts
- Direct labor hours
- New sales leads
- Amount of rework

Find the key numbers for whatever you need to develop a snapshot of events. Design a flash report that you can get every morning or every week that summarizes these numbers. This way you can see where you are and the direction you are going without waiting for financial statements.

Step Three   **Speed up your monthly closing cycle.** If you are not getting statements by the tenth business day each month, something is wrong. Aim for the sixth or seventh day, if possible.

The slower the closing, the more stale the information. View slow monthly closings as a sign that your controller is spending time on financial statements that could be focused on management issues.

Step Four   **Squeeze cash out of your balance sheet.** Start by reviewing your accounts receivable again. Question each account that is past due and do follow up.

Develop a procedure for approving new accounts and steps to take during the collection process. Try to clear up accounts that are well past due, such as those over 90 days old. You may need to be flexible, accepting installment or partial payments. Make sure the person assigned to collections has the skills and time to be effective. In all cases, be persistent.

Reducing inventory levels will also generate cash but, as discussed in Chapter 10, you may need to resolve operating problems before reducing stock. In the short term, review inventory for excess and obsolete items that can be sold off. You may also be able to change some buying patterns to reduce lead times or order quantities.

Other things you can try include looking at your accounts payable to see if payments can be stretched without hurting vendor relations. Consider leasing rather than buying assets or financing large purchases, such as insurance. Use a lockbox to collect checks mailed by customers.

Take a walk-through tour of your inventory. Look for signs of underlying problems. How much do you have on hand? Is it balanced or do you have short supplies of some items and several months' worth of others? How long has it been sitting around; are there items that are just gathering dust?

Step Five

If you are a manufacturer, see if inventory is piled up in specific parts of your building. Are these areas bottlenecks? Are you over-producing certain finished goods or subassemblies? Make sure that valuable inventory is physically secured. Capture scrap as it is incurred and try to measure the cost of rework.

Implement basic controls. Unless your business is very small, ensure that a separation of duties exists for transactions, especially cash disbursements. Make sure that cash accounts are reconciled monthly and that subsidiary ledgers for receivables, fixed assets, and prepaids are agreed to the general ledger balances.

Step Six

Establish logs for sales orders, purchase orders, invoices, and shipments. Develop systems that don't allow transactions to slip through the cracks. For example, trace sales orders to shipments and shipments to invoices to make sure all orders are shipped and all shipments billed.

Keeping logs will also allow you to summarize any open items, so you know your sales backlog and your exposure for outstanding purchase orders.

Put checks and balances or redundant processing in any place where errors can be costly. For most companies, errors are more costly than fraud. No matter how honest your employees, however, controls are still needed.

Computerize your accounting. If your accounting isn't already on a computer, start moving in that direction. This will be a long-term effort but can be done in pieces. Start with basic modules like the general ledger,

Step Seven

accounts payable, and accounts receivable. If your company is fairly small, a checkbook program may suffice and can be up and running in a matter of hours.

Step Eight **Calculate your costs and determine target profit margins.** Are you charging enough for your products and services? Your labor cost is much higher than wages alone. If you bill for services, understand your cost per hour after adding in benefits, down time, travel, and other direct expenditures. How much do you have to charge to cover overhead expenses such as space, support staff, and equipment?

If you sell goods, does your markup cover your handling, holding, and shrinkage costs? If you manufacture, can you trace production costs to units? Should other costs, such as commissions, product development, and customer service be added in and, if so, what are your margins now? Could you outsource the work more cheaply or, conversely, are there operations you could bring in-house? If you can't calculate costs for all products, do it on a sample that includes your best selling items.

If you have already calculated costs, but included allocations of overhead expenses, take a fresh look. Because the allocations can distort costs, looking at direct margins can give you a different perspective on the profitability of certain products.

Step Nine **Run the numbers on new projects.** When new projects come along, run the numbers to see if they make sense. Ask managers to translate vague promises of cost savings or higher sales to hard figures. Determine the net present value. Set criteria, such as a hurdle rate or payback period, that investments must meet to be considered.

Running the numbers not only helps prevent costly mistakes, but provides a basis for choosing among different projects. As with projections, just running the numbers also helps clarify your thoughts about the project and may suggest improvements or alternatives.

Step Ten **Clarify the roles of your key accounting and finance people.** Your key people could include a CFO, controller, accountant, bookkeeper, and outside CPA. Start with your CPA firm. Ask yourself:

- How do their fees compare with what other companies pay? Fees can range widely and are negotiable, so review them periodically.

- Is your CPA firm doing work, like compiling monthly statements or processing payroll, that could be done more cheaply in-house?

- Can you reduce their audit fees by doing more of the year-end work yourself? On the other hand, could they do more for you? CPAs are often very good sources of input on internal controls, systems, and, of course, taxes.

- What is the scope of the CPA's work? Make sure you are clear about whether you need an audit or review and what work will be performed.

- Will you want your CPA to do work beyond taxes and auditing? This work might include evaluating internal controls, providing general consulting, or looking for fraud. Whatever you decide, make sure your engagement letter spells out the scope of work you agree on.

Next, evaluate your internal staff to see if their skills are well matched to what you need done. For example:

- Can they go beyond the mechanics of bookkeeping and accounting?

- Do you need to add someone with more management skills, and should they be full or part-time?

Even more important, discuss with your employees the scope of their duties and how they should apportion their time. Your needs for support in cash management or budgeting may not match how they perceive their jobs. This is particularly true if they have primarily done just accounting. Let your controller know you would like to see less focus on financial statements and more on problems like planning or collections.

Final Words

The bottom line is that whether you are a smaller business owner or a CEO of a large corporation, effective financial management is critical to the success, even survival of companies. A real payback comes with strong financial management when you move beyond doing just basic financial accounting. The payback comes from getting meaningful operating information, improving cash flow, doing planning, and having tight controls. Financial management, particularly in smaller companies, should be very hands-on and requires a strong working relationship between you and your financial managers.

Controllers and accountants who read this book may see how they can expand their roles and apply their financial know-how to operating issues. For nonfinancial business owners and managers, this book should provide the working knowledge needed to work with financial people and information. When you have succeeded at that, you have more than just a grasp of the numbers. You have control.

Endnotes

1. Peters, Tom. *Thriving on Chaos.* New York: Knopf, 1987. p. 402.

2. Richman, Tom. "The Language of Business." INC. Feb. 1990: 44.

3. Crowley, Larry. "Look, Ma, I'm a Businessman." INC. July 1987: 97.

4. Falconi, Robert. (CFO, Planning Systems, McLean, VA) in a letter to the editor, INC. Oct. 1993: 25–26.

Notes

The Appendix

Appendix

Glossary

He uses statistics as a drunken man uses lampposts —
for support rather than illumination.

— Andrew Lang[1]

ABC classification. Inventory management technique that ranks items as "A," "B," or "C" according to their relative importance. Each class of inventory is then controlled differently, with the greatest resources and effort being applied to the high priority "A" items.

Accounts payable. Amounts owed for purchases made on credit.

Accounts receivable. Amounts due from customers for merchandise or services delivered on credit.

Accounts receivable (payable) aging. A listing of open (unpaid) invoices that also summarizes the items by how old (or past due) they are.

Accrual accounting. Accounting method that records revenues and expenses when they are incurred, regardless of when cash is exchanged. The term accrual refers to any individual entry recording revenue or expense in the absence of a cash transaction.

Acquisition cost. What was actually paid to purchase an asset. This is the basis of recording the value of an asset and includes all costs associated with the purchase, such as freight and sales tax.

ACRS. Accelerated depreciation of assets. Permitted by the IRS, this allows companies to record the greatest expense early in an asset's life.

Activity-based costing (ABC). A management accounting approach that attempts to trace all indirect costs, even those in so-called administrative departments, back to the products that generated them. ABC attempts to pinpoint actual cost drivers, rather than simply allocate costs.

AICPA. American Institute of Certified Public Accountants.

Agings. See accounts receivable (payable) aging.

Allocation. Apportionment of expenses or revenues from one category to others, based on an estimate rather than direct measurement. A common example is allocating manufacturing overhead costs to departments or products, based on units produced or labor hours.

Amortization. Similar to depreciation, involves assigning a portion of an intangible asset's cost to an accounting period. Items whose costs are amortized include goodwill, start-up expenses, or a purchased patent.

APB. Accounting Principles Board. A group that oversaw accounting standards from 1959–1973.

Asset. An unexpired cost, something of future value to a business.

Audit. Examination of a company's financial statements by an independent accountant. The result is a signed opinion of whether the statements fairly reflect the company's financial results and position. See also compilation and review.

Audit opinion. Letter signed by an independent auditor and included with a published financial statement. The letter indicates the scope of work done, whether statements fairly present a company's financial position, and if the company has complied with GAAP.

Audit trail. Cross references that enable an accountant or auditor to trace accounting transactions back to source documents. A highly desirable internal control.

Bad debt reserve or write-off. Losses on accounts receivable either estimated to become uncollectible or specifically identified as such, respectively.

Balance sheet. A financial statement that lists the assets, liabilities, and equity of a company at a specific point in time. A basic tenet of double-entry bookkeeping is that total assets (what a business owns) must equal liabilities plus equity (how the assets are financed). In other words, the balance sheet must balance.

Bean counter. Derogatory term for an accountant.

Big Six. The six largest public accounting firms. These firms are international and significantly larger than the next tier of firms.

Bill of material (BOM). Listing of component parts and quantities that go into making a higher-level assembly.

Book value. The value of an asset for accounting purposes. For assets for which depreciation is taken or reserves booked, often expressed as a net book value (see contra accounts). Book value of a company is the excess of assets over liabilities, which is equal to total owner's equity.

Bookkeeper. An accountant, though the term generally refers to someone performing the least sophisticated task, such as recording transactions and simple statement preparation.

Bookkeeping. Any form of basic accounting.

Bottom-up budget. Process where managers propose spending for their departments and their inputs are added together to form the company-wide budget. See top-down budget.

Break-even analysis. A technique for analyzing how revenue, expenses, and profit vary with changes in sales volume. The classic form groups expenses as either fixed or variable with sales and frequently expresses the relationship in graphic form.

Break-even point. The sales level at which revenues equal fixed costs plus variable costs.

Budget. A planned level of expenditures, usually at a fairly detailed level. A company may plan and maintain a budget on either an accrual or on a cash basis.

Capital budget. Spending plan for purchases of property, plant, and equipment. Usually budgeted separately from operating expenses.

Capital lease. A long-term agreement that, because it most closely resembles the financing of an asset purchase, is treated as long-term debt rather than a rental.

Capital stock. A balance sheet account that records the par value of shares sold. Amounts paid in excess of par are recorded to a separate account, such as paid in capital.

Capitalized. Recording of an expenditure as an asset.

Carrying costs. Expenses incurred as a result of holding assets such as inventory and equipment.

Cash basis accounting. An accounting method that does not record accruals; revenues and expenses are recorded when cash is exchanged.

Cash cow. Mature, profitable business or product line that does not require substantial new investment. Not only are most of its earnings converted to cash, but the cash does not need to be plowed back into the business. The cash is available for payouts to owners or reinvestment in growing ventures.

Cash flow. The net receipt or disbursement of cash. Cash flow statements and projections express a business' results or plans in terms of cash in and out of the business, without adjusting for accrued revenues and expenses.

CEO. Chief executive officer.

Certified management accountant (CMA). Accountant who has passed an exam sponsored by the Institute of Management Accountants and met experience and continuing education requirements. Emphasis is on management accounting.

Certified public accountant (CPA). Accountant who has met the criteria for certification, including passing an exam sponsored by the AICPA, and meeting public accounting experience and continuing education requirements. Emphasis is on financial reporting, audits, and taxes.

CFO. Chief financial officer. Generally distinct from a controller due to a concern for financing and treasury issues, not just accounting and control. Smaller companies may not employ a CFO, or the CFO and controller may be the same person.

Chart of accounts. Listing of accounts and account numbers to which transactions are posted.

Closing. Literally, transferring the balance in one account to another. The term most often is used to refer to monthly, quarterly, or annual procedures used to produce financial statements.

CMA. See certified management accountant.

Compilation. Work performed, usually by a CPA, to assemble a company's prepared data into financial statements. No opinion is expressed about the accuracy of the figures.

Comptroller. Another word for controller.

Confirmations. Letters sent to a company's customers, investors, lawyers, and others by auditors to obtain independent verification of account balances and other financial information relevant to the financial statements.

Conservatism. One of the underlying principles of GAAP, which says that given a choice of accounting methods, the one that understates net income or book value is preferred.

Consolidation. Combining the separate financial statements of subsidiary companies with that of the parent to form a single, combined statement. In a consolidation, transactions between the combined entities are adjusted for by eliminating entries.

Contra account. Accounts, such as accumulated depreciation, that relate to, and offset, another account, usually an asset. The balance in the contra accounts is subtracted from the related account to arrive at a net book value.

Contribution margin. Difference between revenue and the associated variable (or direct) costs. An important concept in break-even analysis and last dollar pricing.

Controller. The top accounting and control professional in a company.

Cost accounting. An accounting discipline that focuses on unit costs of producing goods or delivering services. Although some standard techniques exist, cost accounting does not need to conform to external standards and can be adapted to the needs of the individual company. See also management accounting.

Cost center. An entity defined for reporting purposes that is measured on, and only has control over, costs. Other reporting entities include revenue and profit centers.

Cost of goods sold. Costs associated with goods sold during a given accounting period. Usually includes all associated production costs whether direct or overhead.

CPA. See certified public accountant.

CPA exam. Multiple part exam, covering topics such as tax, auditing, theory, and business law that must be passed by accountants seeking certification.

Creative accounting. Derogatory term for accounting methods that, while often permissible, stretch the rules or are used solely to bias the financial statements.

Credit. In accounting terminology, the entry made to the right-hand side of a ledger. Increases in liabilities and revenues and decreases in assets all carry credit balances. Does not necessarily conform to nonaccounting uses of the term, such as selling to a customer on open account or reducing a balance owed.

Credit policy. Guidelines that spell out: how to decide which customers are sold on open account; what the payments terms are; the limits set on outstanding balances; and how to deal with delinquent accounts.

Current asset. Assets that are cash or cash equivalents or convertible to cash within one year, in the normal course of business. Usually includes cash, accounts receivable, inventory, and prepaid expenses.

Current liabilities. Obligations due within one year. Usually includes accounts payable, accrued expenses, and the portion of long-term obligations that is due within one year.

Current ratio. Current assets divided by current liabilities. Used as a measure of a company's liquidity.

Cut-off. The point in time at which transactions become included or excluded for reporting purposes. A cut-off statement — perhaps, sent to customers to verify a receivables balance — would exclude all transactions beyond a certain date.

Cycle count. Periodic test counting of portions of inventory. Cycle counts are frequently done to monitor the accuracy of perpetual inventory systems. They may also substitute for a full-blown physical inventory, provided all items are counted at some time and controls are strong.

Debit. In accounting terminology, the entry made to the left-hand side of a ledger. Increases in assets, expenses, and decreases in liabilities all carry debit balances.

Debt to equity ratio. Used as a measure of leverage and ability to repay obligations, it is equal to total debt divided by equity. There is no consensus, however, on what is included in debt or how to treat items such as preferred stock or deferred income taxes.

Deferred revenue. A liability that arises when a customer pays for goods or services before delivery is complete. One example would be one-year service contracts billed in advance. Under the accrual accounting method, revenue must be booked when the obligation is fulfilled, not when cash is received.

Depreciation. Recognizing part of an asset's cost as an expense during each year of its useful life. Several acceptable depreciation schemes exist including straight-line and various accelerated methods.

Direct costs. Expenditures, such as labor and materials, that vary in direct proportion to units sold or produced.

Double-entry system. A characteristic of modern accounting in which each transaction impacts the balances of at least two accounts and total debits equal total credits.

Earnings. Used synonymously with net income.

Earnings per share (EPS). Total earnings divided by shares of common stock (and equivalents).

EBIT. Earnings before interest and taxes. A popular measure for comparing the earnings power of companies, since it eliminates the impact of capital structure and effective tax rates, two nonoperating factors.

Economic order quantity (EOQ). The optimum (lowest cost) amount of inventory to order at one time. Determined by considering factors such as quantity discounts, rate of turnover, and handling costs.

EDP audit. Branch of auditing focused on computerized systems (electronic data processing) including the accuracy of processing and security.

Elimination. An accounting entry that is used in a consolidation. Eliminating entries reverse the impact of transactions between the related companies.

Equity. Also equal to a firm's net worth. The sum of capital invested by shareholders, plus accumulated earnings retained by the business.

Expenditure. Any purchase or spending, whether the resources acquired are consumed immediately or provide future value. Contrast with expenses.

Expenses. Resources that have been consumed. The time for recognizing an expense in financial accounting is based on when the benefit is received and not when it is acquired or paid for.

Extraordinary item. Expense or income that is considered unusual and unlikely to be repeated. To avoid distorting the financial statements, the financial impact is reported separately, below such items as operating expenses, interest, and taxes, on the income statement.

Fair market value (FMV). Assessment of what an asset is worth in an arm's length transaction. FMV is a common accounting method for valuing both assets and liabilities.

FASB. Financial Accounting Standards Board. Independent board that issues financial accounting policies. Its rulings, which number more than 100, are referred to by number (such as, FASB 33 – Accounting for Changing Price Levels).

FIFO. Method of accounting for inventory and cost of sales in which the first items produced or purchased are assumed to be sold first (first in, first out). The advantage is that this method often reflects how companies actually handle stock; the drawback is that cost of sales in a given period may reflect outdated values.

Financial accounting or reporting. The branch of accounting most commonly used for preparing financial statements and for reporting to investors. Required of public companies and, basically, the standard for most businesses.

Finished goods. Inventory ready for sale.

Fiscal year. Twelve months chosen to comprise a single year for financial reporting. Does not need to coincide with the calendar year. Fiscal months also may differ from calendar months, usually to have month-ends fall on a particular day of the week, such as Saturdays.

Fixed assets. Assets assumed to be retained for at least one year. Generally includes equipment, furniture, buildings, and land.

Fixed cost. Expense that is assumed not to vary with sales volume, or at least within an expected range of sales volume. An important concept in break-even analysis and in distinguishing between gross and contribution margins.

Flexible budget. A budget where variable expenses are projected as a percentage of sales. This allows a budget to be meaningful over a range of sales figures.

Float. Difference between checks you have written and what has cleared your bank. Arises because time elapses from when you write a check to when it is received and deposited.

Footnote. Addendum to financial statements that expands on the figures to ensure full disclosure. Footnotes may explain accounting principles used, provide additional detail, or report on significant events that are not recognized for accounting purposes.

Full disclosure. Financial accounting principle that requires that all information meaningful to statement readers be included either in the numbers, in footnotes, or in a parenthetical disclosure.

Funds flow statement. Name sometimes used for the statement of cash flows.

FYE. Fiscal year-end.

G&A. General and administrative.

GAAP. Generally accepted accounting principles (pronounced gap). Standards by which financial statements are prepared.

GAAS. Generally accepted auditing standards (pronounced gas). Standards by which audits of financial statements are conducted.

General ledger. The main set of accounts from which financial statements are produced and to which transactions are posted.

Going concern assumption. Accounting values presume that a firm will remain in business for at least one year from the date statements are prepared.

Goodwill. Accounting term for amounts paid for an asset over and above its fair market value. Usually arises when a company purchases another business and pays a price higher than the value of the assets alone.

Gross margin or gross profit. Sales less cost of sales, including both fixed and variable costs. Often expressed as a percentage of sales.

Historic cost. What was paid for an asset. The most common way of valuing assets other than cash.

Income. See net income.

Income statement. Also called a profit and loss statement (P&L). Financial report measuring a company's performance over a period of time. The business' revenue and expenses are netted to arrive at net income.

Indirect costs. See overhead.

Institute of Management Accountants. Association focused on issues of management and cost accounting. Formerly the National Association of Accountants.

Internal audit. Auditing performed by a company's own employees. Often functions apart from the accounting department and may examine operations, as well as accounting.

Internal controls. The system of checks and balances that catch and prevent errors from occurring in everyday transaction processing.

Internal rate of return (IRR). Earnings on a project, expressed as an annual percentage return on investment. Related to net present value, which equals zero when the discount rate is equal to the IRR.

Inventory. Goods purchased or manufactured by a company and held for production or sale. Often subdivided into raw materials, work in process, and finished goods.

Inventory turns. See turnover ratios.

Job costing. Method of tracking costs by project or an individual unit of product.

Joint-product costs. Costs for a single production process that yields two or more different products. These costs can't be directly traced to a product and must be allocated.

Journal entry. Any accounting entry made to the general ledger.

Just-in-time (JIT). Inventory and production control philosophy that emphasizes reducing on-hand inventory and improving quality by "doing it right the first time," making manufacturing "demand pulled," and reducing set-up times.

Kanban. Visual system that indicates reorder points for materials or products. Often seen in conjunction with JIT.

Last dollar costing. Analytic approach that focuses on incremental costs when evaluating new products or pricing decisions.

Lead times. Expected time from when an item is ordered from a supplier or put into production to when it is received or completed.

Learning curve. In financial terms, reduced costs as experience in producing a product accumulates. A significant factor in deciding whether to launch a new venture.

Leverage. Relationship between debt and equity used to finance a company. A highly leveraged company has relatively high levels of debt compared to equity.

Liability. An obligation of a company.

LIFO. Accounting method for inventory and cost of sales in which the last items produced or purchased are assumed to be sold first (last in, first out). Advantage is that cost of sales in a period closely matches current period values; drawback is that this method values inventory at outdated cost levels.

Liquidity. Ability of a company to generate cash in a timely manner to meet its obligations. Often measured by quick or current ratios.

Lower of cost or market. How most assets are valued for financial reporting. Assets cannot be written up if market value exceeds cost, but usually must be written down if the reverse is true.

Management accounting. This practice focuses on information needed by internal managers and encompasses the field of cost accounting. Though some standard techniques exist, cost accounting does not need to conform to external standards and can be adapted to the needs of the individual company. Unlike financial reporting, cost accounting can also encompass nonmonetary measures such as quality or productivity.

Management letter. Report written to management by independent auditors discussing weaknesses in the accounting systems and any operating problems noted in the course of their work.

Marginal cost. Incremental cost of producing one additional item.

Marginal revenue. Incremental revenue from selling one additional item. In economic theory, a company should continue to expand as long as marginal revenue exceeds marginal cost.

Market value. What would be paid for an asset in an arm's length transaction. A key concept in valuing assets for financial reporting. See also lower of cost or market.

Materiality. Measure by which decisions are made on what is disclosed in financial statements and how extensive audit tests must be. The key factor is whether the opinion of a reader of the statements would be affected by the added information.

MRP and MRP II. Materials resource planning and manufacturing resource planning, respectively. Two techniques that, with the help of computers, calculate materials, plant resources, and scheduling needed to meet production targets.

Net book value. See book value and contra accounts.

Net income. (also known as net profit or net loss). The earnings of a company over a period of time. What is left after subtracting expenses from revenues.

Net present value (NPV). A measure, in current dollars, of a project's value. Future income and expenses are discounted to adjust for the time value of money and totaled. Theoretically, NPV is the best method for evaluating projects.

Nonoperating income or expense. Items not related to the ongoing operations of a company. Interest income and expense, one-time events, and taxes are examples of nonoperating items.

Operating income. Operating income equals revenues, less cost of sales and all expenses of normal operations. Much like EBIT, operating income focuses on the earnings of the core business.

Opportunity costs. Earnings that might have resulted if cash or other resources had been employed elsewhere. Theoretically, a better measure of cost than simply cash expended. See also sunk costs.

Overhead. Expenses incurred in operating a business that are not directly related to the manufacture of a product or delivery of a service.

Owner's equity. See equity.

P&L. Profit and loss. See income statement.

Paid in capital. Amount paid by investors for stock over and above its par value.

Par value. Stated value of stock. Usually is a minimal value — such as $.01 (one cent) — and has no relation to the market value of the shares.

Payables. See accounts payable.

Payback. Simplistic method of evaluating projects that calculates the period of time needed to recoup the initial investment.

Period expense. Expenses recorded in the period they occur regardless of whether they may benefit or pertain to a prior or later period. Examples include most administrative and selling expenses. R&D and advertising expenditures are good examples of activities that benefit future periods but must be treated as period expenses according to GAAP.

Periodic inventory. Calculation of cost of sales for inventory in aggregate. Standard formula is that cost of sales equals beginning inventory, plus purchases, minus ending inventory.

Perpetual inventory. Tracking on-hand quantities and costs on an item by item basis.

Physical inventory. The counting of all inventory on hand.

Posting. The process of recording entries in the general ledger, either via journal entries or from subsidiary journals, such as accounts payable and receivables systems. Often, the input of entries is a separate process from posting so that their accuracy can be reviewed before permanent changes are made to the general ledger accounts.

Prepaid expenses. Services, goods, and intangibles paid for before the period in which they are received or provide benefit. Accounted for as assets until consumed.

Present value. See net present value.

Price to earnings ratio (P/E). Market value of a company's stock divided by the number of shares (and equivalents) outstanding.

Process costing. Tracking production costs by department or procedure and then allocating to units. Used primarily in continuous, high-volume operations.

Profit. See net income.

Profit & loss statement. See income statement.

Profit center. Department evaluated, for management accounting purposes, by both revenue and expenses generated.

Public companies. Companies whose stock is publicly traded. In addition to the difference in ownership structure, financial disclosure requirements are stricter for public companies than for privately owned ones.

Purchase price variance (PPV). Difference between the standard purchase price of an item and the actual price paid.

Qualified opinion. A negative audit opinion which expresses the auditor's concern over the fairness of the statements. Reasons might include doubts over the survival of a company, lack of conformity to GAAP, or uncertainty arising from a major, unresolved lawsuit.

Quick ratio. Current assets, excluding inventory and prepaid expenses, divided by current liabilities. Like the current ratio, a measure of liquidity.

Ratios. Comparison of financial statement elements, such as price/earnings and return on assets. Often used for financial statement analysis, they are not only very simplistic, but can be severely misleading due to accounting principles and practices.

Raw materials. Inventory category for materials that are inputs for manufacturing.

Realization or recognition. Recording an income or expense item in a given period. This is independent of when cash is actually exchanged and acknowledges that delivery of goods or services is essentially complete.

Receivables. See accounts receivable.

Reconciliation. The process of agreeing internal balances to a detailed listing or independent source. The most common example is balancing a checkbook, which agrees the checkbook register to a bank statement.

Register. A detailed listing that supports or is posted to a general ledger account. Examples include a listing of all invoices (posted to sales) or checks written (posted to various expense accounts) for a period.

Reserve. An estimate of anticipated losses recorded as an expense even though specific losses have not been identified. Usually based on experience, such as the percentage of past due receivables that become uncollectible.

Return on assets (ROA). Net income divided by total assets. Used to measure how efficiently assets are employed.

Return on equity (ROE) or return on investment (ROI). Net income divided by owners' equity. Used as a measure of return on funds invested in the business.

Reversing entry. An accrual entry booked in one month and reversed the next. Used, for example, when an expense is incurred in one month, but routine processing of the item occurs the following month, such as when an invoice arrives after month end). The reversal and the routine entry offset each year leaving the expense recorded in the correct period.

Review. An examination of a company's financial statements that is less rigorous and less expensive than an audit. The review results in an opinion stating whether the auditor is aware of any material modifications that should be made.

Rolling budget or plan. Form of planning that continuously updates budgets and projections so that they always look out a uniform length of time. For example, a rolling budget, revised three months into a year, would update the remaining nine months, as well as the first three months of the next year, so that it remained a year-long plan.

Safety stock. Inventory held over and above minimum requirements to guard against unexpected shortages.

SEC. Securities and Exchange Commission. Body that overseas reporting requirements of all public companies.

Separation of duties. An internal control where responsibility for processing parts of a transaction are assigned to two or more people. This increases the likelihood that errors or fraud will be routinely detected.

Shareholder equity. See equity.

Shrinkage. Difference between book inventory and the value from a physical inventory.

Spreadsheet. Worksheet, laid out in rows and columns used, in various financial projections and calculations. Often refers to a computer application, such as Lotus 1-2-3.

Standard cost. A target or average cost that may be used to value inventory or as a basis for comparing actual costs.

Statement of cash flows. Financial report showing cash provided and used by a company. Required by GAAP, in addition to an income statement and balance sheet, for published financial statements.

Straight-line method. The simplest form of depreciation, where an equal expense is recorded in each year of an asset's useful life.

Sunk cost. Unrecoverable, prior expenditures on a project. These should be ignored when evaluating future decisions.

Top-down budget. Process where top management dictates company-wide spending targets and then asks managers to submit department budgets that are within these targets. See bottom-up budget.

Turnover ratio. Ratio of annual cost of sales to on-hand inventory. Common rule of thumb measurement used to determine inventory management efficiency.

Turns. See inventory turns.

Value added. Difference between what a company pays for items and what they are worth after the company has converted or redistributed the goods.

Variable cost or expense. An expenditure that changes in proportion to increases or decreases in sales or production volumes.

Variance. Difference between actual revenues, expenditures, or productivity and a budgeted or standard target. Usually expressed as favorable or unfavorable.

Warranty reserve. A liability accrued for anticipated expenses to repair products under warranty. See reserve.

Work-in-process (WIP). Inventory in a manufacturing plant that is assigned to production and, usually, found on the production floor.

Working capital. The net of current assets and current liabilities. Net, liquid assets held by a company.

Write-off. An entry reducing the book value of an asset, perhaps for obsolescence or uncollectability.

Endnotes

1. Quoted in the *Manager's Book of Quotations*, p. 390.

Appendix

Index

*Get your facts first, and then you can distort them
as much as you please.*

— Mark Twain

Establish A Framework For Excellence With The Successful Business Library

Fastbreaking changes in technology and the global marketplace continue to create unprecedented opportunities for businesses through the '90s. With these opportunities, however, will also come many new challenges. Today, more than ever, businesses, especially small businesses, need to excel in all areas of operation to complete and succeed in an ever-changing world.

The Successful Business Library takes you through the '90s and beyond, helping you solve the day-to-day problems you face now, and prepares you for the unexpected problems you may be facing next. You receive up-to-date and practical business solutions, which are easy to use and easy to understand. No jargon or theories, just solid, nuts-and-bolts information.

Whether you are an entrepreneur going into business for the first time or an experienced consultant trying to keep up with the latest rules and regulations, the Successful Business Library provides you with the step-by-step guidance, and action-oriented plans you need to succeed in today's world. As an added benefit, PSI Research / The Oasis Press® unconditionally guarantees your satisfaction with the purchase of any book or software program in our catalog.

Your success is our success...

At PSI Research and The Oasis Press, we take pride in helping you and 2 million other businesses grow. It's the same pride we take in watching our own business grow from two people working out of a garage in 1975 to more than 50 employees now in our award-winning building in scenic southern Oregon.

After all, your business is our business.

OASIS PRESS
BOOKS & SOFTWARE

Call Toll Free To Receive A Free Catalog Or To Place An Order

1 - 8 0 0 - 2 2 8 - 2 2 7 5

All Major Credit Cards Accepted

PSI Research, 300 North Valley Drive, Grants Pass, OR 97526 (800) 228-2275 (541) 479-9464 FAX (541) 476-1479

Select The Tools Your Business Needs From The Following Resource Pages

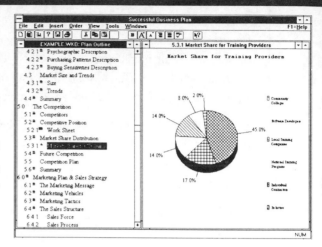

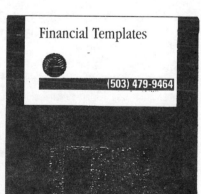

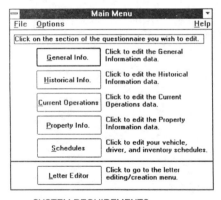
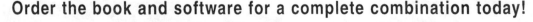

Books that save you time & money

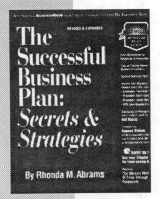

Now you can find out what venture capitalists and bankers really want to see before they will fund a company. This book gives you their personal tips and insights. The Abrams Method of Flow-Through Financials breaks down the chore into easy-to-manage steps, so you can end up with a fundable proposal.

Successful Business Plan: Secrets & Strategies   *Pages: 339*
Paperback: $24.95   **ISBN: 1-55571-194-4**
Binder Edition: $49.95   **ISBN: 1-55571-197-9**

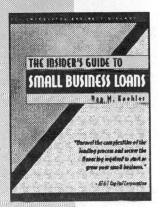

Essential for the small business operator in search of capital, this helpful, hands-on guide simplifies the loan application process. *The Insider's Guide to Small Business Loans* is an easy-to-follow roadmap designed to help you cut through the red tape and show you how to prepare a successful loan application. Packed with helpful resources such as SBIC directories, SBA offices, microloan lenders, and a complete nationwide listing of certified and preferred lenders - plus more than a dozen invaluable worksheets and forms.

The Insider's Guide to Small Business Loans
Paperback: $19.95   **ISBN: 1-55571-373-4**
Binder Edition: $29.95   **ISBN: 1-55571-378-5**

An extensive summary of every imaginable tax break that is still available in today's "reform" tax environment. Deals with the various entities that the owner/manager may choose to operate a business. Identifies a wide assortment of tax deduction, fringe benefits, and tax deferrals. Includes a simplified checklist of recent tax law changes with an emphasis on tax breaks.

Top Tax Saving Ideas for Today's Small Business   *Pages: 320*
Paperback; $14.95   **ISBN: 1-55571-343-2**

Over 200 reproducible forms for all types of business needs: personnel, employment, finance, production flow, operations, sales, marketing, order entry, and general administration. A time-saving, uniform, coordinated way to record and locate important business information.

Complete Book of Business Forms   *Pages: 234*
Paperback $19.95   **ISBN: 1-55571-107-3**
Binder Edition $39.95   **ISBN: 1-55571-103-0**

Books that save you time & money

Learn about the hundreds of ways any business can help secure its future by starting to conserve resources now. This book reveals little-understood, but simple techniques for recycling, precycling, and conservation that can save you money, and help preserve resources. Also gives tips on 'green marketing' to your customers.

Business Environmental Handbook   **Pages: 285**
Paperback $19.95   **ISBN: 1-55571-163-4**
Binder Edition $39.95   **ISBN: 1-55571-304-1**

This exciting workbook explains how a small business can conduct its own market research. Shows how to set objectives, determine which techniques to use, create a schedule, and then monitor expenses. Encompasses primary research (trade shows, telephone interviews, mail surveys), plus secondary research (using available information in print).

Know Your Market: How to Do Low Cost Market Research   **Pages: 177**
Paperback $19.95   **ISBN: 1-55571-333-5**
Binder Edition: $39.95   **ISBN: 1-55571-341-6**

CompControl focuses on reducing the cost of your workers' compensation insurance, not on accident prevention or minimizing claims. This highly regarded book will provide valuable information on payroll audits, rating bureaus, and loss-sensitive points, illustrated with case studies drawn from real businesses of all sizes.

CompControl: Secrets of Reducing Work Comp Costs   **Pages: 159**
Paperback: $19.95   **ISBN: 1-55571-355-6**
Binder Edition: $39.95   **ISBN: 1-55571-356-4**

A wealth of basic, step-by-step marketing information that easily takes a new or experienced business owner through the essentials of marketing and sales strategies, customer database marketing, advertising, public relations, budgeting, and following-up marketing systems. Written in a comprehensive professional way by a marketing consultant, the book features worksheets, a glossary of marketing terms, and a sample marketing plan.

Power Marketing for Small Business   **Pages: 312**
Paperback: $19.95   **ISBN: 1-55571-166-9**
Binder Edition: $39.95   **ISBN: 1-55571-303-3**

Call toll free to order 1-800-228-2275   PSI Research   300 North Valley Drive, Grants Pass, OR 97526   FAX 541-476-1479

No matter what type of business or profession you're in, The Successful Business Library will help you find the solutions you need.

TITLE	BINDER	PAPERBACK	QUANTITY	COST
Bottom Line Basics	☐ $ 39.95	☐ $ 19.95		
The Business Environmental Handbook	☐ $ 39.95	☐ $ 19.95		
Business Owner's Guide to Accounting & Bookkeeping		☐ $ 19.95		
Buyer's Guide to Business Insurance	☐ $ 39.95	☐ $ 19.95		
California Corporation Formation Package and Minute Book	☐ $ 39.95	☐ $ 29.95		
Collection Techniques for a Small Business	☐ $ 39.95	☐ $ 19.95		
CompControl: The Secrets of Reducing Worker's Compensation Costs	☐ $ 39.95	☐ $ 19.95		
Company Policy and Personnel Workbook	☐ $ 49.95	☐ $ 29.95		
Company Relocation Handbook	☐ $ 39.95	☐ $ 19.95		
Complete Book of Business Forms	☐ $ 49.95	☐ $ 19.95		
Customer Engineering: Cutting Edge Selling Strategies	☐ $ 39.95	☐ $ 19.95		
Doing Business In Russia		☐ $ 19.95		
Draw The Line: A Sexual Harassment Free Workplace		☐ $ 17.95		
The Essential Corporation Handbook		☐ $ 19.95		
The Essential Limited Liability Company		☐ $ 19.95		
Export Now	☐ $ 39.95	☐ $ 19.95		
Financial Management Techniques For Small Business	☐ $ 39.95	☐ $ 19.95		
Financing Your Small Business		☐ $ 19.95		
Franchise Bible: How to Buy a Franchise or Franchise Your Own Business	☐ $ 39.95	☐ $ 19.95		
Home Business Made Easy		☐ $ 19.95		
How to Develop & Market Creative Business Ideas		☐ $ 14.95		
Incorporating Without A Lawyer (Available for 32 States)		☐ $ 24.95		
Know Your Market: How to do Low-Cost Market Research	☐ $ 39.95	☐ $ 19.95		
Legal Expense Defense: How to Control Your Business' Legal Costs and Problems	☐ $ 39.95	☐ $ 19.95		
The Loan Package	☐ $ 39.95			
Mail Order Legal Guide	☐ $ 45.00	☐ $ 29.95		
Managing People: A Practical Guide	☐ $ 39.95	☐ $ 19.95		
Marketing Mastery: Your Seven Step Guide to Success	☐ $ 39.95	☐ $ 19.95		
The Money Connection: Where and How to Apply for Business Loans and Venture Capital	☐ $ 39.95	☐ $ 24.95		
People Investment	☐ $ 39.95	☐ $ 19.95		
Power Marketing for Small Business	☐ $ 39.95	☐ $ 19.95		
Proposal Development: How to Respond and Win the Bid	☐ $ 39.95	☐ $ 19.95		
Raising Capital	☐ $ 39.95	☐ $ 19.95		
Safety Law Compliance Manual for California Businesses		☐ $ 24.95		
Company Illness & Injury Prevention Program Binder (OR Get kit WITH BOOK AND binder $49.95)	☐ $ 34.95	☐ $ 49.95		
Secrets to Buying & Selling a Business	☐ $ 39.95	☐ $ 19.95		
Secure Your Future: Financial Planning at Any Age	☐ $ 39.95	☐ $ 19.95		
Start Your Business		☐ $ 9.95		
Starting and Operating A Business in... book INCLUDES FEDERAL section PLUS ONE STATE SECTION —	☐ $ 29.95	☐ $ 24.95		
PLEASE SPECIFY WHICH STATE(S) YOU WANT:				
STATE SECTION ONLY (BINDER NOT INCLUDED) – SPECIFY STATES:	☐ $ 8.95			
U.S. EDITION (FEDERAL SECTION – 50 STATES AND WASHINGTON, D.C. IN 11-BINDER SET)	☐ $295.00			
Successful Business Plan: Secrets and Strategies	☐ $ 49.95	☐ $ 24.95		
Successful Network Marketing for The 21st Century		☐ $ 14.95		
Surviving and Prospering in a Business Partnership	☐ $ 39.95	☐ $ 19.95		
Top Tax Saving Ideas for Today's Small Business		☐ $ 14.95		
Write Your Own Business Contracts	☐ $ 39.95	☐ $ 19.95		
BOOK TOTAL (Please enter on other side also for grand total)				

BLBA1295

Use this form to register for an advance notification of updates, new books and software releases, plus special customer discounts!

Please answer these questions to let us know how our products are working for you, and what we could do to serve you better.

Bottom Line Basics

This book format is:
- ☐ Binder book
- ☐ Paperback book
- ☐ Book/Software Combination
- ☐ Software only

Rate this product's overall quality of information:
- ☐ Excellent
- ☐ Good
- ☐ Fair
- ☐ Poor

Rate the quality of printed materials:
- ☐ Excellent
- ☐ Good
- ☐ Fair
- ☐ Poor

Rate the format:
- ☐ Excellent
- ☐ Good
- ☐ Fair
- ☐ Poor

Did the product provide what you needed?
- ☐ Yes ☐ No

If not, what should be added?
_____
_____
_____

This product is:
- ☐ Clear and easy to follow
- ☐ Too complicated
- ☐ Too elementary

Were the worksheets (if any) easy to use?
- ☐ Yes ☐ No ☐ N/A

Should we include?
- ☐ More worksheets
- ☐ Fewer worksheets
- ☐ No worksheets

How do you feel about the price?
- ☐ Lower than expected
- ☐ About right
- ☐ Too expensive

How many employees are in your company?
- ☐ Under 10 employees
- ☐ 10 - 50 employees
- ☐ 51 - 99 employees
- ☐ 100 - 250 employees
- ☐ Over 250 employees

How many people in the city your company is in?
- ☐ 50,000 - 100,000
- ☐ 100,000 - 500,000
- ☐ 500,000 - 1,000,000
- ☐ Over 1,000,000
- ☐ Rural (Under 50,000)

What is your type of business?
- ☐ Retail
- ☐ Service
- ☐ Government
- ☐ Manufacturing
- ☐ Distributor
- ☐ Education

What types of products or services do you sell?
_____
_____
_____

What is your position in the company?
(please check one)
- ☐ Owner
- ☐ Administrative
- ☐ Sales/Marketing
- ☐ Finance
- ☐ Human Resources
- ☐ Production
- ☐ Operations
- ☐ Computer/MIS

How did you learn about this product?
- ☐ Recommended by a friend
- ☐ Used in a seminar or class
- ☐ Have used other PSI products
- ☐ Received a mailing
- ☐ Saw in bookstore
- ☐ Saw in library
- ☐ Saw review in:
  - ☐ Newspaper
  - ☐ Magazine
  - ☐ Radio/TV

Where did you buy this product?
- ☐ Catalog
- ☐ Bookstore
- ☐ Office supply
- ☐ Consultant

Would you purchase other business tools from us?
- ☐ Yes ☐ No

If so, which products interest you?
- ☐ EXECARDS® Communications Tools
- ☐ Books for business
- ☐ Software

Would you recommend this product to a friend?
- ☐ Yes ☐ No

Do you use a personal computer?
- ☐ Yes ☐ No

If yes, which?
- ☐ Macintosh
- ☐ IBM/compatible

Check all the ways you use computers?
- ☐ Word processing
- ☐ Accounting
- ☐ Spreadsheet
- ☐ Inventory
- ☐ Order processing
- ☐ Design/Graphics
- ☐ General Data Base
- ☐ Customer Information
- ☐ Scheduling

May we call you to follow up on your comments?
- ☐ Yes ☐ No

May we add your name to our mailing list? ☐ Yes ☐ No

If you'd like us to send associates or friends a catalog, just list names and addresses on back.

Is there anything we should do to improve our products?
_____

Just fill in your name and address here, fold (see back) and mail.

Name _____

Title _____

Company _____

Phone _____

Address _____

City/State/Zip _____

E Mail Address (Home) _____ (Business) _____

BLBA1295

If you have friends or associates who might appreciate receiving our catalogs, please list here. Thanks!

Name_____   Name_____

Title_____   Title_____

Company_____   Company_____

Phone_____   Phone_____

Address_____   Address_____

Address_____   Address_____

FOLD HERE FIRST

NO POSTAGE
NECESSARY
IF MAILED
IN THE
UNITED STATES

BUSINESS REPLY MAIL

FIRST CLASS MAIL PERMIT NO. 002 MERLIN, OREGON

POSTAGE WILL BE PAID BY ADDRESSEE

PSI Research
PO BOX 1414
Merlin OR 97532-9900

FOLD HERE SECOND, THEN TAPE TOGETHER

Please cut
along this
vertical line,
fold twice,
tape together
and mail.
Thanks!